Karl Barth
and Radical Politics

Karl Barth
and Radical Politics

Edited and Translated by
GEORGE HUNSINGER

THE WESTMINSTER PRESS
PHILADELPHIA

Scripture quotations from the Revised Standard
Version of the Bible are copyright, 1946 and 1952,
by the Division of Christian Education of the
National Council of Churches,
and are used by permission.

BOOK DESIGN BY DOROTHY E. JONES

PUBLISHED BY THE WESTMINSTER PRESS®
PHILADELPHIA, PENNSYLVANIA

PRINTED IN THE UNITED STATES OF AMERICA

Library of Congress Cataloging in Publication Data
Main entry under title:

Karl Barth and radical politics.

Includes bibliographical references.
CONTENTS: Hunsinger, G. Introduction.—Barth, K.
Jesus Christ and the movement for social justice.
(1911).—Marquardt, F.-W. Socialism in the theology
of Karl Barth. [etc.]

1. Barth, Karl, 1886–1968—Addresses, essays,
lectures. 2. Socialism and religion—History—
Addresses, essays, lectures. I. Hunsinger, George.
BX4827.B3K34   230'.4'0924   76–976
ISBN 0–664–24797–0

Contents

Preface

During 1972, as I was studying at the University of Tübingen, a fascinating debate got under way about the influence of socialist politics on the theology of Karl Barth. The files which became accessible after Barth's death in 1968 disclosed that during his early ministry in Safenwil, Barth was much more active in the socialist movement than had generally been recognized and that in some sense he remained self-consciously a socialist for the rest of his life. The point at issue was whether or not Barth's socialist commitment had had a decisive impact on the shape of his later theology. Although it seemed to me that it had, once the connection was pointed out, competent Barth scholars were raising serious objections to any such view, and the matter seemed far from settled. After returning to the United States, I continued to follow the debate and was surprised that relatively little attention was being paid to it in the English-speaking world. Before long it occurred to me that a translation of some of the principal articles of the controversy might make an interesting and informative volume. The collection at hand contains a representative sample not only of the debate itself but also of the early socialist views which, I am now convinced, were to become absolutely crucial to both the development of Barth's thought and the final shape of his theology. Barth's theological work cannot fully be appreciated at any stage apart from his socialist commitment.

One cautionary word may be in order to readers in the English-speaking world. Barth never conceived of socialism as an "ideology" or a system of ideas. For him socialism was, rather, a series of concrete goals with strong affinities to the kingdom of God. Strictly speaking, therefore, the primary relationship which Barth saw was not between theology and socialism, but rather between the gospel and socialism, or better, between the freedom and love of the living God and socialism. Consequently, Barth did not set out to "prove" a logical relationship between theology and socialism, as between one set of ideas and another, any more than he attempted to "prove" the mystery of the incarnation. If theology was a secondary reflection on the concrete reality of God as proclaimed in the gospel, then socialism commended itself to theology to the extent that socialist goals conformed to those of God for the world. Theology is the conceptual clarification, not the logical deduction, of those goals. The relationship of theology to socialism, therefore, is not the relationship of "theory" to "theory," but rather of "theory" to "praxis."

I would like to acknowledge my indebtedness to the many people who helped make this book possible. I am especially grateful to Prof. Friedrich-Wilhelm Marquardt, who supplied invaluable assistance and support. Above all, my adviser at Yale, Prof. Hans Frei, a *Doktorvater* in the true sense of the term, gave generously of his time, work, and encouragement at every stage of the way. Responsibility for the final product is, of course, my own. I dedicate this book to the memory of my father, who once for a brief time thought he was a socialist, who suffered as a human being, and who died, with questions in his heart, as a Christian.

G.H.

Introduction

GEORGE HUNSINGER

Recently a new book has appeared in Germany whose title translates as *Theology and Socialism: The Example of Karl Barth.*[1] The author, Friedrich-Wilhelm Marquardt, has touched off a stormy debate with his thesis that Karl Barth's theology must be understood as the conceptual side of a lifelong socialist engagement. Among the more surprising corollaries to Marquardt's thesis are these: that Barth was a radical socialist with strong anarchist tendencies; that his theology not only arose from but aims toward socialist action; that revolution was the basic concept for Barth's understanding of both God and society; that Barth's mature Christology provided the final grounding for leftist convictions arrived at earlier; that in Barth's view a church which bears witness to God's kingdom must herself become a revolutionary agent in society. Marquardt regards Barth's thought as laden with intentional political relevance. Far from being peripheral, politics—radical, socialist politics, according to Marquardt—is central and integral to Barth's theology.

The fundamental significance of Marquardt's work is that it sets out to unfold the unity of Barth's entire thought. That is, it attempts to show not only the unity that obtains between Barth's theology and his politics but also the unity of his theology as a whole through its various stages of development. That unity can only be grasped, according to Marquardt, if Barth's theology is understood in its political context as a theology determined by, and determinative for, contemporary history. To demonstrate this unity, Marquardt does not focus, as one might have expected, on Barth's political ethics, but rather on his doctrines of God and Christ. It is thus at the very heart of Barth's theology that he detects enduring socialist elements. Marquardt marshals evidence to show that Barth throughout his life was a radical socialist, who always maintained a critical stance toward politics, but who nonetheless believed that the gospel could not be grasped if its tendency toward socialism were ignored.

Fierce controversy descended on Marquardt's book even before it was published. Submitted as an inaugural dissertation at the *Kirchliche Hochschule* in Berlin, it was rejected by the faculty as "unscientific." In protest against this decision Prof. Helmut Gollwitzer resigned from the staff. The dissertation was then accepted at Berlin's Free University, where Gollwitzer retained a position, and where Marquardt became an assistant professor. After these events the intensity of the controversy did not subside. A conference of Barth's friends and former students was held near Basel, where Marquardt's thesis was debated in his presence by some of the weightiest names in Continental theology. The gathering, often stormy, tended to split into two factions, a "left wing" dominated by Helmut Gollwitzer and Georges Casalis, and a "right wing" dominated by Hermann Diem and Eberhard Jüngel.[2] In the wake of the conference a number of polemical articles then appeared. Those by Gollwitzer and Diem are included in the present volume, along with several others (all of which will be described briefly below).

The reasons for the controversy are complex, and not all of them are related to Marquardt's presentation of his thesis. What makes his work so illuminating and so exasperating at the same time, however, is its rather problematic mix of insight and imprecision. The imprecision is so glaring to some (e.g., Diem) that no insight at all can be credited. The insight is so refreshing to others (e.g., Gollwitzer) that the imprecision hardly bears comment. To my mind, the insight is far more important in the long run than the shortcomings which attend many of Marquardt's judgments. His complicated (and occasionally muddled) syntax, his obscurity of abstraction, and his tendency toward overstatement may well bespeak an insufficiently refined piece of work. But none of this should finally be allowed to overshadow the consistently rich and suggestive level of insight which makes his one of the most important volumes to appear on Barth's theology in recent years.

Despite the various problems his critics have detected, Marquardt's interpretation not only illuminates a neglected aspect of Barth's work (his various socialist involvements) but also affirms in a new way Barth's own view of his theology—that it is thoroughly practical. Like the perennial Weber thesis on Protestantism and the rise of capitalism, Marquardt's view of Barth and socialism promises to serve as an insight which cannot be overlooked and a catalyst to much future research. Moreover, Marquardt's provocative thesis and its corollaries, as presented above, are all inherently plausible, regardless of their need for further refinement. At the very least, they help to explain why it so often seemed that Barth took political differences more seriously than either theological agreements or disagreements. For, as I think Marquardt has shown, Barth did not regard it as a question of taking the one more seriously than the other: Socialism was a predicate of the gospel.

The essays that follow concern first of all the relationship between theology and socialism; second, Barth's views of this relationship; and third, the debate about Marquardt's thesis. The first essay, Barth's "Jesus Christ and the Movement for Social Justice," provides a good example of the early socialist perspective that influenced the development of his theology so decisively. It is interesting to note the way in which Barth had already broken with the tradition of Lutheran inwardness in favor of a more inclusive view of God's sovereignty. It is also interesting that he apparently attempted to concretize Kutter's approach to the socialists by asking about what they want rather than about what "they must."[3] Barth's address elicited a hostile "open letter" from a Safenwil entrepreneur, included next, along with Barth's response.

The second essay, Marquardt's "Socialism in the Theology of Karl Barth," written while his dissertation was still in process, summarizes the position that Marquardt sets forth in his larger work. The appearance of this provocative essay did much to spark the debate that surrounds Marquardt's views. Prof. Marquardt kindly consented to prepare an "Afterword" to his essay especially for this volume.

The next contribution, "Kingdom of God and Socialism in the Theology of Karl Barth," is by Helmut Gollwitzer, the man whom Barth had wanted as his successor at Basel but who failed to receive the appointment because of his radical political views. Gollwitzer's essay may be read as his mature assessment of, and final tribute to, his revered teacher.

In "Karl Barth as Socialist: Controversy Over a New Attempt to Understand Him," Hermann Diem, who has no sympathy for Marquardt's political interests, argues that Marquardt has completely misunderstood Barth's mature Christology. The complicated questions that Diem raises cut to the very heart of the way Marquardt views Barth's later work.

Unlike Diem, who criticizes Marquardt from the "theological right," Dieter Schellong, a substantial young Barth scholar, proceeds in the next essay to criticize Marquardt from the "political left." Schellong's "On Reading Karl Barth from the Left" not only is one of the most thoughtful critical responses Marquardt has received, it also contains many penetrating insights about the political context in which Barth worked.

The essay by Joseph Bettis, "Political Theology and Social Ethics: The Socialist Humanism of Karl Barth," places the Marquardt debate in a setting closer to home by drawing some telling lessons about the theological situation in post-Vietnam America. Bettis also analyzes the political bearing of Barth's theological ethics.

In conclusion, I present my own essay, "Toward a Radical Barth," which evaluates Marquardt's contribution, summarizes the development of Barth's theology, and questions the prevailing views of Barth's relationship to politics.

NOTES

1. Friedrich-Wilhelm Marquardt, *Theologie und Sozialismus: Das Beispiel Karl Barths* (Munich: Chr. Kaiser Verlag, 1972).

2. Cf. Max Geiger, "Karl Barth Tagung auf dem Leuenberg," in Eduard

Thurneysen, *Karl Barth—"Theologie und Sozialismus" in den Briefen seiner Frühzeit* (Zurich: Theologischer Verlag, 1973), p. 45; Markus Barth, "Current Discussion on the Political Character of Karl Barth's Theology," in *Footnotes to a Theology: The Karl Barth Colloquium of 1972,* ed. by Martin Rumscheidt; supplement to *Studies in Religion / Sciences Religieuses,* 1974, p. 91.

   3. Hermann Kutter, *They Must; or God and the Social Democracy,* ed. by Rufus W. Weeks (Chicago, 1908).

Conflict of Opinion

And now to my socialist friends who are present: I have said that Jesus wanted what you want, that he wanted to help those who are least, that he wanted to establish the kingdom of God upon this earth, that he wanted to abolish self-seeking property, that he wanted to make persons into comrades. Your concerns are in line with the concerns of Jesus. *Real* socialism is real Christianity in our time.

KARL BARTH

If in an operation earnings are realized, then the profit belongs solely to the business management itself. Buying, selling, and rational management are the factors that specifically come into consideration here. But what does the worker contribute to any of this? With what moral right do the workers—or better, you and your like-minded comrades, on their behalf—demand a share in something to which they have not contributed in the least?

W. HÜSSY

It is incredible when you want us to swallow the assertion that the worker has "not in the least" contributed to the net profits. Even a child can see that an industrial enterprise would have neither net profits nor profits in general without the participation of the worker. Why does he receive only a wage from the entrepreneur instead of a share in the profits? There is no other reason than the fact that the means of production are the private property of the entrepreneur and that the worker must therefore be glad to receive at least a wage for his work. This inequality and dependence is precisely the injustice that we don't want.

KARL BARTH

Barth's recovery of the two-natures doctrine in his Christology is an objective theological expression for the experience of socialist-Christian solidarity. It forms the organic connection between the Bible and the newspaper, and it generates the two-edged sentence that in Barth's socialist writings occurs again and again: "A true Christian must be a socialist; a true socialist should be a Christian."

FRIEDRICH-WILHELM MARQUARDT

In his personal life-decisions Barth was exceptionally free from bourgeois motivations. But the antibourgeois elan of the Safenwil pastor lost its force when, upon his entering the academic milieu, the previous praxis could no longer be continued. Our classes hold us all tenaciously fast. The counterweight of our ideas cannot offset the influence of our social existence on our consciousness, the bourgeois slant even to a theology antibourgeois in tendency. This antibourgeois tendency would have needed a stronger practical elucidation in order to withstand effectively the "embourgeoisement" of Christianity within the church. How much that tendency in Barth's theology could be overlooked is shown by the surprise and denial which its exposition by Marquardt finds precisely in the circle of Barth's former students.

HELMUT GOLLWITZER

What here approaches us as *Karl Barth tomorrow* has now been made clear. When one recalls the reference in Marquardt's preface to the "antiauthoritarian students" as the "germ cell" of the book, then one will have to grant that the students could be running around with a theologian who is more secure in the saddle than Marquardt when it comes to Christology. Apart from that, however, the question whether the students will "rightly catch sight of" theology (a question that must be raised because of the book's claims for itself) is one that—in view of Karl Barth's theology as Marquardt presents it—can only be answered in the negative.

HERMANN DIEM

It was disastrous that during the period when Nazism was finally in ruins and better stimuli might have been sought for consideration, the writings that Nazism had suppressed still continued to remain invisible so that the intellectual climate came to be renewed precisely under the influence of Heidegger. What did those who studied after 1945, for example, know of *History and Class Consciousness* and of its author's existence [i.e., George Lukács], what did they know of Korsch or Gramsci, of Rubiner or Hiller?—to mention only a few. . . . Marquardt finally situates Barth once again among his contemporaries in their intellectually formative years from approximately 1910 to 1920. Much in Marquardt's polemic can be explained from the fact that he wants to get free from the shadow of a theology under Heidegger's influence in order to be able to catch sight of the impulses of the years prior to *Being and Time*.

DIETER SCHELLONG

I believe there is one explanation for both these facts: the fact that Barth is the theologian par excellence of the twentieth century and the fact that he is ignored in America. The explanation is that Barth's theology necessarily implies a radical socialistic and humanistic ethic that is a direct threat to the liberal capitalist ethic that dominates the American mentality.

JOSEPH BETTIS

The picture which emerges from Marquardt's work is that Barth, from his earliest essays to his final volumes of dogmatics, desired above all else to work out a viable theological solution to the problem of theory and praxis—including political praxis. It was, in fact, the *political* question of theory and praxis which ultimately precipitated Barth's break with liberalism—not merely the theoretical inconsistencies of liberal theology which disturbed him so much in themselves. A look at the chronology of Barth's development in its political context will substantiate this claim.

GEORGE HUNSINGER

1

Jesus Christ and the Movement for Social Justice (1911)

KARL BARTH

I am happy to be able to speak to you about *Jesus,* especially because the initiative for it has come from your side. The best and greatest thing that I can bring to you as a pastor will always be Jesus Christ and a portion of the powers which have gone out from his person into history and life. I take it as a sign of the mutual understanding between us that you for your part have come to me with a request for this best and greatest thing. I can say to you, however, that the other half of our theme lies just as much on my heart: *the movement for social justice.* A well-known theologian and author has recently argued that these two ought not to be joined together as they are in our topic: "Jesus Christ *and* the movement for social justice," for that makes it sound as if they are really two different realities which must first be connected more or less artificially. Both are seen as one and the same: Jesus *is* the movement for social justice, and the movement for social justice *is* Jesus in the present. I can adopt this view in good conscience if I reserve the right to show more precisely in what sense I do so. The real contents of the person of Jesus can in fact be summed up by the words: "movement for social justice." Moreover,

"Jesus Christus und die soziale Bewegung," Vortrag gehalten im Arbeiterverein Safenwil am 17 Dez. 1911, in *Der Freie Aargauer, Offizielles Organ der Arbeiterpartei des Kantons Aargau,* 6. Jahrgang, Nos. 153–156, December 23, 26, 28, 30, 1911.

I really believe that the social justice movement of the nineteenth and twentieth centuries is not only the greatest and most urgent word of God to the present, but also in particular a quite direct continuation of the spiritual power which, as I said, entered into history and life with Jesus.

But against these ideas, there are objections from two sides, and I would guess that both are represented among us gathered here. The one side is formed by so-called *Christian* circles in the narrower sense of the term, with which the majority of bourgeois churchgoers are affiliated. If they read or hear that "Jesus Christ and the movement for social justice" have been linked together, they will protest more or less energetically that Christ is being made into a Social Democrat. "But please don't paint the Savior too 'red,' will you?" a worthy colleague said to me when I told him of my present theme. Then the assertion customarily follows, almost with a certain enthusiasm, that it is completely impossible to associate Jesus with a political party. His person remains nonpartisan, *above* social conflicts, indeed, indifferent to them. His significance is eternal and not historically limited like that of the Social Democratic Party. And so it becomes an untruth and a profanation to draw him into the conflicts of the day, as supposedly occurs in our theme. From the "Christian" side matters can be made still *easier*, however, and that is what usually happens—unfortunately even among many of my colleagues. One points with outstretched finger at this or that gross error or mistake committed by the Social Democratic side. Here the workers beat up a strikebreaker; there someone perpetrated a poisonous newspaper article, abounding in hatred; elsewhere assembly representative Naine made a fool of himself through antimilitaristic tirades; and so on. What does all that—along with all the other irritating things socialists do—what does all that have to do with Jesus Christ? All that obviously has nothing at all to do with Jesus Christ. It has just as little to do with him as those problems found on the free-thinking or conservative side, such as philistine narrow-mindedness, brutal self-seeking, and the self-glorifying exercise of violence. The errors and mistakes of individual persons are found on all sides, and I would not like to point the finger at others.

What concerns us here, however, is not individual persons, but rather the subject matter itself. It is just as cheap as it is unjust to pound away again and again, saying: "Look what the socialists are doing!" It is precisely Christians who ought to know that *we all* fall short when we look at what we're *doing*. When I talk about the movement for social justice, I am not talking about what some or all Social Democrats are *doing;* I am talking about what they *want*. As Christians we should like to be judged by God and man according to what we *want*, not just according to what we *do*. What concerns us, therefore, are not the words and deeds of Bebel or Jaures, of Greulich or Pflüger or Naine, nor even the words and deeds of socialists in Aargau and Safenwil. Rather, what concerns us is what all these persons have in *common*, what is left over after everything personal and accidental, good or evil, is taken into account, what they all with their words and deeds *want*. What they want comes to a few very simple thoughts and motifs, which together amount to a historical phenomenon which is self-contained and independent of the behavior of socialists and the tactics of the socialist parties, and which stands completely *beyond* the controversy of the day: namely, the movement for social justice. I find it difficult to see how it becomes a profanation of the eternal to associate this movement with Jesus Christ. Indeed, we just said that we did not want to talk about what is temporal and accidental in this movement. In the same sense that we are accustomed to linking "Jesus and the Reformation" or "Jesus and Missions," in the same sense we now say: "Jesus and the Movement for Social Justice." We don't want to make Jesus into a German, French, or Aargau Social Democrat—that would be absurd— but rather we want to demonstrate the inner connection that exists between what is eternal, permanent, and general in modern social democracy [socialism] and the eternal Word of God, which in Jesus became flesh.

However, I still need to point out the objection that comes from the *other* side. Among you yourselves, dear friends of the labor union, or perhaps among your comrades in the canton outside, at least one or two persons thought quietly to himself at the announcement of this topic: "Oh, no! Jesus Christ and the movement for social justice! They are still trying to capture us socialists for an antediluvian world view or even for the church." A social-democratic author, Joseph

Dietzgen, has warned against connecting Christianity and socialism, for he sees it as a conservative maneuver. And in fact many a "Christian" approach to socialism does seem like a maneuver designed to "bring the people around" and make them once again into "pious little sheep." While socialism was the means, the Christian church and world view were the actual purpose for which one worked. I would not be surprised if you quietly held a little suspicion toward me as well in this regard. And at this point it would be insufficient to assure you that I really don't want to "bring anyone around." Rather, I must also give you the reason why it isn't so: I must explain why I would like to talk about the inherent connection between Jesus and socialism, and why the purpose of my lecture—that this connection may become clear to you—has nothing to do with your attitude toward the church. Perhaps you will have understood the connection between Jesus and socialism about which I want to speak. Perhaps —and this much I would wish for you—you will enter into a personal, inner relation with this man. Yet, afterward as before, it is still possible to make a wide arc around the church, even around the Safenwil church. The church can help you in your relationship to Jesus, but that is all. At all times there have been persons who have managed without this help. Perhaps you are among those persons. The church has often performed her service badly. That is quite certainly true of our church and of myself. Of the church, therefore, I can only say to you: "She is there in order to serve you. Do what you think is right." The church is not Jesus, and Jesus is not the church.

The same holds true of the so-called Christian world view. If you understand the connection between the person of Jesus and your socialist convictions, and if you now want to arrange your life so that it corresponds to this connection, then that does not at all mean you have to "believe" or accept this, that, and the other thing. What Jesus has to bring to us are not ideas, but a way of life. One can have Christian ideas about God and the world or about man and his redemption, and still with all that be a complete heathen. And as an atheist, a materialist, and a Darwinist, one can be a genuine follower and disciple of Jesus. Jesus is not the Christian world view and the Christian world view is not Jesus. If I would like to interest you in

Jesus today, then I can say to you gladly that I am not thinking of capturing you in order to "bring you around" to Christian ideas. I invite you to put them aside, and to concentrate your attention with me upon the one point we want to talk about: the bridge between Jesus and socialism. I would like nothing more from my lecture than that you all, my dear listeners, would *see* this bridge and attempt to *go* across it, some from this side to that, others from that side to this.

Now let us get into the subject matter. Socialism is a movement from below to above. In the discussion after my last lecture, someone put forth the claim that "we are the party of the poor devil!" As I look at you sitting before me, it seems to me that this indeed says a little too much; even you yourselves will not take it all too literally —but we both understand what was meant. Socialism is the movement of the economically dependent, of those who earn wages working for someone else, for a stranger; the movement of the *proletariat,* as the literature calls it. The proletarian is not always poor, but is always dependent in his existence upon the means and the goodwill of his brother, the factory owner. Here socialism sets in: It is and wants to be a proletarian movement. It wants to make independent those who are dependent, with all the consequences for their external, moral and cultural life which that would bring with it. Now one cannot say that Jesus also began precisely at this point. The reason is quite simply that two thousand years ago a proletariat in the contemporary sense of the term did not exist: There were still no factories. And yet it must strike everyone who reads his New Testament without prejudice that that which Jesus Christ was and wanted and attained, as seen from the human side, was entirely a *movement from below.* He himself came from the lowest social class of the Jewish people at that time. You all recall the Christmas story of the crib in Bethlehem. His father was a carpenter in an obscure town in Galilee, as he himself was during his entire life with the exception of his last years. Jesus was a worker, not a pastor. In his thirtieth year he laid down his tools and began to move from place to place, because he had something to say to the people. Once again, however, his position was fundamentally different from that of us pastors today. We have to be there for everyone, for high and low, for rich and poor; our character frequently suffers from this two-sided aspect of our

calling. Jesus felt himself sent to the poor and the lowly; that is one
of the most certain facts we encounter in the gospel story. Above his
work stands that word in which we can still discern today the fire of
a genuinely social spirit: He grieved when he saw the people, "because they were like sheep without a shepherd" (Mark 6:34). Occasionally, we also hear of rich people who became his followers. If they
did not turn back again after brief enthusiasm, like the rich young
ruler (Matt. 19:16–22)—he knew why!—then in Jesus' presence they
felt more like guests than like those who actually belonged to him.
Nicodemus (John 3:1–2), "a ruler of the Jews," who came to him by
night, is a typical example of this. Indeed, in the last weeks of his life
Jesus even turned to the rich and the educated with that which
moved him—he went from Galilee to Jerusalem—but as you know,
that attempt ended with the cross at Golgotha. What he brought was
good news to the poor, to those who were dependent and unedu-
cated: "Blessed are you poor, for yours is the kingdom of God" (Luke
6:20). "For he who is least among you all is the one who is great"
(Luke 9:48). "See that you do not despise one of these little ones; for
I tell you that in heaven their angels always behold the face of my
Father who is in heaven" (Matt. 18:10). Such sayings may not be
interpreted as words of consolation from a philanthropic man who
spoke thus from on high. "Yours is the kingdom of God!" said Jesus,
and what he meant was this: You should rejoice that you belong to
those who are least; you are nearer to salvation than those who are
high and rich. "I thank thee, Father, Lord of heaven and earth, that
thou hast hidden these things from the wise and understanding and
revealed them to babes" (Matt. 11:25). That clearly was Jesus' own
attitude: He found his friends among the fishermen of the Sea of
Galilee, among the despised tax collectors who worked for the Romans, indeed among the prostitutes of the sea cities. One cannot
reach lower down the social scale in the choice of one's associates
than Jesus did. To him there was no one underneath who was too low
or too bad. And I repeat: That was not a cheap pity from above to
below, but the eruption of a volcano from below to above. It is not
the poor who need pity, but the rich; not the so-called godless, but
the pious. It was at those *above* that Jesus directed his scandalous
saying: "The tax collectors and the harlots go into the kingdom of

God before you" (Matt. 21:31). And again: "Woe to you that are rich, for you have received your consolation" (Luke 6:24). To those *below,* however, he says: "Come to me, all who labor and are heavy laden, and I will give you rest" (Matt. 11:28).

The kingdom of God has come to the poor. But what is "the kingdom of God"? I hear the objection: Social democracy wants only the external, *material* betterment of persons; by contrast, the kingdom of God that Jesus preached is *spirit* and inwardness. Social democracy preaches *revolution;* the gospel preaches *conversion.* The kingdom of God for social democracy is *earthly* and *immanent;* the kingdom of God for Jesus is *transcendent;* it is not called the *kingdom of heaven* without reason. Jesus and socialism are thus as different as night and day. At first glance there seems to be something to this objection. An outstanding and nonpartisan student of socialism, Werner Sombart, has said that the "quintessence of all socialist doctrines of salvation" is contained in the lighthearted poem by Heinrich Heine:

> A new song, a better song,
> I want, O friends, to compose for you:
> We want even here upon the earth
> To build the kingdom of heaven.
>
> We want to be happy upon the earth
> And want to starve no more;
> No more shall idle bellies squander
> What industrious hands have earned.
>
> Enough bread grows here below
> For all the children of men;
> And roses and myrtles, beauty and air,
> And, not least, sweet peas.
>
> Yes, sweet peas for everyone,
> Plant the pods right away;
> Heaven we will leave
> To the angels and the sparrows.

And then one places next to this poem such words of Jesus as these: "Man shall not live by bread alone, but by every word that

proceeds from the mouth of God" (Matt. 4:4); or "Therefore, do not
be anxious, saying, 'What shall we eat?' or 'What shall we drink?' or
'What shall we wear?' For the Gentiles seek all these things; and your
heavenly Father knows that you need them all. But seek first his
kingdom and his righteousness, and all these things shall be yours as
well" (Matt. 6:31–33); or "What will it profit a man, if he gains the
whole world and forfeits his life?" (Matt. 16:26). And then one
juxtaposes social democracy's endless agitation for economic justice
with that scornful reply of Jesus: "Man, who made me a judge or
divider over you?" (Luke 12:14). One then goes on to remark: " 'Jesus
and socialism'—as if the one were not diametrically opposed to the
other!"

Everything now seems to be crystal clear, yet perhaps nowhere else
has Christianity fallen farther away from the spirit of her Lord and
Master than precisely in this estimation of the relation between spirit
and matter, inner and outer, heaven and earth. One might well say
that for eighteen hundred years the Christian church, when confronted by social misery, has always referred to the Spirit, to the inner
life, to heaven. The church has preached, instructed, and consoled,
but she has *not helped.* Indeed, in the face of social misery she has
always commended help as a good work of Christian love, but she has
not dared to say that help is *the* good work. She has not said that
social misery *ought not to be* in order then to summon all her power
for the sake of this conviction that *it ought not to be.* She has
entrenched herself behind a falsely understood saying of Jesus, taken
out of context, which says that "the poor you always have with you"
(John 12:8). She has accepted social misery as an accomplished fact
in order to talk about the Spirit, to cultivate the inner life, and to
prepare candidates for the kingdom of heaven. That is the great,
momentous apostasy of the Christian church, her apostasy from
Christ. When social democracy then appeared with its gospel of
heaven on earth, this very church dared to stand in judgment over
it, because it had denied the Spirit. She referred with smug horror
to the little verse about angels and sparrows, and to similar expres-
sions. She accused social democracy of vulgar materialism, and beat
upon her breast: "Lord, we thank you that we are not as they are, that
we are still idealists who regard spirit as the highest value and believe

in heaven." Thus spoke and wrote the pastors—who would then sit down and eat a hearty midday meal!

The whole picture of the relationship between Spirit and matter, between heaven and earth, becomes completely different when we come to Jesus. For him there are not those two worlds, but the one reality of the kingdom of God. The opposite to God is not the earth, not matter, not the external, but evil, or as he put it in the forceful manner of his day: the demons, the devils who live in man. And that is why redemption is not the separation of spirit from matter; it is not that man "goes to heaven," but rather that God's kingdom *comes to us* in matter and on earth. "The Word became flesh" (John 1:14), and not the other way around! The heavenly Father's love and justice come to rule over all things external and earthly. His will is to be done *"on earth* as it is in heaven" (Matt. 6:10). All those sayings which are often employed against socialism about the unsurpassed significance of the Spirit and its inward testimony are completely right: Jesus knows and recognizes only the kingdom of heaven that is *within* us. But the kingdom must obtain dominion over the external—over actual life—otherwise it does not deserve the name. The kingdom is not *of* this world, but of God. It is *in* this world, however, for *in* this world God's will is to be done. Humanly considered, the gospel is a movement from below to above, as I said. Seen from the divine side, however, it is wholly and completely a movement from above to below. It is not that we go to heaven, but that heaven comes to us.

This kingdom of heaven that comes to earth is by no means "purely spiritual," as is sometimes said. Rather, it is said very simply that we will "sit at table in the kingdom of God" (Luke 13:29). "Blessed are you that hunger now, for you shall *be satisfied"* (Luke 6:21). "Blessed are the meek, for they shall *inherit the earth"* (Matt. 5:5). To all those who have left everything for the sake of the gospel, it is promised that in time they will receive houses and fields a hundredfold once again (Matt. 19:29). The way to the kingdom of God is, however, by no means a merely spiritual and inward imploring of "Lord, Lord!"; rather, "you will know them by their fruits" (Matt. 7:21, 16). Again and again, however, the fruit is nothing but social help in material terms. This supposition of Jesus becomes clear from the great parable of the world's judgment: It is not according to the quality of their "spirit" that persons are separated out to the right or the left. Rather, "I was hungry and you gave me food, I was thirsty and you gave me drink, I was a stranger and you welcomed me, I was naked and you clothed me, I was sick and you visited me, I was in prison and you came to me." For "as you did it to one of the least of these my brethren, you did it to me"; and "as you did it not to one of the least of these, you did it not to me." (Matt. 25:32–46.) The spirit that has value before God is the *social* spirit. And social help is *the* way to eternal life. That is not only how Jesus spoke but also how he acted. If one reads the gospels attentively, one can only be amazed at the way it has become possible to make Jesus into a pastor or a teacher whose goal was supposedly to instruct persons about right belief or right conduct. Power came forth from him which healed them all (Luke 6:19). That was his essential effectiveness. Whether his healings of the sick are explained in a more supernatural or a more natural way, it is in any case a fact that he healed people and that this ability stood far more in the *center* of his life than is usually realized. He was an itinerant preacher who went about doing good and making persons well (Acts 10:38). Many people came to him bringing with them the blind, the dumb, the crippled, and many others, and they put them at his feet, and he healed them (Matt. 15:30). We hear things like this again and again.

I ponder these facts known to every Bible reader and fail to see how one has a right to call social democracy unchristian and materialist because its goal is to introduce an order of society that would better serve the material interests of the proletariat. Jesus by word and deed opposed that material misery which *ought not to be.* Indeed, he did so by instilling persons with the Spirit which transforms matter. To the paralytic in Capernaum, he said first: "Your sins are forgiven!" And then: "Stand up, take up your bed, and walk!" He worked from the internal to the external. He created new men in order to create a new world. In this direction the present-day social democracy still has infinitely much to learn from Jesus. It must come to the insight that we first need men of the future to create the state of the future, not the reverse. But regarding the goal, social democracy is one with Jesus: It has taken up the conviction that social misery *ought not to be* with a vigor which has not been seen since the time of Jesus. It calls us back from the hypocritical and slothful veneration of the Spirit and from that useless Christianity which intends to come only "in heaven." It tells us that we should really believe what we pray every day: "They kingdom come!" With its "materialism" it preaches to us a word which stems not from Jesus himself, yet certainly from his Spirit. The word goes like this: *"The end of the way of God is the affirmation of the body (ist die Leiblich-keit)."*

Something stands in the way of the coming of God's kingdom to earth, says Jesus. Indeed, answers social democracy, what stands in the way is capitalism. Capitalism is the system of production which makes the proletariat into the proletariat, i.e., into a dependent wage earner whose existence is constantly insecure. The materials neces-sary for production (investment capital, factories, machines, raw materials) are the *private property* of one of the co-workers, namely, the boss, the factory owner. The other co-worker (the "worker") possesses nothing but the power of his work, which he furnishes to the factory owner, while the net profits of the common work are accounted as capital—as the factory owner's *private property*. Social-ism declares that it is unjust to pay the one co-worker for his produc-tion so disadvantageously, while the other pockets the full actual gain of the common production. It is unjust that the one becomes a distinguished person, amasses capital upon capital, lives in a beautiful house, and is granted all the pleasures of life, while the other must live from hand to mouth, at best manages to save a little, and, if for one reason or another this is impossible for him, remains a "poor devil," who is consigned finally to charity. This class contradiction, says socialism, is the daily crime of capitalism. This system of produc-tion must therefore *fall*, especially its underlying principle: *private property*—not private property in general, but private property as a means of production. Just as the work is collective or common, so must its net profits be shared in common. For that, however, the boundless *competition* between individual producers must fall; and the state, the whole, must itself become the producer and therefore the owner of the means of production. This in the briefest of words is the anticapitalist theory of social democracy. We could certainly search for a long time until we found a similar theory, or anticipations of one, in the Gospels. We do not want to search for that at all. The capitalist economic system is a modern phenomenon, as is the socialist countertheory. But in these modern phenomena we have to do with a problem that is as old as humanity, namely, the question of *private property.* What was Jesus' attitude toward that? Here is a question we may pose quite legitimately and from that basis infer his attitude toward capitalism and socialism in the present. Let us first take a look around: What does the Christian church say about that? And what about the state, which, through the instruction of a state church, to a certain extent passes itself off as a Christian state? Here we notice that both church and state shroud the concept of private property with an amazing aura of sanctity and unassailability. It has been impressed upon all of us down to the marrow of our bones that what's mine must remain mine. In our penal code, property enjoys far greater protection than, for example, a good reputation or morality. What's mine is mine, and no one can change that! Not only have Christians gotten used to this notion, because temporarily perhaps it could not be otherwise, but they even act as if it were a divine law and have fallen into the deepest dismay regarding the intention of social democracy largely to eliminate private property and to transform private capitalism into social capitalism.

The dismay could well be on the other side. If one lets the words of Jesus say what they really say without watering them down or weakening them, then one finds that precisely the notion that 'what's mine is mine' is condemned with a greater force than perhaps found anywhere in all of socialist literature. Jesus is more socialist than the socialists. You know the saying: "It is easier for a camel to go through the eye of a needle than for a rich man to enter the kingdom of God" (Matt. 19:24). Here clever theologians have made the discovery that the eye of a needle is not really the eye of a needle, but a Palestinian name for a narrow gate through the city wall. A camel could pass through such a narrow gate only with great difficulty; thus a rich man, if otherwise virtuous, could supposedly enter the kingdom of God, albeit with great difficulty. Thus is the Bible watered down! No, no, the eye of the needle is and remains the eye of the needle, and Jesus really wanted to say that a rich person, a possessor of worldly goods, does *not* enter into the kingdom of God. You know the story of the rich man and poor Lazarus. It nowhere says that the rich man committed some sort of particularly evil deed and for that reason ended up in hell and torment. No. Rather, his fate was the consequence of the contrast—of the class contradiction—in his life, which consisted in the fact that he was rich and had it good, while Lazarus was poor. "Now he is comforted here, and you are in anguish" (Luke 16: 19–31). And it is not accidental that we are reminded of modern capitalism when we hear of the rich man (Luke 12:16–21) whose land brought forth so plentifully that he no longer had room to store his crops and who decided to tear down his barns to build larger ones. Why shouldn't he? His profits were certainly his property! And we hear nothing more evil about him than that he was so satisfied in his possessions. Yet the parable continues: "Fool! This night your soul is required of you; and the things you have prepared, whose will they be?" (v. 20). Then there is the rich young ruler (Matt. 19:16–22) who had kept all the commandments from his youth. Jesus said to him: "One thing you still lack. Sell all that you have and distribute to the poor." But when he heard this he went away sorrowful, for he was very rich. Moreover, there is the entire section from the Sermon on the Mount, which begins with the words. "Do not lay up for yourselves treasures on earth" (Matt. 6:19), where we hear that such gathering of treasure turns the inner light in man into darkness; where we are placed before the great Either/Or: "No one can serve two masters; for either he will hate the one and love the other, or he will be devoted to the one and despise the other. You cannot serve God and mammon" (Matt. 6:24). One can only be continually amazed if one realizes how easily Christendom of all confessions and types has glossed over these words, while it has often been so zealously strict and precise in dogmatic questions which had no meaning at all in the life of Jesus. Jesus rejected the concept of private property; of that, it seems to me, there can be no doubt. He rejected precisely the principle that what's mine is mine. Our attitude toward material goods should be that of the famous steward in the parable (Luke 16:1–12): "Make friends for yourselves by means of the mammon of unrighteousness." We should not possess it, but we should be "faithful" with it. And "being faithful" in this context means quite clearly: We should make others into its common owners. As private property it is and remains precisely the mammon of unrighteousness. The fact that this was Jesus' belief is finally most clearly illuminated by the position which he himself adopted in practice, and which he also enjoined upon his disciples. There was a man who declared that he was ready to follow Jesus wherever he went. Jesus answered him: "Foxes have holes, and birds of the air have nests; but the Son of man has nowhere to lay his head" (Luke 9:57–58). Indeed, the abolition of private property goes farther: His mother and his brothers called to him as a crowd was sitting around him. But he no longer knew of any familial bonds that had some personal, private value in themselves: " 'Who are my mother and my brothers?' And looking around on those who sat about him, he said, 'Here are my mother and my brothers!' " (Mark 3:31–35.) The same held for his disciples: "Take no gold, nor silver, nor copper in your belts, no bag for your journey, nor two tunics, nor sandals, nor a staff" (Matt. 10:9–10). Do we want once again to wriggle off the hook by saying that these words apply only to those who were missionaries in the earliest era of the gospel, or do we detect in them the heartbeat of the gospel itself? It says to us: Thou shalt become free from everything that begins with "I" and "mine," absolutely free, in order to be free for social help. Do the two go together, Jesus and capitalism, the system of boundlessly increasing private property? Joseph Dietzgen, mentioned earlier—by his own words a despiser of Jesus and Christianity—says at one point: "The real original sin, from which the human race has suffered up to now, is self-seeking. Moses and the prophets, all the law givers and preachers of morality together, have not been able to liberate us from it. . . . No fine phraseology, no theory and rule, has been able to abolish it, because the constitution of the whole society hangs on this nail. Bourgeois society depends upon the self-seeking distinction between 'mine' and 'yours,' on the social war, on competition, on the defraudation and exploitation of the one by the other." This despiser of Jesus has understood Jesus *correctly.* Jesus' view of property is this: Property is sin, because property is self-seeking. What's mine is absolutely not mine!

However, social democracy does not only say that the material situation of the proletariat must become a different and better one. It does not only say that for this purpose human work must cease being a way merely to increase private capital. Rather, it seizes and employs a means to lead this goal to realization. The means is called *organization*. The historic programmatic text of socialism, the Communist Manifesto of 1848, concludes with the famous words: "Proletarians of the world unite!" Socialism proceeds from the *solidarity* that is actually already imposed by the capitalist system. In distinction to the crafts of the old guild type, modern factory work is collective work under conditions of solidarity. Twenty pairs of hands and more take part in producing a single shoe! Now socialism wants to bring to the worker's consciousness this (in itself necessary) solidarity as the source of his power and progress. He should learn to think collectively, solidarily, commonly, socially, just as he has actually been long since working socially. He should become a class-conscious worker. It is customary in this context to speak of the "battalion of workers." The individual worker can achieve nothing, but the battalion of workers will in an unremitting assault bring down the fortress of capitalism. To be a socialist means to be a "comrade" in consumers unions, in labor unions, and in political parties. He ceases to be an individualist, to be something for himself. He takes seriously that fine Swiss saying: "One for all, and all for one." As a socialist, he no longer thinks and feels and acts as a private person, but rather as a member of the forward-striding, fighting totality. Solidarity is the law and the gospel of socialism. Or to speak once again with Joseph Dietzgen: "Conscious and planned organization of social work is what the longed-for savior of the modern period is called."

As Christians we will at first be inclined to say that the gospel and the Savior of the New Testament are something quite different. There what is concerned is not a matter of the masses, but of the individual soul. Do we not hear from Jesus' lips of the shepherd who leaves ninety-nine sheep in the wilderness to go after the one which is lost, until he finds it (Luke 15:3–7)? The socialist call to solidarity and Jesus' call to repent and believe the gospel stand in rather strange contrast to each other. Unfortunately, in fact they really do—not for Christ, however, but for those who call themselves by his name. It is thus also one of the current misunderstandings that religion is a means of making the individual quiet, cheerful, and where possible blessed in the midst of the anxieties of life. Because Jesus said, "When you pray, go into your closet" (Matt. 6:6), we act as if Christianity as a whole were a matter of the closet, and indeed of *our* private closet. One finds oneself together with other persons in the church in order to secure the consolation and joy of the gospel, but the community extends no farther: Religion beforehand and afterward remains a matter between God and the soul, the soul and God, and only that. This attitude is found today especially among the Christians of Germany, above all to the extent that they stand under the influence of Luther. They then distinguish themselves without exception by a complete failure to understand social democracy. In that regard we Swiss, even if we don't realize it, are brought up differently through our Reformers, Zwingli and Calvin. To these men, religion was from the outset something cooperative, something social, not only externally, but also internally. It is therefore no accident that among us, Christianity and socialism have never come to the kind of rift that exists between them in Germany. Rather, with ever-increasing clarity one begins from both sides to become aware of the correlation, indeed of the *unity* between them.

This unity is found already in Jesus. We believe, without wanting to derogate others, that we understand Jesus better than our fellow Christians in Germany. Certainly, Jesus wanted to bring the heavenly Father to the soul *and* the soul to the heavenly Father. But what do we pray: 'my Father' or 'our Father'? Isn't that the whole point? For Jesus there was only a social God, a God of solidarity; therefore there was also only a social religion, a religion of solidarity. In Jesus' view, do we have eternal life in a secluded retreat or in the *kingdom of God?* Does the *gospel* really say that *I* attain life, eternal life, blessedness? What does Christ say? "Whoever would save his life will *lose* it; and whoever loses his life for my sake and the gospel's will *save* it" (Mark 8:35). It is not for our own sake that we are called; it is not for the sake of the soul's self-seeking that we are to repent, be converted, and believe in God. Rather: "Follow me and I will make you become fishers of men" (Mark 1:17). "You are the light of the *world.*" "You are the salt of the earth." (Matt. 5:13–16.) Against the Pharisees, who took piety with the utmost seriousness, Jesus directed the saying of the prophets: "I desire mercy, and not sacrifice" (Matt.

9:13). God's law is blotted out when we want to be pious instead of practicing *love* (Matt. 15:3–6). "Woe to you scribes and Pharisees, hypocrites! for you tithe mint and dill and cummin, and have neglected the weightier matters of the law, justice and mercy and faith" (Matt. 23:23). There is no other greatness before God than the greatness of helping others: "Whoever would be great among you must be your servant" (Matt. 20:26). All this does not stand *beside* faith in God the Father in heaven as something added onto it afterward; rather, it is inextricably bound to it. In answer to the question, "Which commandment is the first of all?" Jesus named two: "You shall love the Lord your God with all your heart," and "you shall love your neighbor as yourself." (Mark 12:28–31.) From this awareness of the collective, solidary, communal, social God, the rule of corresponding action follows of itself: "Whatever you wish that men would do to you, do so to them" (Matt. 7:12). And Jesus added: "This is the law and the prophets." God's love should flow into us in order to transform us in love into human beings again. And now we look once again from Jesus' words to his life. We step here into the most sacred area of our faith. Above our religion stands the sign of the *cross*. This sign stands first over the life of Jesus: "The Son of man . . . came not to be served but to serve, and to give his life as a ransom for many" (Mark 10:45). He gives up his life unto death, not for his own sake, or for the sake of his own eternal happiness, but rather in order to help many. You know the story of how Jesus washed his disciples' feet: "I have given you an example, that you also should do as I have done to you" (John 13:4–19). You know the words of institution at the Last Supper: "Take, this is my body"; and "This is my blood of the covenant, which is poured out for many" (Mark 14:22–24). This was the climax and end of his life, an act of *faithfulness* to his disciples. Have we understood the word of the cross when we so conduct ourselves as if there were something in life even higher than the *giving* of one's life for others, than this consciousness of solidarity which makes the neighbor equal to oneself? Indeed, this word of the cross is a scandal and folly, just as it was at the time of Paul (I Cor. 1:18). Let him take it in who can, that one must lose one's life in order to find it, that one must cease being something for oneself, that one must become a communal person, a comrade, in order to be a person at all. "But to those who are being saved the word of the cross is the power of God." I find something of this power of God in social democracy's idea of organization. I also find it elsewhere, but here I find it more clearly and purely, and here I find it in the way in which it must be worked out in *our* time.

And now, in conclusion, allow me a few personal words which I would like to say to you as a pastor of this community.

First, to those friends present who up to now have related themselves to socialism in an indifferent, reserved, or *hostile* way: At this moment you are perhaps feeling somewhat disappointed and upset, so that it would not be inconceivable that one or another might go out from here and report: "He said that the socialists are right." I would be sorry if anyone said that. I repeat once again: I have spoken about what socialists *want*, not about the manner in which they *act* to attain it. *About what they want, I say: That is what Jesus wanted, too.* About the manner in which they *act* to attain it, I could not say the same thing. It would be easy for me to come up with a broad critique about the manner in which the socialists act to attain it. But I fail to see what good such an easy exercise would accomplish. Therefore, I have not said that the socialists are right! Nonetheless, I do not want to say that you nonsocialists should now go home comforted and reassured. If you feel upset, then that is good. If you have the feeling that "Oh, no, Christianity is a hard and dangerous matter if one gets to the roots of it," then you have rightly understood me—or, rather, not me, but *Jesus*. For I did not want to tell you my view, but the view of Jesus as I have found it in the Gospels. Consider, then, whether as followers of Jesus you ought not to bring more understanding, more goodwill, more *participation* in the movement for social justice in our time than you have up to now.

And now to my *socialist* friends who are present: I have said that Jesus wanted what you want, that he wanted to help those who are least, that he wanted to establish the kingdom of God upon this earth, that he wanted to abolish self-seeking property, that he wanted to make persons into comrades. Your concerns are in line with the concerns of Jesus. *Real* socialism is real Christianity in our time. That may fill you with pride and satisfaction about your concerns. But I hope you have also heard the rebuke implied in the distinction I have made between Jesus and yourselves! He wanted what you want—as you *act* to attain it. There you have the difference between Jesus and yourselves. He wanted what you want, but he *acted* in the way you have heard. That is generally the difference between Jesus and the rest of us, that among us the greatest part is program, whereas for Jesus program and performance were one. Therefore, Jesus says to you quite simply that you should carry out your program, that you should *enact* what you *want*. Then you will be Christians and true human beings. Leave the superficiality and the hatred, the spirit of mammon and the self-seeking, which also exists among your ranks, behind: They do *not* belong to your concerns. Let the faithfulness and energy, the sense of community and the courage for sacrifice found in Jesus be effective among you, in your whole life; then you will be true socialists.

However, the unrest and the sharpening of conscience which Jesus in this hour has hopefully brought to us all should not be the last word in this beautiful Christmas season. I think we all have the impression that Jesus was someone quite different than we are. His image stands strangely great and high above us all, socialists and nonsocialists. Precisely for that reason he has something to say to us. Precisely for that reason he can be something for us. Precisely for that reason we touch the living God himself when we touch the hem of his garment. And if we now let our gaze rest upon him, as he goes from century to century in ever-new revelations of his glory, then something is fulfilled in us of the ancient word of promise which could also be written of the movement for social justice in our day: *"The people who walked in darkness have seen a great light."*

POSTSCRIPT *(An exchange of letters: A Swiss entrepreneur vs. Karl Barth)*

Open Letter to Mr. Karl Barth, Pastor in Safenwil
Safenwil, February 1, 1912

Dear Pastor:
    Yesterday I became aware of the lecture that you gave on December 17, 1911, within the confines of the Safenwil labor union. In a long rabble-rousing speech, garnished with an incredible number of

religious quotations, you attempted to "enlighten" your listeners. Permit me to concern myself with this speech for a moment:

As to the abundance of philosophical and sophistical considerations, the majority of your listeners have probably not retained much. What will stay with them, however, is the following passage, which I reproduce word for word: "Private property must fall—not private property in general, but private property as a means of production." By this you want to say that the private property of dependent earners must be assured, whereas that of independent earners must be confiscated and distributed. According to this, however, as soon as any dependent earner, by the power of his intelligence and his spirit of work, raises himself to become an independent earner, he will have to come to ruin in favor of those who remain dependent.

Your further observation that "in our penal code property enjoys greater protection than a good reputation or morality" sufficiently demonstrates the correctness of my interpretation of your remarks. Of course, you were shrewd enough to place them on the lips of a generality: "what socialism wants." Since you have underscored them so heavily, however, they in any case represent your own inwardly highest thoughts and pious wishes.

Socialism is, as you say, a movement from below to above; in accordance with that, though you simply forget to mention it, you are also asking for a countermovement from above to below. Many of the greatest employers of all time were dependent earners in their youth; therefore, when the time is ripe, they will have to be pulled down, according to your theory, so that they do not get too high. To judge how many hundreds of thousands of families would then be unable to maintain a comfortable existence who now enjoy one is something I leave to those who have a more objective judgment and whom I even find among the people whose heads you are now trying to confuse.

Therefore, you want not only to eliminate the independent earner but also forcefully to limit the upward mobility of the dependent earner, whose lot lies so much upon your heart—an upward mobility which no one obstructs for him and also which no one can obstruct for him. Thus, you would nip all initiative in the bud. But who, then, will pull the cart? The wheels will not turn by themselves, and those who pull the cart must have a certain elbowroom, otherwise the cart will not budge from the spot, especially not for those who grasp the wheels, nor for those who sit inside.

That is thus your ideal of a future state! My dear pastor, you are still very young. Therefore, let an older man say to you that even in the twentieth century there is still a difference between theory and praxis that even the most ancient, and hence today no longer pertinent, Bible sayings do not help to remove.

What you want, after all, has already been tried in practice, yet the attempts actually ended in a few years in a miserable fiasco. I remind you only of Zion City. That was a communist state under the mantle of religion. Why didn't you enlighten your listeners about cases like that?

So much for the general aspects of your lecture, which sound more like castles in the air. In them, however, I find a more concrete desire, which, for now, rests content with the distribution of the net profits. In this regard permit me to say the following: The occasional profits are absolutely necessary to the factory owners in order to compensate for the unavoidable and sometimes enormous losses which accompany downturns in business. For if the owners wanted to distribute the profits in good times, the latter would soon be dissipated and then in times of need could no longer be procured, even if you demanded counterjustice from the side of the workers. Have you ever thought about that?

Furthermore, the cost of a manufactured article does not consist merely in wages. In its production, material is also necessary as are machines and a lot of other things. Besides, industry has long since been forced to take wages into account as it has paid for these things. In the most favorable cases for the workers, therefore, nothing is deserved in addition to wages.

If in an operation earnings are realized, then the profit belongs solely to the business management itself. Buying, selling, and rational management are the factors that specifically come into consideration here. But what does the worker contribute to any of this? With what moral right do the workers—or better, you and your like-minded comrades, on their behalf—demand a share in something to which they have not contributed in the least? My dear pastor, from an educated person in general, one *may* require that he express himself in public only about matters which he has fully mastered. From a pastor in particular, however, one *can* require that he adopt a mediating role and that he not seek, with means that fly in the face of all healthy human understanding, to sow discord between employer and employee.

The majority of listeners were not able to analyze the internal value of your speech. They thus took what was said at face value. You know that, and you count on it; that is the strange part of the whole story.

One more thing. If you ever again have the desire to vent your intractable rage about capitalism, then do not implicate industry. For capitalism and industry are two entirely different things. I would have given you credit for knowing that.

Respectfully yours,
W. Hüssy

From: *Zofinger Tagblatt*
     February 3, 1912

Answer to the Open Letter of Mr. W. Hüssy in Aarburg
Safenwil, February 6, 1912

Dear Sir:

My December lecture to the Safenwil labor union prompted you on February 1 to go on the warpath against me and to sling something at me. I am letting you know that you failed to hit your target. And because at the same time you have told me with such a refreshing clarity what you think of me, you will certainly not take offense if despite the prevailing coolness, I enter the fray in my shirt sleeves rather than my frock coat and reply with equal clarity.

First of all, for a prelude, you level the charge against me, as groundless as it is crude, that in a calculated way I offered something to my listeners "at face value" which was really something else and that just that is "the strange part part of the whole story." Herr Hüssy, to those kinds of *insults* pulled out of thin air, I will make no reply; they are among the arrows which missed the mark, but hit the archer. You call my lecture a "rabble-rousing speech" with the purpose of "sowing discord between employer and employee." In reality I spoke completely objectively about capitalism as such and meticulously avoided every personal reference to specific capitalists. Through your "open letter" *you* linked yourself and your name with the general interest; you have thus given a point to my lecture which it was not supposed to have. I regret this, but *you* carry the *full* responsibility for it. I did not bid you to feel affected and to let everybody know about it.

You hold out before me the few years by which you are older than I, and on that basis admonish and instruct me in the tone of a schoolmaster. With this you make yourself look ridiculous, for your "open letter" inspires me and others with no great respect for your seasoned wisdom. You advise me, in my capacity as a pastor, that I should "adopt a mediating role." Indeed, just as *you* understand it, right? That would be convenient. With your permission, however, as a pastor I am faced with a different program regarding which I owe *you* no accounting. You can state with amazing certainty that the majority of my listeners did not understand my lecture, and you even specify exactly what they managed to retain. I would admire you for your sagacity, but I must reply that *you* at any rate, Herr Hüssy, have understood *nothing at all* in my lecture. I seriously doubt whether you read the whole thing. The number of "religious quotations" was far too great, and you found it far too difficult ("too philosophical and sophistical," as you would say). You nowhere touch upon the basic ideas of my lecture, but from everything that I said only a few sentences about private property made any impression on you. To be sure, you have even misunderstood these; but they apparently struck the red terror into your breast, as if we wanted to start the great "redistribution" tomorrow. And *on the strength of that* you took up your pen.

That was the prelude. Now comes the main piece. I said that "private property as a means of production must fall," and this upset you. You construed it as follows: "The property of the independent earner must be confiscated and distributed." Herr Hüssy, may I lend or mention to you a few good books from which you could obtain information about the essence of modern socialist theory? Or must I let my reply expand into a treatise on the matter? I can only say to you that with this interpretation of my remarks you prove to be unanswerable, for you haven't the faintest grasp of the meaning of my ideas, which are quite familiar to anyone even slightly acquainted with the subject matter. You behave as if in the passage in my article which you retained, you thought about socialism for the first time. I fear that is really the case, your protests are so pathetically naïve. May I remind you of what you preached to me at the conclusion of your "open letter" about "educated persons"? But I would gladly inform you, to the extent that it can be done briefly. Where in the world did you find expressed in my lecture the view which you ascribe to me that what is at stake is the "confiscating and distributing" of private property? At most, this is the kind of thing one says to little children when one wants to make them afraid of the "red menace." And how could you possibly make the mistake of connecting socialism with the communism of Zion City? Have you never heard anything about the *nationalization* of the means of production? Since you seem to know nothing about it, let me tell you what it means according to the wording of the official program of the Swiss Social Democratic Party. It means that society takes over both the means of production (i.e., investment capital, factories, machines, raw materials) and the management of production. It means the "replacement of the capitalist economy, whose purpose is to produce profits, by a collective economy whose purpose is to meet social needs." The contemporary economic system is an anarchy from above. For "every capitalist stands under the compulsion dictated by competition to be constantly intent upon reducing the price of his product and expanding his market, and thus upon beating his competitor before his competitor beats him. Since, however, this feverish economic activity has the realization of profits as its purpose, without considering social needs, it necessarily leads to overproduction and to periodic crises." Must I remind you, Herr Hüssy, of the consequences of these effects for the people as a whole and especially for the working class? You speak of the hundreds of thousands of families who have maintained a "comfortable existence" through the present system. Good, accepted that it is so, yet over against these hundred thousands there are millions for whom the opposite is true. (I would note that you could have found this entire explication in somewhat different words in my lecture, if you had read it correctly.) We therefore want the nationalization of the means of production through which we expect to regulate production and thus to avoid those deleterious effects. How? From something of that sort you fear that the individual's "upward mobility" will be "obstructed," that "initiative" will be "nipped in the bud," indeed, even that "his intelligence and spirit of work" will be thwarted, or at any rate that his "elbowroom" will be restricted, don't you? Indeed, if by "upward mobility" you mean the way of the careerist who walks over others' heads, and if by "elbowroom" you mean the freedom to jam one's elbows into others' ribs in order to get ahead, then your anxiety is certainly justified. Here I am of the opinion that at some point this sort of thing must and will cease. I believe, however, that persons can be instilled with work, initiative, and freedom such that they will gladly and willingly place them in the service of the whole, just as is now done out of merely private interests. Am I not a dreamer, Herr Hüssy? You see, I am of this opinion because I believe in the moral progress of humanity. Instead of the word "progress" here, I could also use another, deeper word. But you would presumably consider it as "no longer pertinent today." Yet in my view it is too good for a newspaper article. What has led me as a pastor to place myself on the side of socialism (for definite reasons I do *not* belong to the *party* for the time being) is precisely this: that in the idea of a socialist "state of the future," which you like to ridicule, I find expressed the belief in progress away from economic egoism toward an economic sense of community. In this respect I am at one with a great number of Swiss Christians and pastors. If you would only declare that you do not believe in this progress, then the situation between us would be clear. Everything else is incidental.

However, besides this "castle in the air" you would also discover in my lecture a "more concrete desire," namely, one which, "for now, rests content with the distribution of the *net* profits." I can only shake my head in amazement at the abyss of noncomprehension disclosed by the phrase "for now" which you use here. You mean that "for now" only the net profits will be distributed, whereas later on, under the spell of castles in the air, there will come that great confiscation when everybody will stick his share of the common

wealth in his pocket and go home to have a good time. Haven't you
noticed that what you so crudely call the "distribution of the net
profits" is precisely the *final goal* of socialist thought and not something "for now"? Haven't you noticed that this concerns the salient
difference between capitalism and socialism? The net profits of the
common work of the entrepreneur and the worker now become the
private property of the former, because he is the private owner of the
means of production. That is the essence of the capitalist economic
system. (You know quite well that all *industry is organized capitalisti-
cally;* and when you charge at the end that I have confused the
difference between capitalism and industry, you are engaged, objectively, in a totally pointless splitting of hairs.) Socialism fights against
this economic system, and rightly so, because the net profits which
become part of the private wealth of the entrepreneur are by no
means equivalent to his contribution to the common production. The
business management, which as a rule is in his hands, is the ultimate,
and therefore certainly an extremely important, aspect of the production process. But it is only one aspect among many. It is incredible
when you want us to swallow the assertion that the worker has "not
in the least" contributed to the net profits. Even a child can see that
an industrial enterprise would have neither net profits nor profits in
general without the participation of the worker. Why does he receive
only a wage from the entrepreneur instead of a share in the profits?
There is no other reason than the fact that the means of production
are the private property of the entrepreneur and that the worker must
therefore be glad to receive at least a wage for his work. This inequality and dependence is precisely the injustice that we don't want. At
this point you raise the long-known objection that the net profits
from the good years must compensate for the losses of the bad years
in business. Indeed, do you really believe that after the nationalization of the production processes, the net profits would then be distributed without remainder among the managers and workers so that
there would no longer be reserve capital, as there commonly is even
now in all state operations? But even apart from that, this objection
is simply a clever deception and does not amount to a reason. Or
would you seriously contend that the capitalization of the net profits
is useful and necessary simply to compensate for bad business years?

My dear Herr Hüssy, that would be believed in *Safenwil* by no one!

In conclusion, a word about your tired *expression* that there is a difference between theory and praxis. (Even you yourself wouldn't have the boldness to designate this commonplace as a thought?) Thereby you want to say that praxis should be as unencumbered as possible by theory. Coming from you, this wish is quite intelligible. What you mean by praxis is *private profit;* what I mean by theory is *justice.* You are quite shrewd to remove private profit as far as possible from justice and to explain away certain unfortunate Bible sayings as "ancient and thus today no longer pertinent." But we intend to wait and see whose light will burn longer, that of your shrewdness, which separates theory from praxis, or that of socialism and the Bible, which replaces private profit with justice.

You can keep on writing "open letters" to me, Herr Hüssy, if you feel the urge to do so; but you can depend on the fact that such efforts will not stop the march of things in the world—in the long run not even in the region of Zofingen. The outcome of the recent parliamentary elections in Germany might have reminded you of what is "pertinent today," to use your term. May I give you a piece of advice? It would simply be not to cling to your present reactionary position so stubbornly that you can no longer come out of it. You are indeed older than I am, as you observe, but certainly still young enough to develop better judgments. I sincerely wish that for you.

Respectfully yours,
Karl Barth, pastor

From: *Zofinger Tagblatt*
     February 9, 1912

2

Socialism in the Theology of Karl Barth

FRIEDRICH-WILHELM MARQUARDT

In this essay I will present four theses:

I.   Karl Barth was a socialist.

II. His theology has its life setting in his socialist activity.

III. He turned to theology in order to seek the organic connection between the Bible and the newspaper, the new world and the collapsing bourgeois order.

IV. The substance of his turn to theology was the construction of a concept of "God."

I. *Karl Barth was a socialist.*

Barth twice joined the Social Democratic Party, both times at moments when party membership was difficult. The first time, at the end of 1915, he joined the Swiss Socialist Party while it was still radical, that is, before it split into communist and revisionist wings. The reason: he now wanted to criticize the party from within for having lost its radical socialist principles; previously he had advanced this criticism only under religious-socialist auspices. He was troubled,

From "Sozialismus bei Karl Barth," *Junge Kirche* 33 (1972), pp. 2–15. Translated and reprinted with the kind permission of the author and the journal.

for example, by the question of national defense and militarism on which the party, after August 4, 1914, had reneged.

The second time, in 1932, he joined the German Social Democrats when the victory of the National Socialists was discernible. In January 1933 he insisted on staying in the party against the leadership's recommendation that publicly prominent figures should leave. Tillich followed this advice, observing that socialism was entering into a new phase, in which its existential shape was changing, and no longer needed the form of a party. Barth defended his membership on the grounds that for him socialism was not an ideological, but a political and practical commitment, in other words, one that was concrete. In contrast to Tillich, he understood his socialism in terms of *praxis,* not in terms of religious and social theory.[1] Shortly afterward, *Reichsminister* Rust demanded that Barth refrain from "organizing cell groups," thereby proving that he (Rust) was acquainted with Barthian activities. Barth expressly informed Rust that party membership was integral to his entire work. Barth's dismissal from the university, therefore, was not only a result of his refusal to take the state-imposed oath (a matter on which he was willing to compromise), but was—and this has never been sufficiently stressed—a result of his socialist recalcitrance.

As a rule, Barth's opposition to National Socialism is seen only in the light of the church struggle. In fact, however, it was politically motivated. In 1932, with unparalleled radicalism, he entered into the Dehn affair,[2] turning a purely academic-political matter into a full-blown political cause. On February 15, 1932, in the morning edition of the Frankfurt daily newspaper, he spoke out publicly under the headline "Why Not Fight All the Way?" He placed himself in the line of fire beside Dehn and sharpened the debate by citing from a speech by Hitler. He tried to raise political consciousness by moving from a particular case to a discussion of society and National Socialism.

Immediately following his expulsion from Germany, Barth continued to pursue his anti-Nazi activity—as documented, for example, in "A Swiss Voice"[3]—activity that several times brought him into conflict with the Swiss censors. Toward the end of the war, he also worked actively in the Swiss section of the communist-led "Committee for a Free Germany."[4] The documentation of this collaboration has yet to be made public. Even before the German collapse, Barth wrote letters to Germany that stressed this involvement and urged others to join. In Basel he worked closely with the committee's communist leaders, including Teubner, Goldhammer, Fuhrmann, Wolfgang Langhoff, and Dr. Karl Mode. His editorial assistant, Charlotte von Kirschbaum, became the Confessing Church's delegate to the committee.

Since the existence of this Confessing Church delegation has never before been made public, and since on the surface it seems incredible, this fact is of particular interest. It was apparently a self-delegation by Barth and von Kirschbaum on behalf of the Confessing Church. Perhaps this delegation suggests something of how Barth envisioned the future. Indeed, the committee worked in Germany during the period after the collapse, and it is conceivable that Barth was seriously convinced the Confessing Church should have a voting representative on the steering committee of this communist organization. If so, that would be highly significant for his understanding of the political function of the Christian community. We will come back to this function later.

From this perspective Barth's famous or infamous attitude toward Eastern European communism also takes on a political aspect: that of his socialism. Barth was no neutralist—either with respect to the church, which he wished to place "between East and West," or with respect to state and society. His "No" to Soviet imperialism was of equal importance with his "Yes" to a "more than Leninist"—or left-wing—socialism.

II. *Barth's theology has its life setting in his socialist activity.*

Barth's socialism, regardless of its closer theoretical definition, was *socialist praxis.* I am currently deciphering the remainder of Barth's socialist speeches and preparing them for publication. They permit a more precise view of how his theology began, although in general this view was already available. Barth's theology is in fact rooted (as Barth was aware on the theoretical level) in his political involvement *(praxis).*

The relation of Barth's theology to his praxis has up to now been insufficiently and, in my opinion, even falsely described. Here one endlessly encounters the quotation of his so-called "anxiety at preaching": "As pastors we should talk about God. Yet because we are men we cannot talk about God. We should recognize these two things— our obligation and our inability—and so give God the glory." That is from the Elgersburg lecture "The Word of God as the Task of Theology"[5] from October 1922. Since then it has been said again and again, "That is not only the starting point, but also the sum and content of Barth's theology."

But this view leaves two essential points unnoticed. The first is that very early on in the *Church Dogmatics,* Barth no longer remains only a theologian of revelation and the Word of God. When he elevates the person of Jesus Christ to prominence, he removes "revelation" decisively to the background. With the sacraments, furthermore, he displaces the Word of God (read: sermon) from its dominant position in theology and ecclesiastical practice.

Equally unnoticed is the second point, which cuts in the opposite direction, that prior to October 1922—and this essentially means prior to the second edition of *The Epistle to the Romans*—Barth was already a theologian. The way he posed questions in his early theology, and the conditions under which he did so, are not well known. His questions were broader in scope, theoretically more precise, and even structured in a completely different way than most of us are aware.

Here I would like to pause for a moment with some remarks on Barth's theological reception in Germany. Barth's theology has been subjected to a series of the strangest misunderstandings from which any intellectual work in our time has had to suffer. There are several reasons for this:

1. During the Hitler period in Germany, the *Church Dogmatics* was only available in two volumes, I/1 and I/2, that is, in the doctrine of the Word of God. The subsequent volumes that appeared prior to 1945—the doctrines of God, predestination, and creation—remained unknown.

2. The known volumes were immediately appropriated for practical use in the struggle of the Confessing Church. Their theoretical content—the relativization of revelation and the Word of

God, accessible only to theoretical reflection—was almost completely lost.

3. The popular impression that emerged from the Confessing Church's use of the *Church Dogmatics* is the impression of Barth that prevailed, especially in the institutional church.

4. Bultmann's praise for the second-edition *Romans* conferred academic drawing-room respectability upon Barth; thereafter, the second-edition *Romans* became the key to interpreting him.

5. Only the Barth of that work became academically respectable. The idealist dialectic between God, world, and man—the greatest common denominator of all modern theology in Germany even to the present day—seemed to find a particularly drastic expression in that book. As a result, it seemed to provide a kind of founding charter for that theology.

6. When the first-edition *Romans* was rejected by Bultmann and others, that in effect meant the banning of social consciousness from modern German theology.

7. In that way the elements in Barth's thought which were disturbing to German idealism were rejected.

8. The second-edition *Romans* was a public success in Germany because of its supposedly antirevolutionary tendency. It was enjoyable as modern theology in an expressionist and existentialist vein with a seemingly antirevolutionary twist. It was the book of the newly democratic Christian bourgeoisie, especially of the younger generation, to which the work was expressly directed.

9. In Germany, Barth's relation to politics has been interpreted in two ways: at worst, as antirepublican decisionism (Marsch and others) or as advancing conservative revolution (Scholder); at best, as socialist revisionism and social democracy. In the first instance, Barth is still considered to be worth something theologically; in the second, he is thought to have been disposed of long ago.

As a pastor, Barth's primary problem (as his unpublished writings show) was not merely the anxiety of preaching. It was not merely the theme of God's Word vs. our talk about God. Rather, it was the problem of belonging to that socially comprehended religious organization, the church.

In a report from January 24, 1916, he poses the following list of questions:

"1. Is ours a worthy calling or must we regard it as an absurdity? 2. Should we continue the church's tradition or break with it? 3. Is the organization of 'religion' either possible or desirable? 4. Is 'religion' itself legitimate or should it be overcome by another relation to God?" He answers with postulates: "Instead of pastors, free bearers of the spirit; instead of tradition, new forms (socialism); instead of organized religion, practical work; instead of religion, experience of God."

He asks about another, "nonreligious" relation to God, but in so doing he is more to the point than Bonhoeffer, for he asks how to overcome religion as organized and transmitted. Unlike Bonhoeffer, he constructs no theory about the development of intellectual history as ending the religious era. Rather, he projects a practical assignment, that of overcoming the past; and he designates the new form that will replace church tradition as "socialism."

Barth's attitude toward religion and socialism can be illustrated by a few practical examples. One time at the synod in Aarau, he made the following motion: Resolved that "as a Christian exercise, the synod's customary worship service is inwardly incompatible with the synod's spirit as an administrative arm of the state. From here on the worship service will be abandoned." The reason for this ideological unmasking: the deception of such worship. "Everything, above all regarding the state, is here taken a hundred times more seriously than God. The synod should come clean on this and draw the consequences. If we can't be genuine prophets, we should at least avoid being false ones." This is apparently the opposite of "revelation positivism"; it is an ideologically critical relation to sermon and worship.

The "free bearers of the spirit," who in Barth's postulate would replace pastors, are neither the "divine men" of Hellenistic gnosticism nor the "religious geniuses" of Schleiermacher. They are, rather, socialists who remain true to the Christian community. That, it seems to me, is where the accent lies in Barth's activity as a pastor. The essential work of his pastorate, besides sermons, talks, and confirmation instruction, consisted chiefly in his union and party activity.

Preserved in his files are outlines of speeches and discussions, often held on a weekly basis, with workers and party members. Barth not only participated in organizing three unions in Safenwil, where he was a pastor, but also in setting up the organizational groundwork throughout the Aargau region.

To this period belong the following documents: reports on the political situation, which continue through the First World War (especially from the decisive year 1917); historical material on the position of European socialist parties on militarism and national defense (about which Barth once taught a seven-week course); research for a critical history of the Bally shoe firm and the Sulzer munitions factory, where many Safenwil workers were employed, and, in particular, where Christian self-understanding had to confront the social conditions dictated by factory owners; a sixty-page exposé, "The Worker Question," which analyzes and comments on material gathered from newspapers, books, and encyclopedias regarding the social, economic, and cultural plight of the European labor force—with special reference to conditions in Safenwil.

As the high point of these materials, Barth unequivocally affirms the class struggle, the strike, and the revolution; he rejects the owners' tactic of bringing in "scabs," or strikebreakers. Several times he attended conventions of the Swiss party as a delegate. At the end of each day he would jot down his impressions: these notes have been preserved. In 1919 he was present at the first international socialist conference after the war, held at Bern. Under the title "Dictatorship or Democracy?" the questions of the party's complicity in the war and of its relation to bolshevism were discussed. Under the same title, Barth's notes repeatedly refer to the same themes. Although, at the end, the Swiss socialists did not join the Third International—a fact that the Swiss religious socialists boast about even today—Barth at any rate did not go along with them. Instead, under the heading "Bolshevism," he reveals a critical but sympathetic stance toward the October revolution.

Between 1913 and 1922 his socialist activity had three primary focal points.

1. Before the war broke out in 1914, Barth worked to radicalize the social consciousness of individual party members. He attacked

several tendencies: the emergence of petit-bourgeois resignation; a socialism of reports and meetings; the egoistic motivation for socialist decision in which personal improvements were sought, but not the comprehensive and radical goal of world revolution. He also stood against an undisciplined and constant complaining about conditions that did not lead to concrete revolutionary activity, against alcohol as a supposed means of salvation (Barth joined the Blue Cross, an abstinence organization, and actively propagandized its cause), and against hatred of the class enemy—as he tried to sharpen the responsibility the revolutionary takes for the bourgeoisie.

In short, prior to the war (1914), Barth exemplified the radicalizing possibilities of moral and ethical indoctrination. He was motivated by what he called "the glowing coal in Marxist dogma," namely, the revolutionary goal of world transformation. In the first-edition *Romans* (1919), he then described this ember as "unfortunately extinguished." Yet it once awakened in him the hope for the "resurrection of a socialist church in a world become socialist."

2. Barth was profoundly disillusioned by the outbreak of the war. Indeed, the reason for this was not merely the bankruptcy of bourgeois liberals, especially in the universities (that is, of Harnack and all Barth's German teachers, including Martin Rade).

> This brings us to Barth's attitude toward historical-critical theology: It was directly related to his disillusionment about that theology's social and political failure. Society and politics were criteria to him for the meaning of historical criticism (as can also be shown in other contexts). The remark from the first-edition *Romans* belongs here: "The historical critics, it seems to me, need to be more critical!" Barth rejected the concept of history current in academic, bourgeois theology (whether idealistic, individualistic, or ontological). Instead, he adopted a dynamic and materialist concept of history—one which saw reality in social and economic terms.

A good example is the analysis of eighteenth century theology in his volume on Protestant thought.[6] Another example, from the second-edition *Romans* is the concept of *Urgeschichte*, which meant not supernatural, but revolutionary history. When academic theology rejected Barth's concept of history and condemned his exegesis and thought as unhistorical, it revealed two things: the extent of its absolute incomprehension, and the extent to which its own bourgeois preoccupations were threatened by the subversive meaning of Barth's concept of transcendence.

Barth and Eduard Thurneysen[7] were disillusioned not only by academic liberalism, but at least as profoundly by empirical social democracy. Barth has left behind him about ten lectures on the theme of "Socialism and War." When the socialist international succumbed to defending the various fatherlands, Barth took it as an unmistakable sign that the glowing coal in Marxist dogma had gone out. Science, socialism, and Christianity—the three great "spiritual powers" of Europe—were all part of the same total failure, and the hour was ready for a completely new beginning.

3. This disillusionment led to Barth's ultimate radicalization as a socialist, which between 1917 and 1919 brought him into conflict with Leninism. That was the third phase of his early relation to socialism, and it remained definitive. In the first-edition *Romans*, the exegesis of Romans 13 was implicitly and explicitly a debate with the Lenin of *State and Revolution*. In November 1918, at roughly the same time as the Swiss and German revolutions, Barth was exegeting Romans 13. Lenin's pamphlet had just appeared in translation, and Barth responded to it in his commentary.

In rejecting every metaphysics of the state, Barth stands in agreement with Engels and Lenin. Despite the words "from God" in Rom. 13:1, he describes the state as a "highly fortuitous setup," and refuses, with Lenin, to grant it a "transcendent status as the highest immanent order": "Thou shalt refuse it the elevation, seriousness, and importance of the divine." "We fight it fundamentally, radically." The "present state" is "not to be improved, but to be *replaced;* the forces of injustice above and below, overcome" by the forces of justice. He always refers to the concrete state of the present—not the state in general, but the state of bourgeois society. Even as a "state of laws" it is an agent of evil—"organized and systematic coercion by one class against another, one part of the populace against another." It will not wither away but must be overcome.

Barth describes himself as "more than Leninist," because he rejects Lenin's notion of the dictatorship of the proletariat. Instead, he adopts the anarchist position attacked by Lenin in *State and Revolution*, that is, the position of "left-wing socialism," which Lenin was later to call "a childhood disease." Barth did not reject the dictatorship of the proletariat because of the violence that necessarily went with it—of a Christian rejection of violence he at that time could only have spoken ironically—but because Lenin was insufficiently radical and wanted merely to replace the state with the state.

Lenin's revolutionary tactics wanted "to deal with people as they are at the moment"—hence the dictatorship of the proletariat. Typically anarchist and consistent was Barth's counterproject: the new man, here and now, whose possibility Barth did not doubt for a moment. This new man became the object of Barth's thinking and acting. The radicalization of the individual[8] should serve the radicalization of the group to which the individual belongs. It should serve to create the objective conditions for a radical, total revolution. It should work toward a situation in which the state is no longer necessary, a situation that can come into being—under the liberated conditions of the revolutionary goal—even during the course of the struggle.

If the socialist proletariat fails in this task, then among others the Christian community must learn to exist as "the agent of the new" and so as the "agent of society." This was where Barth's ecclesiology had its origin. In the thought and life of this "more than Leninist" anarchist party-comrade, who at the same time was the pastor from Safenwil, the Christian community became the agent of revolution.

I am not concerned to debate with Marsch and others whether this concept of a revolutionary agent was an illusion or not. Personally, I do not believe that it was, but that in the future even among us, as is already true at many other points on the earth today, it will be the only vital form of the empirical Christian community. My only concern here is to sketch Barth's anarcho-socialist profile. That profile permanently determined his open relation to the Soviet Union —a relation that was generally positive, while tempered by a definite anarchist negation. (In his files there is an as yet undeciphered report on Kropotkin!)

It is important to point out that Barth's later so-called doctrine of the state in no way attempts to justify the state and that if so interpreted, it is falsely understood. Take, for example, his 1946 essay "The Christian Community and the Civil Community."[9] There he viewed the civil community entirely from the standpoint of the Christian community. The problem was to set up a relation between Christians and the state at all. After *Romans* and the Nazi period, Barth found this extremely difficult. At any rate, this "justification" really relativized the state by setting it in relation to the community and to its own eschatological negation.

Apart from its anarchist starting point, Barth's entire contribution to ethics, including his ethics of marriage, cannot be understood at all. It is not for nothing that his theology is a theology of freedom. As such, it cannot go along with that seesaw called "freedom and civil obligation," whether conceived in bourgeois-Hegelian or Marxist-Leninist terms. By "true freedom," rather, his theology means the onset of absolute freedom under the conditions of the here and now. It means the realization, instead of the endless promise, of freedom.

Nor can Barth's commentary on Romans 13 in the second-edition *Romans* be understood apart from his radical-socialist background. The content of that commentary is the "censure of the red brother." Up to now, if this political content was even recognized or seen as interesting, it was explained in one of two ways: (1) as an antirevolutionary turn, a transition away from Lenin to Dostoevsky, Nietzsche, and Kierkegaard—from revolution to literature; or (2) as the basis for a transition to socialist revisionism. Nothing could be falser than that!

The correct view is that in 1922 Barth apparently wanted to give a chance to the Weimar Republic, which had meanwhile come to power (in other words, just the opposite of what Scholder attributes to him, that he was among those who wanted it to fail). The correct view is that he now urged cooperation, short-term "remedies" and "small steps." The correct view is also that—he did not expect otherwise—the bolshevist revolution of 1922 led no farther than the counterrevolution of the White Guard. The experiences in Russia— the nonchoice between revolutionary and counterrevolutionary— contributed directly to the context of *Romans* in its second edition.

It would be an error, however, if Barth's cooperation with social democracy were taken as his fundamental position. It was purely tactical. Its point was subversion. It had no other purpose than to exploit the given circumstances for its own unbroken theological-socialist goals. He censured "the red brother"—not to negate him, but to fight against the revolutionary "hot air," "pathos," "bullhead-edness," and "metaphysics" which at that time promised more than could be delivered. To him that was a completely typical sign of persons not yet liberated.

After 1919 Barth fought as he had prior to 1914 for the radicalism of real revolutionaries, against the unradical way of making a revolution that would only replace one establishment with another. Indeed, it is precisely in the second-edition *Romans* that one reads that the existing order, the Establishment as such, is evil—even the existing order of a still pseudo-revolutionary establishment. Empirically, this is no longer a party viewpoint, whether Social Democratic or Independent Socialist or Communist. On the other hand, Barth could not content himself with anarchistic individualism. So once again he places the Christian community in the radical-socialist role, even up to the demand—which may be read in the first-edition *Romans*—that the community, if need be, participate in street fighting from the barricades.

Barth's support for social democracy after 1919 remained revolutionary, but he could not see the bolshevist revolution as yet a genuine one. From this assessment of the political situation, he drew theological consequences. He joined the "more than Leninist" revolution to its theological complement—the religious-socialist idea of the "revolution of God."

It would, however, be methodologically false to locate the origin of Barth's theology in this neat configuration. For Barth, "God's revolution" was no mere stopgap for the failures of the bolshevist revolution as it ossified into an establishment.

I cannot here undertake a discussion of the intellectual sources from which Barth's theology comes. Kant, Hegel, Marburg theology, Harnack's historical criticism, the Blumhardts, and Kutter all belong to his lineage. What they contribute, however, is no more than the elements. The real origin of Barth's theology was his theological existence in Safenwil. As such, that existence was socialist praxis. In the over five hundred sermons that remain from the Safenwil period, Barth worked out the unity between his faith and his deeds. These documents are the genesis of his theology.

III. *Barth turned to theology in order to seek the organic connection between the Bible and the newspaper, the new world and the collapsing bourgeois order.*

Here I will only call attention to a few facts. Barth first began really to formulate his ideas as he encountered the proletarian situation directly. He first experienced this situation as a vicar in Geneva and a pastor in Safenwil. His theology originated as he conceptualized from this experience.

> It is part of the "pre-Barthian" heritage of liberalism that Barth first grounds his theology in experience instead of in revelation. That he did this consciously can be seen in a statement from 1914: "Experience, praxis, or whatever one wants to call it, is obviously the source of all religious utterances." Apart from the fact that it was actually formulated by Barth, this sentence is interesting, because it equates the religious concept "experience" with the left-Hegelian and Marxist concept "praxis." Barth's previously cited postulate, "instead of religion, an experience of God," is thus to be understood: praxis as the overcoming of religion. What kind of praxis is at stake here cannot, in view of the above, be in doubt. We will, however, theoretically explicate the fact that Barth's theology arises from social action. Barth often reflected on the theory-praxis relation.

Kutter's religious-socialist outlook included a religious interpretation of the proletarian situation—a situation which he both deplored and idealized. Some essential components of religious-socialism were: 1. The proletariat was in such desperate straits that remedies could no longer help, but only the overthrow of all relationships—thus revolution. 2. "God's revolution" was a concept formed to threaten the bourgeoisie and to make them notice the proletarian situation. 3. The concepts "mammon" and "mammonism" did not designate individual cases of moral corruption, but rather the dominant and oppressive capitalist system. 4. The religious socialists used Biblical ideas and images to analyze society in a way that today seems pre-scientific. Kerygmatically, however, this method served to communicate the proletarian situation to bourgeois society.

To the extent that Barth drew upon religious socialism, he sharpened the issues through a twofold distinction: First, he did not explicate the proletarian situation from the outside, and hence he did not interpret it religiously. Instead, he established solidarity; indeed, he identified himself with the proletariat in a very definite way, as we shall see. For him it was not a matter of interpretation but of transformation. Second, he did not use isolated religious views and concepts when he did theology. Rather, he focused on Biblical passages in their *whole* contexts in order to bring together the Bible as a whole with society as a whole in its contemporary details. In Safenwil the proletariat was the material of Scriptural exegesis.

This brings us to Barth's understanding of the relation between exegesis and society. As Barth experienced and asserted more than once, contemporary conditions create new exegetical situations. As Thurneysen put it: Though he and Barth already knew the Bible, August 1914 and November 1918 were moments in their discovery of the Bible.

1. "It happened as something basically very simple: The Bible struck us in a completely new way. It was already familiar to us, but we read it through certain filters and interpretations. When the theology and the world view which created those filters were shaken, the interpretations began to fall apart."

What he means is:

a. Treating the Bible as a "world of literature," that is, as a superstructure and a function of ideology instead of as a basic phenomenon.

b. Supporting exegesis through those socially determined "opinions" that were already at hand—whether "bourgeois or religious socialist, critical or conservative."

2. Instead of that, the discovery of the Bible was "completely dominated by an interest in the concrete situation in which with all of our contemporaries we found ourselves enmeshed." The discovery arose through an awakening of political interest.

3. Barth on November 11, 1918: "How is one now to create abundantly, to interpret, to illuminate, to find and open up paths —and how meagerly flow the little brooks of knowledge. . . ." "If only we had turned to the Bible sooner, we would now have firm ground under our feet! One broods by turns on the newspaper and the New Testament and sees very little of the organic connection between both worlds to which one should now be able to give a clear and powerful witness." (The origin of the two-natures doctrine: Bible and newspaper!)

4. In 1948 on Hungary, Barth expressed some quite parallel sentiments: If "political relationships change, then Christians will simply take that as an occasion to read the Bible anew. . . ." "And quite certainly this: a new understanding of Scripture . . . is the community's decisive participation in the change of the political order." The concrete consequences of political change: an occasion for the church to revise the basis of its actions, a summons to new concentration, an "exercise of new witness." The background: Just as in 1914–1918 so in Hungary, the church failed in the prophetic role to which it was undoubtedly called and equipped. It proved itself "incapable of understanding, illuminating, and interpreting the political situation." (Hence it was incapable of doing theology of history [*Geschichtstheologie*]—not only retrospectively through "a prophetic assessment of previous events," but also prospectively through "a prophetic assessment of the consequences of such a change.")

Behind this relationship between exegesis and society, which cannot here be analyzed further, a systematic principle exists which Barth had already formulated at Marburg: "We strive energetically to express the inexhaustible powers of the Christian religion in the directions that are particularly important to us." This is the systematic principle typical of Marburg and Wilhelm Herrmann: *tua res agitur* ["the subject matter concerns you"]. "To us, religion is experience as grasped strictly individually."

Even during his liberal period, however, Barth places a completely different construction on this principle. The duty to which he sees himself obligated as a liberal theologian is this: By starting from experience as grasped strictly individually, "we interact clearly and positively with the theoretical side of human cultural consciousness." A few years later Barth's concern then shifts from the subjective to the objective side of human culture—to the "culture of objective social values." His concern shifts, that is, from consciousness to society.

Bultmann and Barth both started out from liberal premises. However, whereas Bultmann interpreted Scripture in terms of individual existence and its ontological structure (being and time), Barth did so in terms of historical existence and its social structure (man in society, the social history of the human species). Barth thus moved in a completely different direction—from Marburg to Feuerbach and Marx, from liberalism to socialism instead of to existentialism. Barth and Bultmann hold differing views of historical criticism, because they hold differing views of history and reality.

In Barth's view, historical criticism of Scripture focuses on the difference between the times; yet it must treat that difference in prospect as well as in retrospect. It must direct itself not only to the historical problem but also to the problem of social criticism. Barth can place himself on the same plane with Paul, because the historical-*critical* difference that binds him to Paul is of far greater importance than the merely *historical* difference that separates him from Paul.

As gauged from the future, we find ourselves with the Bible in the *same* time and the same struggle for a new world—a world which the Bible promises and which we postulate from present reality as something most urgently desired. Exegesis has to take both differences—retrospective and prospective—into account. Under the primary impulse of the future, however, the structure of exegesis is formed not by faith and existential understanding, but by love, hope, and the salvation of all men (the human species).

As an example of social exegesis, Barth's commentary on Romans 13 in both editions of *Romans* has already been mentioned. The "substance" of that commentary is Lenin and the bolshevist revolution. Another important example is Barth's exegesis of Rom. 8:9–15 [*sic*][10]—the text of the anxious straining of the creation, which waits for the revelation of the sons of God. This apocalyptic text was already standard material in the writings of the two Blumhardts: The elder Blumhardt applied it to the straining of those enslaved body and soul by sickness and sin; the younger then transferred it to the straining of the oppressed proletariat for freedom. In this form it made an impact on religious socialism and eventually on Barth, who could use it in the latter sense.

For, as religious socialism had done, Barth directly connected the Bible's apocalyptic-eschatological proclamation with the situation of the contemporary proletariat. Indeed, the reverse was true: The atrocious situation of the proletariat interpreted the real content of the Biblical-apocalyptic eschatology. It was an exegetical fact. It filled the apocalyptic forms with content. In Barth's Safenwil sermons and Thurneysen's Leutwil sermons, Biblical eschatology and the proletariat were mutually and really present to each other. Barth grasped this basically religious-socialist thesis with particular precision.

For Barth, the straining and waiting, the orientation of the proletariat toward the future, was not merely a negative concept. It was not merely an abstract "non-being" or "not-yet-being." The burning issue of this situation, rather, was the radical need for transformation. The will to transformation was a positive factor which, under the pressure of negation, persisted and grew. This situation was only understood by one who saw glowing in it the Marxist dogma of revolution, and freedom welling up to an explosion.

Translated into theological language, this view of eschatology and society meant that Barth did not understand the proletariat in terms of an abstract *Heilsgeschichte* in the Old Testament sense. He did not view the situation merely "toward God." The proletarians were not merely the people who walk in darkness; rather, they were the people who in darkness have seen a great light. The theological basis for this interpretation is the movement of the Holy Spirit, which has already descended on the world, and the dynamite of the resurrection, which has already exploded all frontiers and negations. The power of the resurrection was the deepest actual ground of political unrest.

Like Bultmann, Barth cited Augustine's *cor inquietum:* "Our hearts are restless until they rest in Thee." But even in the context of Augustine's life, the ground of this unrest was not merely mystical, neoplatonic, and purely individualistic. From an ideologically critical standpoint, the conditions of the *civitas terrena* in his own day certainly played a role. Barth interpreted this ground of unrest wholly in social terms: The proletariat was not only the occasion, but also the subject of the call to freedom, which was the concern of Barth's theology. Theology did not build upon general human phenomena, as for Bultmann, but upon limited and concrete social situations.

A second highlight in Barth's understanding of apocalyptic is this: The suffering creature waits for the revelation of the sons of God—in other words, for us. Here Sartre's philosophy of the prospective is anticipated. The whole proletarian situation holds us first and foremost in prospect. We stand beside the proletariat: They are the first to be hit by the misery of capitalism, and we are the first to enter into solidarity with them. This unity does not arise from romantic, arbitrary preferences, but from the objective situation as it ferments toward the future. The young Barth retrieves the concept of solidarity from the language of the socialist struggle and makes it into a standing concept of his theology. "Solidarity" designates the identity of social situations between the proletariat and "us."

In that "we pastors" belong to the proletariat as the first to share in their situation, we are motivated not by eros and agape, nor by *diakonia* and "home missions," but rather by the objective conditions. Our straining and waiting toward that which we label by the ominous word "God" is the inner side whose outer side is proletarian unrest. Our waiting for God between the times has the same objectivity as the unrest of the revolutionary proletariat. The concept of solidarity provides the common context of reality—a socially determined reality—which unites the proletariat and Barth's developing theology, "comrade" Barth and "brother" Barth. As one can show from all periods of his work right up to the last month before his death, Barth was conscious of this context and of the peculiar character of his concept of religion.

It is a fairy tale and a superstition, created by Harnack and therefore believed even to the present day, that Barth was a Marcionite, a schismatic, or the like. The opposite is true. Barth's recovery of the two-natures doctrine in his Christology is an objective theological expression for the experience of socialist-Christian solidarity. It forms the organic connection between the Bible and the newspaper, and it generates the two-edged sentence that in Barth's socialist writings occurs again and again: "A true Christian must be a socialist; a true socialist should be a Christian."

IV. *The substance of Barth's turn to theology was the construction of a concept of "God."*

The idea of a "turn" is correct, both biographically and materially. Barth was not always a theologian, nor at the outset did he intend to be one. He became a theologian in about 1916 in the process of his work on Romans. Prior to that he reflected theologically on his activity, but he did not yet construct a theology on the basis of it, in other words, he did not seek the concept of his praxis.

In general that is how Barth constructed his theology. This is indicated, for example, by Harnack's critique, which today is everywhere warmed over, that Barth confused the lectern with the pulpit. It is also instructive to take into account the opposite charge, made by Kutter, Ragaz, and Menniken, that Barth fled from activism to dead theology, from the "reality" of God to the mere "Word" of God.

Barth was seeking the primary concept of theology, the concept of God. As mentioned above, however, he understood "concept" in the Hegelian sense—not as a positive, technical definition, but as the intellectual ground of open-ended experience, a ground that as such opens up new experience. In his concept of God, Barth did not abandon the dialectic between theory and praxis—he explicated it.

1. The foundation of this God-concept was, above all, the experience of transcendence that Barth gained and depicted in solidarity with the workers. His "God" did in fact bear the marks of transcendence, but not the transcendence of Plato or Marcion, nor that of an ideal concept or of an ideology of revolution. It was, rather, the transcendence of the real revolutionary situation where human beings were oppressed by the class-structure of capitalist society. If "God" were not grasped in relation to this social reality, then nothing of "God" was grasped at all.

2. Social experience determined Barth's theology so strongly that his "logic of God" was developed from a critically conceived "logic of (bourgeois) society." In the context of the experience of transcen-

dence, his concept of God as the "Wholly Other" did not directly refer to God's ontology as something beyond and aloof. Rather, it set God in connection with the Wholly Other of the new man, the new world, and the new age—in other words, with the contents of revolution.

The logic of social reality prescribed the significance of the "Wholly Other" in a further sense. Society, Barth wrote, though "full of cracks on the inside, is from the outside a reality contained in itself—without any opening to the kingdom of heaven." "Society is now dominated by its own logos" whose content is society as a whole.

In this society one experiences himself "as up against the totality of being and happening, as up against something alien: as suffering, as succumbing, as asking and receiving no answer, as protesting and rebelling without power, totally incapable of doing anything but crying out—or falling into silence." All this, moreover, is socially concrete: "in the insanity of our cities, and the obtuseness of our villages, in the banal violence of our most primitive drives and in the ideological naïveté of our knowledge and conscience, in the pointlessness of the circulation of world history."

This alienated social totality corresponds negatively to Barth's concept of the divine "as something whole and closed in itself—a kind of new, different reality vis-à-vis the world." The totality of God is defined here as the reverse image of the social totality; the "logic of God" becomes the reverse image of the "logic of society."

An ideological critique of this concept of God would be irrelevant, because the concept of God here is consciously constructed as the reverse image of society. How can a truly theological concept arise from a merely ideological one? It can arise through the function which "God" as the contrary of society has with respect to society. His totality, unity, and otherness vis-à-vis the world have a twofold sense. First, a God described in this way "cannot be instructed, tacked on, or accommodated . . ." There is no *aggiornamento* (assimilation) with society, no adjustable theology—it is thus a theology of revolution. Second, the God who is not to be accommodated wants "to overthrow and set right." That is the meaning of the concept of the Wholly Other. The "logic of God" overthrows the "logic of society"—this society as a present reality, not society in general. Even God's logic is a social logic, but that of another society, one not yet attained, not even in the Soviet Union.

3. In the same context, but in another place, Barth lays a new foundation for the tradition of God's absoluteness. He grounds this tradition in terms of a particular human experience—the experience of the person who loses himself in the culture of objective social values, but who also proceeds to receive the only meaningful assignment of his life. ("Faith in a Personal God," 1914.)[11]

4. The same material connection between God and society can be found once again in a striking observation, with which I conclude my report:

What in 1914, under the influence of liberal theology, is called God's "personality" later becomes, in the *Church Dogmatics*, God's "love" and God's "freedom"—in other words, the "concept" of God as he "who loves in freedom."

In Barth's early thought, however, the concept of "love in freedom" appeared as the "idea of a totality of good activity." Love in freedom was the guiding idea of his ethics, the "concept of the ethical object." It answered the question, "What are we to do?" It was the goal of human action, which Barth could also describe as the "image of the thousand-year kingdom." (He allowed a measure of chiliasm in his ethics, but not an abstract *Heilsgeschichte.*)

He thought of love in freedom "in this sense: as a task, not an object of desire; as a goal, not a termination of moral struggle; as that which enthusiast, idealist, communist, anarchist, and (despite all genuinely Lutheran teaching)—note it well—even Christian hope envisions as a reality here on earth: freedom in love and love in freedom as the pure and direct motive of social action, with a community constituted in justice as its direct objective."

Barth's concept of God, in other words, elaborates the ethical and social goal of human action. Its visible content is "putting an end to tutelage, or, rather, to the exploitation and oppression of man by man, putting an end to class differences and to national boundaries, to war, to coercion and violence in general. It means a culture of the spirit instead of a culture of things, humanization instead of reification, brotherhood instead of universal hostility." This is a programmatic socialist goal as the content of a Christian-chiliastic ethics. It is also the content of what, for Barth, "God" is—not what God "means," but what he "does" and "wants" and therefore "is."

In the *Church Dogmatics*, Barth speaks of "God" (again operating with the concept of totality) as the one who is "all in all" and who as such concerns the "totality" of human existence. God is "the fact that not only newly illuminates, but also really transforms reality." That is Marx's eleventh thesis on Feuerbach applied to the concept of God: God is not a basis for interpreting the world, but the fact which really transforms it. Hence the concepts of reality and of facts are aligned with the *empirical* content of Barth's concept of God.

My thesis is this: The *Church Dogmatics* subjects the dogmatic tradition of Christianity to the canon of a socially reflected concept of God. Those who think that it establishes a theological ontology of transcendence are wrong. Those who see that it is essentially political even in its theological details are correct.

This interpretation agrees with the 1932 foreword in which Barth justifies "undertaking a dogmatics at the present time": "I am firmly convinced that we cannot reach the clarifications, especially in the broad field of politics, which are necessary today and to which theology today might have a word to say (as indeed it ought to have a word to say to them!), without having previously reached those comprehensive clarifications, in theology and about theology itself, with which we should be concerned here."[12]

In other words, just as in 1914–1918 Barth saw his discovery of the Bible, so in 1932 he saw the task of dogmatics as thoroughly situated in a social and political context. Indeed, dogmatics was not merely the foundation for an ethics derived from it only subsequently. Like the Bible, dogmatics itself is to be read politically, however it may appear in detail. "For I actually believe," Barth continues, "that a better church dogmatics (even apart from all ethical utility) might actually make a more important and weightier contribution even to questions and tasks such as German liberation, than most of the well-intentioned material which so many, even among theologians, think they can and should produce when they dilettantishly take up such questions and tasks."[13]

In other words, political prognosis directs Barth's dogmatics. Why that can be so, can only be known when one discovers the socialism in the theology of Karl Barth.

AFTERWORD *(Special to the American translation)*

Written to get discussion rolling, this paper was drafted in 1968 for a conference of Protestant campus ministers in Germany. The apodictic form was chosen in order to provoke thought and disagreement and in that way to highlight the background of Barth's theology, which had previously been considered too little or not at all. For too long Barth had been regarded as a theologian without a history and as the patriarch of a neo-orthodoxy that severed all ties to culture and society. His political texts were taken as *parerga* ["side issues"] having no relation to his Scripture exegesis and his dogmatics.

The latter view is false; it has been surpassed by historical facts, some of which are presented in my paper. The meaning of these facts will be debated for a long time to come, certainly also in America. Eventually, many of the more provocative conclusions in my paper may come to be modified or set aside. The facts themselves, however, will not simply vanish.

The editor of this book has seen fit to present American readers with the more provocative, less scholarly form of my thesis about how theology and socialism are connected in Karl Barth. I am thankful that after six years I have been given an opportunity to make a few additional remarks.

During those years I have been steadily pursuing further the questions raised in my paper. Through this subsequent work, particular problems have been differentiated and, above all, elaborated. At the same time, however, the basic question about the impact of sociopolitical praxis on the development of Karl Barth's theology has only been made more precise, not pushed to absurd limits. In my book *Theologie und Sozialismus: Das Beispiel Karl Barths,* I have issued an initial and comprehensive presentation of the problem. Some of the essays collected in the volume at hand are critical reactions to my book, others carry the discussion further. In particular, Gollwitzer's essay below may be seen in the closest relationship to a splendid article by Paul Lehmann entitled "Karl Barth, Theologian of Permanent Revolution" (*Union Seminary Quarterly Review* 28 [1972–1973], pp. 67–81). Here an intellectual kinship in understanding Barth already exists, a community of work in the interpretation of Barth which stretches across the ocean. At this I can only rejoice.

Since the completion of my book, my work has proceeded in two basic directions:

1. The remarkable fact had to be explained that only a few weeks after assuming his pastorate in Safenwil, Karl Barth also began extensive activity as a socialist speaker. This activity persisted during the entire period from 1911 to 1919. The question is this: What were the inward intellectual conditions which made it possible for Barth to view public political engagement as a meaningful and even necessary part of his preaching and pastoral activity? What basic theological factors could have motivated him as a pastor to undertake concrete political efforts?

This question led me back from the Karl Barth of Safenwil to the Karl Barth of Geneva and to his publications between 1909 and 1911. Previously, they had seldom been examined in terms of their practical political significance. In fact, however, they contain "the conditions for the possibility" that practical political activity could have repercussions upon Barth's theology. For in Geneva, Barth created a scientific-theoretical, religious-philosophical framework which overcame the old Kantian-Schleiermacherian opposition between "religion" and "science"—the "two kingdoms" theory of German idealism. This framework was to govern his entire theological work to come. In the Geneva publications, "religion" was set in a theoretically clear relationship to the "cultural consciousness" of bourgeois society. Religion does not fit in with the normative processes of this culture as they were understood after Kant—logic, ethics and aesthetics. Neither does it enter into competition with them, nor yet does it separate itself from them. It "actualizes" them. Theology has not only a task with regard to the church but also a "task with regard to humanity." Namely, theology establishes the "connection to reality" that scientific consciousness with its abstractions from reality is not capable of establishing. Our forms of consciousness are determined by the conditions in bourgeois society under which our sensibility, our understanding, and our actions are developed. These forms have devolved into norms and abstractions. They no longer grasp the connection to concrete particulars, to manifold, spontaneous, and free life, to "reality." Here religion can help. It can do so, but not by setting up a new world of its own of anarchistic lawlessness and freedom. God is "not a second reality" that can be conceived as "separate from what is presumably real here and now," as even the later Barth could still say (CD IV/3, 489 rev.).[14] Religion can help, rather, "in a regulative fashion." From the "boundary" of the unconditioned realm in which freedom operates, religion can grasp the totality of reality quite differently than can the individual sciences in the lack of consciousness characteristic of their division of labor. Religion can do this because, into the stagnating society which exhausts itself in mechanical or dialectical norms, religion can bring modes of orientation, goals, a *focus imaginarius*, which Kant deemed both possible and desirable. At the same time, religion does not destroy the "limitations of humanity"; it enters into these limitations, and within them it discloses to humanity goals and modes of orientation which the normative processes and social necessities of culture would never reach. Religion with its eschatological vigor can help society to achieve vitality and social-scientific consciousness to establish "a connection to reality."

To the Barth of Geneva, however, this function does not mean that religion merely sets up utopian and imaginary goals for society. Religion sets to work, rather, within the processes of the present. It mobilizes, as Barth says in Geneva, the "agents of culture." These are the religious individuals in whom is being realized the entire regulative contribution of religion to culture. That is to say: Religion is "immediate self-consciousness." It liberates the individual from the determinative forces of society and the laws of scientific consciousness. It is effective only in individuals, where "in-dividuals" means those who are undivided, that is, who are liberated from the psychological, social, and logical consequences of the division of labor in society and who actually live concretely and historically, unfettered by abstract norms. As Barth put it in Geneva: "Faith and historicity of culture become synonyms."

The fact that only individuals could be "agents of culture," however, did not sanction for Barth a liberal "religious individualism." In Geneva, Barth had already abandoned that piece of bourgeois tradition called "religious individualism," thereby paving the way for his socialist decision in Safenwil. Precisely those who believe are those who know what persons stamped by bourgeois and scientific consciousness notoriously do not know: that they live and "are being lived." Those who know this exalt their individuality to the "transindividual" plane and then experience, in reverse, that transindividual life takes root in their individuality. "None of us lives to himself, and none of us dies to himself" (Rom. 14:7). However, Barth defines the "transindividual" plane strictly "within the limits of humanity," not as the concern of individual persons, but as the concern of all persons, as a "social fact." Those who believe "receive" and "transmit," i.e., they lead their lives in a social context, and the *"unde* and *quo"* (source and goal) of all their life activities "is human society, human beings." The essence of faith is its active and passive activity in a transindividual social context. Moreover, the social process is the context of tradition in which alone we receive Jesus and the kingdom of God. The God who is "Wholly Other" encounters us only through the medium of transindividual society. Through the passive and active activity of those who believe, religion is enabled to regulate the normative consciousness of culture and to place it in "connection to reality."

From this theory of science and culture in Geneva, it is only a short and logical step to the Safenwil praxis of a socialist pastor and theologian. In Barth, therefore, theology and socialism are not merely accidentally and biographically connected; nor, on the other hand, can the relation be determined, in a vulgar Marxist sense, as a simple reflection of praxis within theology. Rather, the relation is determined in fundamental and theoretical terms. The middle term between Karl Barth's theology and his socialism, his sermon and his politics, is a clear scientific-theoretical conception of the connection between religion and cultural consciousness. It confers a necessity upon this conception which belongs to the essence of Barth's theology and without which one cannot understand that theology in Barth's sense.

2. In the discussion of my thesis, it has been very much contested whether "socialism" remained an ongoing motif in the political criterion of Barth's theology or whether his socialism was confined to his early period. H. Gollwitzer's essay [reprinted in this volume] has contributed further material regarding the meaning and persistence of socialist elements in Barth's development. Meanwhile, I myself have investigated Barth's *political* motivations in relation to his stance during the German church struggle of the 1930's ("Theologische und politische Motivationen Karl Barths im Kirchenkampf," *Junge Kirche*, May 1973, pp. 283–303). My study shows that in contrast to the German theologians of the Confessing Church, Barth's motivations in the fight against the Hitler regime were by no means only ecclesiastical and theological. He constantly argued from the standpoint of a comprehensive political resistance, which brought him into deep conflict with his German brethren. This conflict was made all the more difficult, however, by the fact that Barth employed Marxist modes of argumentation to evaluate fascism as the necessary and final stage of bourgeois-liberal society, which, to the pastors of the Confessing Church, often German-nationalist in orientation, must have seemed especially strange.

It must have seemed equally strange when Barth participated very actively in the Moscow-led "National Committee for a Free Germany," an instrument of communist popular-front politics, on which a detailed article has now appeared in East Germany (Heinrich Fink, "Karl Barth und die 'Bewegung Freies Deutschland,' " *Standpunkte* 2 [1974], Beilage zu Heft 9, pp. 28–30). That Barth in this regard was thoroughly conversant with the economic categories of Marxism is shown by the little example of his reply from the year 1912 [reprinted in this volume] to the Safenwil entrepreneur W. Hüssy, who had protested in the name of his economic interests against Barth's lecture "Jesus Christ and the Movement for Social Justice." More materials on this aspect of socialism will appear when the remainder of Barth's early writings are published.

I am well aware that to many theologians in Anglo-Saxon countries, socialism and Marxism as themes of Christian theology will seem like an old European perversion. In their countries, the Marxist traditions are not so deeply rooted as on the European continent.

Also lacking is the broad intellectual-historical background which Marxism possesses in the philosophy of German idealism. In contrast to the continent, even the student revolution did not lead to a Marxist renaissance in the United States, whereas in German social philosophy, there ensued a renaissance of both Hegel and idealism. In the great essay on Hegel in his history of Protestant theology, Barth foresaw this (p. 417) with the observation that theology "certainly has no occasion to assume an attitude of alarm and hostility to any renaissance of Hegel which might come about," for Hegel is "a great problem and a great disappointment, but perhaps also a great promise" (p. 421). Barth himself was deeply rooted in the world of idealism, and his socialism thus stands in an intellectual-historical context.

In conclusion, then, it may be important to point out that the theme "theology and socialism in Karl Barth"—however much it may be influenced by the student movement and the renaissance of Hegel and idealism—does not arise in Europe out of historical and aesthetic diversion. In Europe as in America there are students and friends of Karl Barth who are deeply involved in the class struggles of their society and for whom the question of how to understand Barth's theology is of vital and practical significance. It is of both scholarly and political interest to rescue Karl Barth from the clutches of conservative or liberal social forces which misuse his theology as an apolitical legitimation for existing relationships or for the glossing over of real political conflicts through a cheap reconciliation. The World Council of Churches in Geneva can attest especially of the German churches, which today once again like to place themselves in the light of Barthian theology, how great an antiprogressive potential their abstract theological consciousness represents for the churches in the world. It is thus also of ecumenical interest to retrieve Barth from the twilight into which he has fallen together with such churches. And finally, the working class and the proletariat of all parts of the world are distinguished from the Western bourgeoisie by the fact that they simply cannot turn their backs on the great traditions of humanity. Where the bourgeois class in the profusion of even its intellectual wealth can without serious reservations declare that God is dead, where it can "demythologize" and rationalize the Biblical traditions to make them suitable for bourgeois self-consciousness, where it simply emasculates and abandons dogma and dogmatics, at such points there lives in Barth as in the poor of this earth, who indeed cry out not only for bread, but also for spirit, a knowledge of the indispensability of every particular historical moment of truth. Precisely in the most alienating features of dogma, Karl Barth himself saw the most far-reaching promises for us persons. In that way as a theologian he was completely unbourgeois. He did not clear difficulties away; he broke them open. Precisely that is the hermeneutic of the poor. They do not disrupt, neither do they despise. They knock to see whether it will be opened to them and whether there is something there "for the present day." And if not, they simply wait.

Friedrich-Wilhelm Marquardt

November 14, 1974

NOTES

1. EDITOR's NOTE: See below, pp. 116 f., note 10.

2. EDITOR's NOTE: In 1928, Günter Dehn, the pastor of a church in a working-class district of Berlin, gave a lecture entitled "The Church and the Reconciliation of Nations" ("Kirche und Völkerversöhnung," *Christliche Welt* 45 [1931], 194–204). In this lecture Dehn spoke out on Biblical grounds against the glorification of militarism and war. After a year of controversy and attacks by the right-wing press, he was censured by the ecclesiastical hierarchy on trumped-up charges. Two years after the lecture, Dehn received a call to a chair in practical theology at the University of Heidelberg. When a theology professor revived the earlier controversy, the call was withdrawn.

Dehn then received a similar call from the University of Halle, where several even more radical candidates for the position had already been rejected. When Dehn began his lectures, the hall was filled with hundreds of right-wing students who disrupted him and made it impossible to proceed. Dehn had to be provided with a police escort by the university.

Barth, whom Dehn had referred to in his 1928 lecture and who was a friend of Dehn's, first tried to arouse academic support for him, but then entered the fray with the article cited here by Marquardt after Dehn was attacked in the press by theology professors E. Hirsch and H. Dörries. This division among the ranks of the theologians marked one of the opening rounds in the church struggle. See E. Bizer, "Der 'Fall Dehn,' " in *Festschrift für Günter Dehn,* ed. by W. Schneemelcher (Neukirchen, 1957), pp. 239–261.

3. Karl Barth, *Eine Schweizer Stimme 1938–1945* (Zurich: Evangelischer Verlag, 1945).

4. EDITOR'S NOTE: For further documentation, see Friedrich-Wilhelm Marquardt, *Theologie und Sozialismus: Das Beispiel Karl Barths* (Munich: Chr. Kaiser Verlag, 1972), pp. 50 ff.

5. Karl Barth, "The Word of God and the Task of the Ministry," in *The Word of God and the Word of Man,* tr. by Douglas Horton (Harper & Brothers, 1957), pp. 183–217.

6. Karl Barth, *Protestant Theology in the Nineteenth Century* (Judson Press, 1973).

7. Thurneysen figures prominently here and could almost always be mentioned as well; these matters at least have the benefit of two witnesses!

8. He speaks of the individual, not the "individualist." Exactly like Lenin, he warns against individualism prior to revolutionary outbreaks, and criticizes it as a squandering of revolutionary energy and a defusing of the objective revolutionary situation.

9. Barth, "The Christian Community and the Civil Community," in Karl Barth, *Community, State, and Church: Three Essays,* ed. by Will Herberg (Doubleday & Company, Inc., 1960), pp. 149–189.

10. EDITOR'S NOTE: Marquardt is apparently thinking of Rom. 8:18 ff.

11. Karl Barth, "Der Glaube an den persönlichen Gott," *Zeitschrift für Theologie und Kirche* 24 (1914), pp. 65–95.

12. Karl Barth, Foreword, *Church Dogmatics,* Vol. I/Part 1 (Charles Scribner's Sons, 1936), p. xiii.

13. *Ibid.,* p. xiii (revised).

14. EDITOR'S NOTE: Quotations from the *Church Dogmatics* follow the authorized English translation, published by T. & T. Clark and Charles Scribner's Sons. Where marked "rev.," the translation has been revised for greater clarity within a given context.

3

Kingdom of God and Socialism in the Theology of Karl Barth

HELMUT GOLLWITZER

I

Perhaps—as F. W. Marquardt contends in his second book on Barth —it happened like this: A young Christian, deeply moved by the gospel from childhood on, was to study theology and become a pastor. His journey through the liberal theology of his teachers was intellectually fruitful, but changed nothing about the fact that for him the gospel was something simply astonishing, the alpha and omega of his thought. As an assistant pastor in Geneva he encountered, for the first time massively, the misery of the industrial proletariat, the "social question." Through the voices of religious socialism—Christoph Blumhardt, Leonhard Ragaz, Hermann Kutter—it became clear to him that this gospel not only concerned the salvation of the individual before God but also a world upheaval, a world revolution. God does not want this old world, whose atrocious conditions became so vivid to Barth in Geneva. God wants the kingdom of God, a new world, a new society: that is what was at stake in the entire contents of the gospel. This new reality could also be called "socialism"—not as an ideology but as a condition to be realized. "Jesus is the movement for social justice."[1] "Socialist" is thus, it must be said, a predi-

From "Reich Gottes and Sozialismus bei Karl Barth," *Theologische Existenz heute,* Nr. 169, hg. Karl Gerhard Steck (Munich: Chr. Kaiser Verlag, 1972). Translated, abridged, and reprinted with the kind permission of the author and the publisher.

cate of the gospel. God wants socialism. The true socialism is the kingdom of God—both as the goal of God's history with man, and as the present movement on earth here and now. Where the kingdom of God is at stake, there socialism is always at stake as well. Where socialism is at stake, moreover, there God's kingdom is always already at stake.

In the Aargau industrial village of Safenwil, where Barth held his first pastorate from 1911 to 1921, this was taken seriously. There he spoke and practiced these perceptions with ever-increasing clarity. He treated his pastoral office in the way that many church officials today fear left-wing theology students will do: He combined the Sunday sermon with weekday political agitation. He did not feel that being a pastor obligated him to political restraint. On the contrary, precisely *because* he was a pastor, he had to be in the forefront of the class struggle. His involvement in social problems and political action was as important to him as his theological work, which never relaxed in intensity. The two were not in conflict with each other. He did not see his life in the pastorate as an ellipse with two foci, and even the question of which was primary and which secondary he would have rejected as totally beside the point. On Sundays as on weekdays he confronted one and the same subject matter, that of being a Christian, of the gospel, the subject matter of God. Theology and national economy, sermon and politics, belonged indissolubly together. The politics interpreted the sermon; the sermon interpreted the politics. Both had to occur at the same time; otherwise each was falsified or at least highly misleading. Even during periods when, as he confessed in the preface to the second edition of *Romans*, his community saw him more at his desk in theological work than in their homes, he did not neglect political activity. Rather, after the October revolution of 1917 in Russia and the Swiss general strike of 1918—two historical events which stirred him to the core—he became a party-convention delegate in the swirl of the Swiss Social Democrats' fiercest policy struggles. In 1915 he had joined the most leftist party of the time, the Social Democratic, and was always active in the party's left wing. That was why he was so stirred by the struggles over the party's direction: He belonged to the left-wing Social Democrats, who, precisely because of their profound socialist convictions, could not support their party's joining the Third International. In Safenwil he established three unions, organized strikes, traveled up and down the country as a party speaker, offended the factory owners and the well-to-do in his community, urged his presbyters to join the party, formed a "red" presbytery, was decried (and is still remembered today) as the "red pastor," and, when called to a theological professorship in Göttingen, took pains that the community could be turned over to a pastor at least as red as he.

Did his transition to an academic post mean a break with what had gone before, as if it were all a mistake, or did he even betray his former cause? Did directing all his energy to theological work mean he had renounced his previous convictions? Ragaz, who shortly before had abandoned his professorial chair in Zurich because of the sterility of pursuing academic theology, feared precisely that. So did many others, who reproached Barth, saying that he now wanted a depoliticized theology and even reaction in the church. Barth was to insist again and again that he wanted nothing of the kind. But why did what once stood in the foreground now recede to the background? The Safenwil material, still to be evaluated, confirms and demands Marquardt's interpretation of Barth's course, unless—against Barth's own statements—one wants to understand the change as a break, a renunciation, or even a betrayal on the part of the newly appointed professor.

Two great disappointments with the socialist movement forced him to a new orientation: the participation of the European socialist parties in the wholesale slaughter of the First World War and the rise of Leninist centralism after the Soviet revolution, which he had greeted with enthusiasm. The disappointment at his German teachers, who had succumbed to the madness of nationalism, strengthened the desire, which he had already felt in the years prior to the war, to find a better theological foundation. With his friend Eduard Thurneysen, he expounded Paul, read Luther and Calvin, and then Kierkegaard. From his identification of God's kingdom with true socialism he was not to stray, not at this point, and, as I would like to assert, never. That God's socialism always infinitely surpasses whatever we men can create as socialism was something he already knew, just as he also knew, however, that this does not exclude, but includes, our

struggling for a revolutionary transformation of the present ungodly
social order into one which better corresponds to God's socialism.
Such a socialism he considered possible, because the gospel—this he
learned from the Blumhardts—is aimed toward a bodily, worldly
realization. That against which and for which God struggles, according to the gospel, is that against which and for which—with appropriate distance of the creature from the Creator—we, too, must struggle. That constitutes the practical shape of the analogy—the *analogia
fidei*—on which he was always to insist.

But now with his daring identification of the kingdom of God and
socialism he saw a danger. It made a difference whether we perceive
an identity between God's kingdom and socialism, or whether we
identify our socialism (as idea, movement, and finally achieved condition) with God's kingdom. In the first instance we follow the movement of the gospel, serving, believing, and obeying its promise. In the
second instance we exploit God for our own purposes and then have
—in only a seemingly revolutionary way—simply a new aspect to the
old sins of the church and the religions: the utilization of God to serve
our own respective interests (a new aspect also evident in bourgeois
cultural Protestantism). The result would not be revolution, but a
new enslavement of man. The warning against reversing the divine
identity between God's kingdom and socialism into an equation of
our deed with God's deed—the warning against "brazen identifications"—pervaded the second edition of his *Romans*. (During the last
years at Safenwil, he wrote the second edition in daily dialogue with
world events, with the news from Russia and the struggles over the
direction of the Swiss Social Democracy; and through that work he
was to become famous at one stroke and receive an endowed chair
in Reformed theology at Göttingen.) The general public heard only
this warning from the previously obscure figure and understood it as
a renunciation of his former social-revolutionary activity. Why didn't
he correct that impression by continuing his activity? Suddenly become famous, why didn't he encounter the theological, ecclesiastical,
and other publics now aware of him, as a socialist speaker and a party
member at the same time?[2] Apart from personal reasons, various
factors account for this: Without adequate academic preparation, he
faced the difficult task, whose demands he took very seriously, of

filling a chair in dogmatic theology. He was enmeshed in the fiercest of debates concerning his new theological discoveries. As a Swiss in Germany, he considered it right—at least at first—not to be politically active. Above all, he was also—much like Karl Marx—a man of solidity, a fundamental thinker and worker. The rambling talk of the world improvers who were then posing as socialists was just as foreign to him as the theological liberalism which called itself Christian, but which stemmed more from the humanistic spirit of the time. That sort of theological liberalism had already separated him from the religious socialists. A theologian's socialism without a solid theological foundation was to him a way of losing everything through a lack of substance. A church so instructed would fail to provide both the world and socialism with the very substance which the church and only the church was supposed to bring to them. He had now discovered something of that substance by placing himself before the Bible; and he did this in a way he had not learned from his liberal teachers: by placing himself before the radical contents of the Biblical writings, precisely in their strangeness, without premises conditioned by modern culture. He aligned himself with Jeremiah and Paul (and then also with Luther and Calvin) against modernity, rather than with modernity against the Bible and the Reformers. To find and lay a solid foundation for Christian thought and action—that was why he now had to become a professor of theology, that was his political task.

For he was not turning away from contemporary political and social problems when he turned toward a more solidly grounded dogmatics and toward research into the theological tradition so slighted by liberalism. His disappointments taught him that the road to a socialist society that could be an earthly analogy *(Gleichnis)* to God's kingdom, would be a *long* road. Now he began in his own manner "the long march through the institutions." Who should be the agent of revolution? The Marxist camp would agonize over this question again and again. The Western European proletariat had abandoned its revolution, the socialist parties had variously failed, and the Soviet way seemed increasingly dubious. How did things stand with the Christian church? For centuries she had been an exponent of the existing order, of restoration, indeed of reaction. In and through her, however, was and is transmitted, as brokenly and impurely as ever, that gospel of God's kingdom through which Barth had become a socialist. She stood therefore—despite the reactionary role she had long played in society—under the demand of the gospel to be a social-revolutionary force, even if not *the,* yet in cooperation with others, *an* agent of revolution. If others fail, degenerate, or grow weary, she must hold high the banner of the gospel's revolutionary transformation. Should it be more hopeless to work for such a renewal of the church from the core of the message entrusted to her than to work for the renewal so necessary to socialist organizations? Previously, Barth had expressed himself in a sharp, polemical distance to the church, but had always known himself as a man of the church. Now he poured all his energy into the task of renewing the consciousness of the Christian gospel's explosive contents. He no longer did this by way of political agitation, but by way of renewing the church through a sermon no longer adapted to the needs of bourgeois man —through a nonmodernist, radical, and Biblical sermon. So little did he hope any longer in direct political work, so decisively did he set all hope upon this kind of church renewal, that in the '20s he sometimes warned his friends—for example, those of *Neuwerk*—against further squandering their energies in work with the socialist party; all energy was to be dedicated to transforming the church. He saw himself called to the task of theoretical construction, to concentrated reflection on the contents of the Christian message, on the Bible, on the meaning of the great statements of the dogmatic tradition. He took the theoretical task seriously because he knew what disastrous consequences could arise for individual and social life from misinterpretations of the gospel. He became a radical and Protestant, yet ecumenical theologian, investigating the whole breadth of confessional traditions for tendencies that pointed beyond the church's accommodation to the existing order, her loss of a truly revolutionary function. He sought tendencies that stood opposed, as he did not hesitate to say, to the church's embourgeoisement. What seemed to many a self-contained intellectual work, a mere interpretation, was always reinterpretation for the sake of transformation—of the church as well as the world. His work was always directed toward a new Christian praxis, and indeed toward none other than that which he engaged in at Safenwil.

That no other praxis was at stake, that leftist politics was always intended, he was now to make pointedly clear in his continuing sharp criticism of the church, in his opposition to the nationalist students in Göttingen, in the "Dehn affair," in his joining the SPD [German Social Democratic Party] in 1932, and finally in his fight against national socialism. After 1945 he made it clear in his attitude toward the East-West conflict, against the politics of the cold war, against German rearmament, against nuclear testing, and for a better understanding of the Christian task behind the Iron Curtain. He seldom used the word "socialism," but when he did it was always with a significant accent. It was too shopworn, too discredited, too much fallen under the suspicion of ideology still to be employed without being misunderstood. It could no longer be used as a shorthand formula for that toward which God's activity was directed and for the new human activity which it initiates. He thus assumed the appearance of having changed from a socialist bent on destroying the present system of exploitative power relationships into a Social Democrat whose resigned pragmatism stuck within the system and sought only isolated improvements. However, if, guided by Marquardt's work, we consider these political attitudes not only in the context of Barth's ethical reflections, but also in the context of his dogmatic work—his doctrines of God's attributes and of reconciliation—then from there a line of continuity emerges which points far beyond such a diffident pragmatism. This pragmatism did not displace the earlier tendency toward social revolution; rather, it was the consequence of historical experiences, resulting from the confrontation between the socialism of God's kingdom and resistant historical realities. It was a pragmatism that constantly pressed beyond itself, hence a socialist pragmatism.

II

After imploring Western Christianity to "keep itself 'leftist' " over against those who represent the social disorder of class society—"that is, to confess that it [the church] is fundamentally on the side of the victims of this disorder, and to espouse their cause" (CD III/4, 544 rev.)—Barth thus, for example, concludes his 1951 discussion of the work situation in class society and the class struggle, with these words:

> The Christian community can and must *also* espouse various forms of social progress or even of socialism—always the form most helpful in its

specific time and place and in its specific situation. Yet her decisive word cannot consist in the proclamation of social progress or socialism. It can only consist in the proclamation of God's revolution against all "ungodliness and wickedness of men" (Rom. 1:18). That means, however, that it consists in the proclamation of his kingdom as it has already come and comes (CD III/4, 545 rev.).

One senses the distance from his attitude in the Safenwil period. Side by side with advocating a system-destroying socialism, it is now possible to work for social progress within the existing system—yet he does not forget immediately to add: "at least in immanent opposition to the system" *(ibid.).* Reformism and revolution no longer stand in exclusive opposition. Moreover, the content of proclamation may only be political within and beneath the "decisive word," the proclamation of God's kingdom. (At that time he said this in view of the particular temptation of Eastern European churches to conformism.) But even here the unity is retained undiminished between proclaiming the kingdom of God and participating in the "relative countermovements" against the distortion of man and work in class society. The relation between the "decisive word" and espousing social progress is like the relation between center and circumference, origin and consequence, grace and living from grace. Those who suppose they agree with Barth when they separate the "decisive word" from what he meant, in order to protect its priority, have removed themselves far from Barth.

The crassness of equating the deeply Christian-motivated demands of today's young theology students that the church be socially engaged, with the demands of the misguided SA students of 1933, who were nationalist, anti-Semitic, and fascist, would have been just as foreign to Barth as the equation between national socialism and communism, which even in the shrillest days of the cold war he never accepted, because in spite of everything communism perceived the social problem "with a completely different seriousness" than the West.[3] He distinguished as to *content* where others who appealed to him operated with a comfortable formalism, and the criterion for his distinction was the "direction and orientation" derived from the gospel, which rejected fascism while recognizing in socialism an "affinity" to the gospel.

To relegate all this to "ethics," as if that were a realm separable from dogmatics, or to understand this as the writer's subjective political tendency, as if he spoke here in a less binding way than in his dogmatic reflections, would be completely foreign to Barth's richly elaborated basic premises. The "unity of dogmatics and ethics" (CD I/2, §22, 3) is nothing but the theological program for the knowledge practiced in Safenwil: God is concerned about the kingdom of God; the kingdom of God is the true socialism; therefore, the socialist movement is a "reflection" of God's kingdom (thus in a Safenwil lecture). This he had not heard from Wilhelm Herrmann; this was the deepest break with Marburg. The break with Marburg occurred not only because there Wilhelm II's war was acclaimed and the treaty with the Armenian-murdering Turks defended,[4] but even more because there the separation between dogmatics and ethics was ratified: For the difficulties into which the demands of autonomous ethics bring us, dogmatics supposedly directs us to the sources of consolation and power; the "moral instructions of Jesus" are thus subordinated to our changed moral consciousness and no longer have much to say to us. Barth rejects this late-Protestant form of distinguishing between law and gospel. He rejects the supposition that "the truth of the Christian religion . . . consists in this, that, properly understood, the doctrine of Jesus Christ, and the way of life that corresponds to it, has the secret power of making man inwardly capable to strive for and attain the goals and purposes which he otherwise elected autonomously" (CD I/2, 336 rev.).

Against this, Barth directs the full energy of his view on gospel and law: The gospel itself gives the goal, contents, and direction of human action and not only the power for goals gained or imposed from elsewhere. But why then doesn't socialism belong to such "autonomously elected goals and purposes"? By appealing to the sixth article of Barmen, with the "autonomously elected" goals of the German Christians of 1933 in mind, present-day Barthianism defensively tends to raise this objection against a position equivalent to that of the Safenwil pastor, and in Safenwil this question was already perceived and taken seriously. Was the unity between God's kingdom and socialism, in which the young pastor lived, anything more than a "brazen identification," a new form of "secularization"? Could this have been avoided in any other way than through a return to Herrmann's separation of dogmatics and ethics with its good old Lutheran tradition? The contradiction on which Wolfgang Huber sees Barth impaled was acutely perceived by Barth himself: "He condemns the German war-theology because it brings the 'sinful necessity' of war into connection with God, and he demands that God be completely left out of the question on this matter; yet he himself claims God in justifying social democracy; it is the only political direction which takes God 'politically seriously.' "[5] For a time in the following years, reading Luther, Barth would test his conviction, even entertaining Luther's distinction between law and gospel. But the impression of the message of the kingdom of God and its coincidence with the social question was too strong. He would not let himself be silenced in this way. And so in those years when the capitalist world, whose inhumanity he recognized in Safenwil, showed its full possibility for brutality in fascism, Barth came to discover the unity between gospel and law. This insight was nothing but a theologically clarified resumption of the unity perceived in Safenwil between kingdom of God and socialism. The images from the Safenwil period were to recur. The unity perceived was based on "reflection" and "analogy" *(Gleichnis),* not "identity" (that would have allowed the reversal which the second *Romans* wanted to prevent). Yet the rejection of "identity" did not intend "lack of identity" but rather that "analogy" to God's kingdom be the earthly order of society which the Christian community espouses.[6]

With the Safenwil thesis, "Jesus is the movement for social justice," this breakthrough could not in the long run have been accomplished. It sounded too much like a naïve attempt to legitimate one's own decision through a venerable historical example, or even more like an attempt to anchor one's own attitude in something absolute. That, however, would have been the illicit reversal to which every suspicion of ideology is exposed. If there really is, as the Safenwil pastor was convinced, an ineluctable momentum leading from the socialism of God's kingdom to action within the socialist movement, if Jesus "is" in *this* sense the movement for social justice and the God revealed in him is in *this* sense a socialist, if that remained valid and uncontested despite the now clearly perceived "infinite qualitative

difference"[7] between Creator and creation, between the true socialism of God's kingdom and the always impure socialism of human
politics, then simply to assert as much was insufficient. In order to
protect this assertion from all "brazen identifications," which in the
history of theology and church are so abundant, it had now to be
grounded theologically—that is, exegetically and dogmatically, in the
"concept of God," as Marquardt says, in the working out of the
Christological basis to the message of God's kingdom, as for Barth,
after all, that naïve Safenwil thesis already suggested.

If God's commandment—which aims toward our parable-like correspondence to God's kingdom—is already contained in the gospel,
and is only to be discovered and grounded there, then it must first
of all be found in God's own action, and God is to be recognized in
this action as he is "first of all in himself." To that end is necessary
the doctrine of the Trinity, which is introduced in the prolegomena
of *Church Dogmatics*, but is only fully developed in the doctrine of
reconciliation. It is the doctrine of the Trinity that first provides the
solidly Christian foundation for that earlier naïve assertion and for
the equation—at first more or less instinctive—of God's kingdom
with socialism: The "humanity of God" (1955), the "humanism of
God"[8] is not God's arbitrary action, but God's self-revelation; "God's
being is in becoming"—namely, the becoming of his kingdom—
which occurs in the threefold parousia of Jesus Christ (CD IV/3,
§69, 4), whose second form, the operative form of the Holy Spirit,
is the "age of the church," the arena of our struggle as shared by
Jesus, who is the victor on his way toward, and leading the way
toward, his revelation.

Now the foundation is laid; now the community no longer receives
the content and goal of her earthly activity from anywhere else. She
no longer needs to establish them "autonomously," but only to follow
the "humanity of God"—and she knows what she has to do here on
earth. How can she still allow the sovereignty of the world to stand
unchanged if within the activity of God himself sovereignty and
servitude are reconciled as he makes himself a slave so that man
might be redeemed from bondage (CD IV/1 and 2)? From the unity
between God's mercy and justice, how is "logically a very definite
political problematic and task" not to follow: "a political attitude

decisively conditioned by the fact that man is made responsible for all those who confront him as poor and miserable, that he for his part is summoned to espouse the cause of justice, and indeed to espouse it for those who suffer injustice"? (CD II/1, 387 revised in the context of the doctrine of God's attributes.)

For everything that is believed must be put into practice. "Only the doer of the Word is its real hearer" (CD I/2, 792). There is therefore *"no* ethics from the *ultimate* standpoint which we must adopt in Christ. There is only the *movement* of God to which, in every single moment, there must correspond on our part a quite definite recognition of both the situation and our necessary action following from it."[9] The entire theological work to come was a commentary on this Safenwil statement, and it served to determine the Christian and ecclesiastical activity which was "necessary" on the basis of the gospel, and thus which was no longer simply congenial or arbitrary. What guides this theology is "the category of praxis"; this theology is "simply the *theory of this praxis"* (CD II/2, 548 rev.). Praxis belongs inseparably to "pure doctrine." The praxis which aims toward "social progress or even socialism" is inseparable from the "decisive word" of the "proclamation of God's kingdom as it has already come and comes" (CD III/4, 545). "The proclamation of the church is pure doctrine when the human word spoken in her offers and creates obedience to the Word of God in confirmation of the Biblical witness to revelation" (CD I/2, 743 rev.). For man "in his action and in his human speech about God . . . is required to be the platform for this work" (CD I/2, 758 f. rev.)—i.e., for that "movement of God" of which the first-edition *Romans* spoke, the movement of the "politics of God," as Barth might well have said with Paul Lehmann. Therefore, "within the life of the church" falls "the decision about the purity or impurity of her doctrine . . . not least in her attitude toward state and society" (CD I/2, 770 rev.). As Barth never tired of stressing, the community is not an end in itself, not a little flock of the saved in Noah's ark while all those around her drown. She is "the provisional representation of the whole world of humanity justified in him [Jesus Christ]" (CD IV/1, 643), and as such she has only "a *relative, provisional,* and *teleological* exclusiveness" (CD IV/1, 666 rev.). She is totally directed toward her coexis-

tence with the rest of humanity (CD IV/3, 826). "She is elected
from the world that she might perform the service which the world
most needs" (CD II/2, 196 rev.). If man's future in Jesus Christ is
God's kingdom as a life in freedom, service, and community, then
the Christian community is "the place of great anticipatory joy in
view of all men and all creation, or else she is not the Christian
community" (CD IV/3, 812 rev.). This anticipatory joy will also be
worked out in the manner of her present struggle, in that she reckons
all men, even her opponents, unconditionally to God and overcomes
the craving of men for that reversal, for that transmutation of their
goals—even, for example, of socialism—into religion, the impulse of
the state "unceasingly absorbed in progress towards its own deification" (CD I/2, 759 rev.). That is how, as a theological thinker and
teacher, the former pastor of Safenwil, through a long intellectual
journey, answered the questions that had arisen for him through
sobering historical experiences regarding the connection he had perceived between God's kingdom and socialist activity. That is how he
set his hopes on the Christian community, against all appearances,
as the agent of the necessary revolution; and that is how he wanted
to equip her for this mission. He changed language, disposition, and
style of thought. He became more soberly pragmatic than he once
was about politics, but he never abandoned the radical and revolutionary orientation for work in society that he had received from the
message of the kingdom of God. He described the proper "order of
the community" (CD IV/2, §67, 4) as the orientation of an anarcho-
socialist, decentralized, democratic group—not so that the community thus ordered would smugly exist as an island or a sect in a society
whose order was completely different, but so that she would create
externally an "*exemplary* law" that could have "repercussions and
correspondences" in the outside world and that might result in "a
certain corrective to the law at work in the world" (CD IV/2,
719–726).

> In the form in which she exists among them she can and must be to the
> world of men around her a reminder of the justice of the kingdom of God
> already established on earth in Jesus Christ, and a *promise* of its future
> manifestation. *De facto*, whether they realize it or not, she can and should

show them that there already exists on earth an order based on that great transformation of the human situation and directed towards its manifestation. To those outside she can and should not only say, but also demonstrate by deed, that worldly law in the form in which they regard it as binding and outside which they suppose that they cannot know any other or regard any other as practicable, has already ceased to be the last word and cannot enjoy unlimited authority and force; that *things can be different*, not merely in heaven but on earth, not just some day but even now, than those to which they think they must confine themselves in the formation and administration of their law. (CD IV/2, 721 rev.)

The long journey of the socialist pastor who became a theologian thus brought forth two things. First, the contention that the God of the gospel wants socialism led to a penetrating consideration of evangelical talk about God and to its Christological and Trinitarian contents and foundation; yet this reflection was always aimed toward determining what the kingdom of God is, the kingdom of God in heaven *and* on earth, transcendentally *and* immanently, as a prototype of the grace to be imitated in praxis here and now (CD II/2, 576 ff.). Second, the search for the revolutionary agent defined the Christian community as such, and gave her direction for her social action following from the highest and no longer questionable authority, from the revelation of this God himself in his Word, namely, Jesus Christ. This is what has persisted. This is the unity of Barth's theology through its various, living phases, progressing in constant self-correction. This is also the unity of theology and politics in Barth on which he insisted so tenaciously and on account of which, even in isolated questions, he was ready, often impatiently and distrustfully enough, to take a political disagreement as an occasion for turning theological agreement into something problematic.[10]

Nonetheless, the "infinite qualitative difference" of the kingdom of God as the true socialism, which the second-edition *Romans* insisted upon, is never forgotten. "What man does on his own" is never the "break" through which the new is really realized and the old really abolished. "The little revolutions and attacks by which they [the powers of history] seem to be more shaken than they really are can never succeed even in limiting, let alone destroying, their power. It is the kingdom, the revolution, of God which breaks, which has already broken them. Jesus *is* their conqueror" (CD IV/2, 544 rev.). That is incomparably more skeptical than what the Safenwil pastor used to say about human revolutions. Historical and political experience is worked through here just as much as the knowledge of faith. But the skepticism here plays an ancillary, not a predominant role; it is meant to sober but not hinder "little revolutions" (CD IV/2, 545 rev.). For "there is only one possible answer to the insight really gained about the imperfection of all human activity, and that is to set to work anew."[11] The profundity of the crisis befalls precisely the "revolutionary titan," who is depicted as "far more godless, far more dangerous, than his reactionary counterpart—because he is so much nearer to the truth."[12] But this is not to say that the radical crisis of the Word of God lumps them all together indiscriminately, whether reactionaries or revolutionaries, capitalists or socialists, democrats or fascists, into a night, "when all cats appear gray" so that there would be no distinction in terms of praxis, and a Christian could adopt any of these positions according to preference or even remain in neutrality, as Barth at that time was immediately and readily misunderstood to be saying.[13] Here there are distinct "affinities" and "resemblances" to the gospel,[14] whose contents are not cancelled, but are directly confirmed through the criticism of us men by God's Word. Here there is, on the basis of the "analogy" to God's kingdom, a "direction and orientation" that is to be pursued in obedience, not only by individual Christians, but by the entire Christian community in "choosing and deciding."[15] Barth did not simply ignore Tillich's criticism that the radicalism of the "theology of crisis" could issue in a neutrality that disavowed every distinction in relative truth among the possible human positions;[16] he reckoned with it in his own way.

III

The words "revolution" and "analogy" *(Gleichnis)* are not imprecise terms; they are meant to be taken literally and seriously. "Revolution" means a fundamental transformation, a decisive qualitative difference from what has preceded. The discontinuity is greater than the continuity; the transformation embraces the whole, not simply particulars; the substance, not simply incidentals. It is a transformation so radical that it cannot be forged by the old powers; only new powers can produce it. Justification and rebirth must be understood as revolution in the strict sense, not as reform. In that sense the theology of the Reformers has stood the test in contrast to the anthropological reformism of scholasticism and of Erasmian humanism, and in that sense Barth adhered to it. He attacked Emil Brunner so vigorously because in him he saw a regression to this reformism: "Or should one hope for an angel from heaven who would call to Brunner through a silver trumpet of enormous dimensions that II Cor. 5:17 is not a mere phrase which might just as well be applied to an automobile that has broken down and then been successfully 'repaired'?"[17] Reformism thinks in terms of the permanence of the system; revolution is a transcending of the system. A revolutionary attitude reaches out for the qualitatively new in the light of which the *status quo* appears as the old which can and ought to be overcome, as that which can no longer be regenerated by its own powers. For Barth the qualitative leap was decisive, whereas Brunner focused abstractly on the permanence of the "formal personality." Barth did not deny that, but contended it is not something independent in itself, that it appears as such only when considered in abstraction, that it retains its (quite relative) value only in the concrete context of the old or new being. Thus Barth maintained that in Gal. 2:20 Paul, "despite this permanence, speaks not of continuity but of discontinuity, or rather of the divine miracle of the continuity of his existence both without and with, both outside and within, Christ."[18] Only the old comes out of the old. A qualitative renewal of man cannot be attained through individual repairs, nor is it the result of the strivings of the old man who "can swim well enough to help his deliverer by making a few good strokes."[19]

The radicality of the Reformation doctrine of grace contains an image of revolution that was to remain decisive for Barth from the moment (beginning with reading Calvin in Geneva) he discovered Reformation theology—and this paralleled his discovery of socialism and the social question! From then on he saw all revolutions that do not fulfill the conditions of this image of revolution as only "little revolutions." He would criticize them principally from the left, as Marquardt correctly sees, that is, on the basis of even greater expectations and claims which are to be set in place of that which dares to call itself revolution.

This way of criticizing revolution, however, was made possible and intelligible only through two revisions that Barth applied to the notion of revolution as found in the Reformation doctrine of grace.

1. The revolution of the individual (which Reformation thought aimed at in continuation of the earlier doctrine of grace) was brought into connection with the revolution of humanity, as a particular case within a universal horizon. This was done via the religious-socialist tradition, especially through L. Ragaz's appropriation of the Blumhardtian message of the kingdom of God and through H. Kutter's criticism of pietism. The narrowing of eschatology to the individual's renewal by the word addressed to him in grace, as occurred in the Bultmann school, was never accepted by Barth, nor was the narrowing of renewal to a new self-understanding, found already in Melanchthon's doctrine of imputed justification. To speak with Marx's eleventh thesis on Feuerbach, that would simply be a new interpretation, not a transformation of existence. Existence and humanity must, however, be materially transformed—indeed, to a revolutionary extent. Under the influence of the religious socialists, Barth conceived of "the kingdom of God" in material, universal, and social terms. The meaning of the eschatological promise is "God's victory in the *materiality* of the whole creation,"[20] hence reconciliation between man and nature, and the redemption of both to *"bodily glory."*[21] In consequence, we "truly no longer need to stare at the external world as a strange and hostile objectivity and power of destiny," because *"we* are called and enabled one day to become the mediators and aides of the world destroyed by us, one day to speak the redemptive words and to do the liberating deeds which nature expects from her Creator."[22] Thus even now "the world with her great misery crowds into our horizon," and even now the spirit is "given to us that we might strongly call for *more* Spirit to enter the world, for a continuation of the Spirit's outpouring on *all* flesh."[23] The Spirit "puts us to work, and into conflict, with an unredeemed world whose ungodly elements are opposed to his glory"; therefore there is "no remaining in inward community with God. That would be a quenching of the Spirit. That would be the old individualistic

abomination of pietism, whose false paths and blind alleys we have escaped in Christ."[24]

Barth was never to repeat that in the same way. His eschatological reflections in the second half of CD IV/3, probably because of their relation to the doctrine of reconciliation, remained limited to the future of man. But his turning away from J. T. Beck does not imply that he also turned away from the Blumhardts, who also influenced the cosmic perspective of the first-edition *Romans* and whose hope Barth was then to take up so decisively in CD IV/3 (§69, 3: "Jesus Is Victor"). Precisely in this section, however, Barth went on to describe the victorious way of Jesus Christ as a "story of conflict." Participation in the conflict may not, of course, be "confused" with human ideas of progress—the warning of the second-edition *Romans* is not absent here! "At this point there can be no reversal. The victory of Jesus Christ, and thus what can seriously be called the victory of light over darkness, can never be inferred from any victories of humanity—never at any rate with real certainty" (CD IV/3, 264 rev.). But even here this warning does not mean that Christians should withdraw from the struggle for the progress of humanity. For as "parables of the kingdom" such ideas of progress, often so easily despised by a "strict Christianity," belong to those "true words" [*extra muros ecclesiae*] which are included, not excluded, by the one Word of God called Jesus Christ (CD IV/3, 124 ff.). Although Christians should have no "illusions as to the antithesis between the kingdom of heaven and those of this earth" (CD IV/3, 122), it does not follow that they must regard godlessness and paganism as "insurmountable walls"; rather, they have to reckon with "true words . . . even from those fronts" and to participate in their realization. In the list of "true words" which Barth presents, socialism is implicitly mentioned as "the disquiet, not to be stilled by any compromise, . . . at the great disorders in state and society, and at the human beings who are inevitably crushed by them" and as "the iron decisiveness of will to attack just these great disorders" (CD IV/3, 125 rev.).

2. Barth was unable to develop his concept of the kingdom of God. It may be supposed, however, that in the eschatological part of the *Church Dogmatics* he would have taken up the concept of the first-edition *Romans*. That is, he would have presented the hope for God's

kingdom as a cosmic fulfillment, as a reconciliation of man and nature, and as social in magnitude—as a new community among men. He would not have presented it simply as a perfection of the individual's life or as the eternal life of the individual in communion with God. In other words, his image of the kingdom of God would have been not only vertical but also horizontal. This may be inferred from the second revision to which he subjected the eschatological image of revolution in the Reformation doctrine of grace: The Reformation's outlook toward the transcendent fulfillment was not simply individualistic—*justus in re* instead of the present *justus in spe* (Luther)—but it remained almost without consequences for social life and political ethics. For Barth, however, the term "kingdom of God" fell increasingly within the purview of the latter arena (thus resuming his Safenwil ideas). That the social arena was "in need of and capable of analogy" to God's kingdom became the foundation of his political ethics.[25] What he thought about the "kingdom of God" may thus be inferred from what he here calls "analogy to the kingdom of God." To him the eschatological reservation did not entail withdrawal from the world. He drove no wedge between transcendence and immanence so as to make hope for the transcendent kingdom of God irrelevant to the shaping of this world. Nor did he drive a wedge between God's action and human action in such a way that what God does is *eo ipso* not to be done by men.

As to the difference between divine and human action, Barth indeed passed through the strict school of the Reformation doctrine of grace. Therefore, there are statements from the first-edition *Romans* which he would no longer repeat, where he pressed beyond the old antithesis between *gratia* and *opus hominis*. This reconsideration was a sign that he no longer spoke in dialogue with the Marxists and their objection to the potentially quietistic consequences of Reformation theology, but rather in dialogue with Tridentine Catholicism, which in the '20s he took more seriously than did any other Protestant theologian. In that context he saw his main task as the outlining of the Reformation position, which modern theology had so vitiated through natural theology and semi-Pelagianism.

In the first-edition *Romans*, Barth came to recognize that the Pauline doctrine of grace did not mean man was condemned to a lasting passivity. That view seemed to have been what resulted when the doctrine of grace was renewed by the Reformation; at any rate the fathers of the Council of Trent had that impression. The same impression was to recur when the doctrine of grace was renewed in the twentieth century by dialectical theology. Barth was later to explain "that as a description of grace, the formula 'God everything, man nothing' would not merely be a 'terrible simplification' but rather complete nonsense" (CD IV/1, 89 rev.). Thus he distanced himself from a misunderstanding that was also prevalent about him and which he tolerated more readily in the '20s.[26]

The antithesis between grace and the self-creation of man is overcome by an understanding of grace that better corresponds to the gospel. It is not apart from and against the reign of grace, but precisely through its presupposition, its presence, and its powerfully renewing effects that the bold proposition of the self-creation of man can be advanced without illusion.

That is how Barth had already described the relation between divine grace and human action in the two editions of *Romans*, and how he was to maintain it in the clamping together of dogmatics and ethics, in his writings on political ethics, and finally in his meditation on the second petition of the Lord's Prayer (in the still unpublished part of IV/4): By the word of grace, man is called to be a co-fighter with God; what the Creator fights against, the creature in his struggle must also fight against—a fight, of course, which would be senseless and hopeless, indeed ungodly arrogance, did it not occur under the presupposition of the divine struggle. What God alone can do is not the task of the creature. If the creature should want to take God's task into his own hands, then this *sicut Deus* (Genesis 3) would be his ruin. It is now certain, however: "Because *he* [God] has made the controversy with it [*dem Nichtigen*] into *his* affair, nothingness *cannot* be an eternal adversary, it can have *no* permanent existence" (CD III/3, 362 rev.). On the human plane, this disempowerment of nothingness, which has already occurred, does not mean quietism, however, but fearlessness and irreverence toward evil (363 f.). It means "to make a new beginning"—to make use, "by the obedience of Christian faith," "of the freedom which directly excludes the anxiety, legalism and pessimism so prevalent in the world." The

"Christian perception" that the evil in the world can be overcome must distinguish itself from other, more optimistic perceptions, not by greater pessimism (that is only a necessary *stage* in the "recognition of nothingness"), but by the fact that this perception is in a position to demonstrate that evil has been overcome, a position that is *"stronger,* because grounded—*braver,* because in exercise and proclamation of the freedom given to us—and *more consistent* because not done as a venture but in simple obedience" (364 rev.).

Against this background, the concepts of "parable" *(Gleichnis)*[27] and "correspondence" display a central significance in Barth's theology. It is indicative of academic theology's idealist way of thinking that it is not these concepts, but their correlate from the theory of knowledge—the concept of analogy—which has held the center of attention in the discussion and interpretation of Barth. In reality the entire direction of Barth's thought leads to *praxis:* to faith as the praxis-determining element, not to faith as the enabling of dogmatic utterances—the latter is only a stage on the way to praxis. *Analogia fidei* corresponds at the theoretical level to "parable" at the level of social praxis; the former is necessary in that it grounds and secures the correct occurrence of the practice of the Christian life.

After a long trek leading from Safenwil to the shattered Europe of the second postwar era, from "Jesus is the movement for social justice" to the "It is finished" of the doctrine of reconciliation, "parable" is now the concept that remains as the final outcome of the differences between the first edition and the second edition of *Romans,* between identification and the infinite qualitative difference, between the Lutheran *est* and the Reformed "however."[28] *Negatively,* what the concept means is this: no identification. The post-Safenwil Barth would always be allergic to identifications, and this allergy has generally come to be known as the chief distinguishing mark of his theology. Even Luther's dictum that the Christian should be and can be "another Christ" to his fellowman is too much for Barth; he suggests that it be abandoned. Between the great hope and the little hopes, the great revolution and our little revolutions, the socialism of God's kingdom and our socialisms, the difference must be observed and honored as fully as possible. God is God, and man is man—that remains the primordial datum of creation, the strict limit to creation which is not canceled even by redemption. For that limit is not canceled even in the *unio personalis* of the Son of God and man (cf. the *Extra Calvinisticum* against the Lutheran understanding of the *communicatio idiomatum*), as all Feuerbachian identifications and reversals serve constantly to warn us and must constantly be resisted. Redemption does not cancel this limit, but reconciles us to it, by ending our resistance to it through love. "The glory of the creature is this, to be lowly in relation to God" (CD III/3, 171 rev.). More glory than this we no longer desire, for our glory consists precisely in being a parable, a correspondence, to the glory and love of the Creator. Hence even the form of our social life is not "an anticipation of God's kingdom," as if even now a fragment of God's kingdom were realized.[29]

In the infinite distance of the creature from the Creator, increased by the distance of the sinner—even the justified sinner—from divine righteousness, our immanent realizations *follow* God's kingdom always as mere imitations, always pervaded by sin, always without claim to identification, always dependent upon the grace of forgiveness and election.

Positively, the concept of "parable" means this: What ought here to take place in social affairs is capable of "reflecting" the kingdom of God "indirectly as a mirror-image."[30] Here the eschatological reservation loses the paralyzing effect it has exercised for so long. Here what occurs is not only the relativization of the political so favored (and of course frequently necessarily) by Christian social ethicists, which, when all is said and done, is merely the theological form of liberal pluralism. As Barth said quite clearly in his essay "The Humanity of God," all his negations are spoken simply for the sake of positive positions. The eschatological reservation here no longer produces that great indifference toward all human choosing and deciding, be it to the right or the left, which submerges everything into the triviality of a merely aesthetic crisis that only appears to be radical. It does not annul the "direction and orientation" which the model of God's kingdom gives us, as if the course of this direction served only to preserve us from the arrogance, autonomy, illusions, and despair indicated by the *eritis sicut Deus*. Rather, "parable" shows how the kingdom of God is conceived here: not individualistically and spiritually, not merely as a symbol whose picture of social fulfillment (rejected by the Old Testament and thus very inauthentic) is the individual's perfection through his affirmation by God. Rather, whoever is guided by the concept of parable in "The Christian Community and the Civil Community" to carry out the specific determinations of choosing and deciding from below to above by analogy to the kingdom of God, that person receives a vision of brotherly human society filled with salvation in communion with God: precisely that vision which—in the midst of the Safenwil misery of the women who contracted abdominal disease through factory work—caused the Safenwil pastor to become not only a social reformer, but indeed a socialist. The kingdom of God is God's act, apart from our act, but for our act it is the living ground, the goal on ahead, the material orientation, not merely a consolation with the Wholly Other in earthly misery. Eschatology does not brake, but propels, our activity. "The transcendent is the power in our midst" —so Barth was to quote Ernst Troeltsch in Tambach,[31] and so it was to remain.

After 1945 the priority of socialism was to become explicit in Barth's thought once again, yet very subdued (for it was the time of Stalinism) and with reservations toward the course of his friend J. L. Hromádka, who correctly perceived, however, that this was not a rejection or lack of solidarity.[32] From this period until the end of Barth's life, hardly a writing of his can be found in which some passage or other does not indicate that "direction and orientation" which in "The Christian Community and the Civil Community" in regard to the order of the state he describes as a "tendency" toward democracy (section XXIX), and in regard to the "social question" he describes with an enumeration of various socialist possibilities (section XVII). Hence Marquardt is correct when he observes that "anything other than a socialist criterion obviously does not come into question here."[33] It is right when, in his letter to Eberhard Bethge about the latter's 1968 biography of Bonhoeffer, Barth concedes his own political restraint during the '20s, but speaks at the same time of "the direction I silently presupposed or only incidentally stressed: ethics—co-humanity—servant church—discipleship—socialism—peace movement—and hand in hand with all that, politics."[34] A certain regret, a self-critical question, may be detected in these words as to whether he ought to have stressed this more forcefully. They are, however, a clear indication given shortly before his death of how he wanted his course to be understood: not in the least as a different way contrasted to the intentions and socialist engagement of the Safenwil pastor, but as the continuation, deepening, refinement and theological grounding of the course begun at that time with all too little resources. That the gospel concerns the world, but with every word it speaks enters into conflict with the existing society, that it places us into this very conflict and *in* this society equips, mobilizes, and obligates us to pursue progressive change—this idea persisted to the end.

IV

Much remains open; many questions arise anew. This man's spirit cannot be reduced to a simple or a single formula. About the rash question, often raised as a defense mechanism, of what socialism really means here, nothing more will be said. Marquardt has clearly worked out what content and what nuances the concept had for Barth. The lack of consistency about it is not so great as it appears in face of the conflict of the many socialisms. For they are all close together when it comes to the notion and promise of the goal: Socialism means not merely certain social reforms, certain improvements within the capitalistic system of production, but rather a society in which all members are assured an equal share in the commonly produced social product, and in which the control of production is in the hands of the producers—a society which is thus as egalitarian as possible, one which is constantly destroying the material privileges that continually accumulate and which is constantly building up a material democracy. Socialists consider such a society possible (even under the presupposition of earthly imperfections) and urgently necessary. The conflicts among socialists concern the course of transition to this goal, the means and the methods, the strategy and the tactics for the period of transition. Karl Barth knew what he was saying when he spoke of socialism.

1. Certain questions can be raised about the phrase "only inciden-

tally stressed" (in the letter to E. Bethge). Marquardt's presentation, and even more the Safenwil documents, evoke astonishment even among those who knew Barth well. In conversations between him and many partners, this was not something "only incidentally stressed"; it did not come out at all. Whether they belonged to the smaller or larger circle of friends, the obligation to social engagement taken for granted among Christians was common to these conversation partners. Also taken for granted was the aversion to expressly propertied, bourgeois political parties, especially when they passed themselves off as Christian. But among these friends it was not a point of consensus that the gospel pressed toward the dismantling of bourgeois society. One moved about more in the vicinity of social-democratic reformism. It is immediately objected that the first sentence of Marquardt's book should say: "Karl Barth was a social democrat"; not "Karl Barth was a socialist." If, as Marquardt and I maintain (in connection with which we can also call upon our own memories, of course), a continuity can be shown to extend from Safenwil to the end of Barth's life, then why didn't Barth himself make this so apparent that a controversy about it would be impossible? Why did he treat his Safenwil engagement in such a way that, while certainly never hidden, it was yet less manifest than his theological work at the time, so that, previously downplayed and suppressed, it must only now be discovered?

In the transition to Göttingen, the aversion to liberal theology, with which religious socialism was connected, was certainly a factor. As long as there was no clarity at the center about "the decisive word" which it was the particular task of the Christian community to speak both to the world and to socialism, socialist activity could only be a way of losing everything through a lack of substance in which a birthright would be sold for a mess of pottage and the church would remain in debt to the world by failing to provide what the world most needed. The call to subject matter, especially the subject matter of the church, made dogmatics more necessary than ever. The bridges to religious socialism were thus brusquely broken off, as if religious socialism were nothing more than a variety of cultural Protestantism. Even in 1933 (in "Abschied," his final article on departing from *Zwischen den Zeiten*), Barth was still to boast that "already in 1919" he had "basically rejected the course of the religious socialists" and to deny every "theological and ecclesiastical affinity to Marxism, liberalism, etc." How inappropriate that was he himself confessed in 1938 in "Church and State" ("Rechtfertigung und Recht") and in 1946 in "The Christian Community and the Civil Community," in which such an affinity was now asserted positively. Indeed, through "incidental" assertions in all his publications and through his political positions, he again and again indicated his conviction that the theological and the political are inseparable. Yet for a long time he apparently considered the following a sequence to be possible and necessary: theological clarification first, and only then the turn to the political. In 1938, in the midst of his agitation against national socialism, he unfolded plans to us at the "Bergli" for an international theological journal to be named simply *Doctrina;* but now there was no longer a sequence, but rather a mutual and simultaneous influence, as the rest of his life then showed. However, previously he seems to have been thinking within the schema of such a sequence and therefore took into account that dialectical theology might have a depoliticizing effect. When, in a letter of January 9, 1924,[35] Bultmann communicated to him that at a lecture given by F. Siegmund-Schultze in Marburg "the followers of Karl Barth" declared themselves to be people "who had emancipated themselves from social duties," that seems to have stimulated no alarm on his part. He seems to have been quite in agreement with the thesis Bultmann defended there "that the mission of the church can only be the proclamation of the Word," and he showed no need to express some kind of solidarity with Siegmund-Schultze's work as well. When in retrospect Paul Tillich spoke angrily of "the Barthian indifference toward social matters" and stated that "among the young theologians Barthian theology emptied of its meaning the problem of 'the church and a humanistic society' and in particular of 'the church and the proletariat,' "[36] then the latter—at least in large measure—turned out to be true.[37] The political consequences of that phase were later to concern Barth, but at that time apparently not.

2. It is also remarkable that Barth was one of the few theologians of his generation who for a time at least had eagerly read the writings of Marxist theoreticians from Marx through Kautsky to Lenin.[38]

Since this was only a limited study, some important Marxist recognitions penetrated only insufficiently into his consciousness. As is traditional in theological social ethics, his vital interest in politics and his political positions were to remain fixed upon the state, upon the politics of government. That state and politics are based on a conflict of social interests—the class conflict—and that a critique of political tendencies and decisions must be driven farther, to their social presuppositions, and must thus become a critique of the political economy, this he did not notably come to say through his Marxist studies. So his protests against Nazism, against the cold war, and against West German rearmament were to remain on a moral plane, where they certainly also belonged, but where, however, they remained blind to the genuine causes as long as they were not supplemented by a recognition of the most powerful, counteracting social factors—which of course were also to influence the church to which Barth particularly addressed himself.

In the Safenwil lectures Barth speaks positively of the "glowing ember of Marxist dogma"[39]—of the socialist eschatology—as the best possession of the worker's movement. In 1948 he says the same thing when he speaks of the eschatology "which Karl Marx gave to his followers as the supreme good and as the appropriate driving motive for socialist action on the way to it" (CD III/2, 388). The relation between Christian ethics and Christian eschatology (analogy! [*Gleichnis*]) takes up much the same theme. The reason it becomes more subdued is connected with historical experience, with the Christian recognition of sin, and with the eschatological reservation: the "infinite qualitative difference" remains. Yet the hope for the kingdom of God should, according to Barth's assurances, be an incentive, not a hindrance. The passage from CD IV/2 cited above (p. 90) clearly indicates how little even the later Barth is willing to be paralyzed by the eschatological reservation in his socialist vision that *"things can be different . . . even now"* (CD IV/2, 721 rev.). However, the subdued tone is often so pervasive that earthly hope seems to be suppressed. Thus, for example, Barth once describes the Christian community as a community which transcends peoples, races, and classes (CD IV/3, 898–901). Unexpectedly, he equates—forgetting socialist insights—the class structure of society with the separation of men into peoples and races, and he gives the Christian community simply the function of working against the absolutizing of class differences and of making parabolically clear "if only from afar, their negation" (CD IV/3, 900 rev.). Here the negation is apparently conceived, however, as one that is only eschatological. Hence the community "has to erect the sign in the midst of the class struggle which points unmistakably to its goal and end and thereby also to its hidden meaning." What is probably meant by this "hidden meaning" is only the class struggle from below, the proletarian aspect. That does not prevent Barth, however, from instructing the community that she need not express herself either positively or negatively about capitalist or socialist ideas. Rather, she must "energetically address" capitalists and proletarians alike "that as men they are called children of God" and thus belong together—a rather idealist form of address, it seems to me, with a harmful reconciliation of classes through an ideology of social partnership as a consequence, as long as it is not immediately added that because "things can be different even now," the community must work against class separations and toward the overcoming of class society.

3. The Safenwil pastor stood simultaneously in ecclesiastical and socialist praxis. The one demanded from him the other. That the theology professor withdrew from socialist praxis is unavoidable in our society with its division of labor. It is, however, also a danger— as was probably not hidden from a man as clear about the unity between theory and praxis as Barth. The espousal of social democracy, his joining of the SPD in 1932, was a sign of such praxis,[40] as was his participation, toward the end of the Second World War, in the national committee for a "Free Germany" in which he consciously and affirmatively cooperated with its communist members. Yet the academic-bourgeois milieu has an undertow, of whose corrupting effect Ragaz had already warned him. What no longer stands before one's eyes loses its immensity; what is no longer connected to one's own activity becomes an object of aesthetic rather than practical judgment. To distinguish between external questions and questions placed before the disciples by their Lord is something Barth taught as an important methodological principle for theological thought. In baptism a being-grasped occurs which must be taken

seriously in thought—as he said already in 1931 in his letter to Karl Heim.[41] The Safenwil pastor understood his joining the party as obedience to his baptism, and at the same time as a step parallel to baptism across the Rubicon which separates bourgeois parties from the workers movement. That, despite his background, he belonged to the one and not to the other had to be made externally and actively visible. That is why he refused to leave the SPD in the summer of 1933. But regarding socialist praxis something seemed possible to him —at least after 1933—that never seemed possible regarding ecclesiastical praxis: the reduction to a minimum. Yet, as scarcely another theologian has said as clearly as he, an absence of practical responsibility has its effect on thought. It is difficult for thought by its own resources to counteract the repercussions upon it from the milieu and its class-bound character. The young pastor's involvement with the proletarian struggle for liberation no longer took place in the same clear way later on. That is linked to the development of this struggle and to its defeats. Soviet communism did not turn out to be a convincing realization of socialism. The true left became homeless; even apart from their sectarian characteristics, the little groups of scattered Trotskyites and other Marxists critical of the Soviet Union offered no alternative for a political praxis concerned with political effectiveness.

Despite its embourgeoisement, therefore, the social democracy still came into consideration as a political organization worthy of a socialist's support, especially because the socialist fire was not quite extinguished within it, as the controversy about the building of battle cruisers showed in 1928, in which Barth concurred decisively with the left. The discouraging situation of the socialist movement in the decades since the First World War must not be forgotten when asking about the possibilities of political praxis for a man whose whole energy was directed toward the renewal of theology and church. In addition there was Barth's firm conviction, bolstered by his transition from Switzerland to Germany, that what was now urgent for the Germans was the exercise, previously neglected, in the bourgeois democracy only just attained. He saw it that way in view of the right-wing tendency of the German middle class after the First as well as after the Second World War. Because of his concern for this

first, now necessary, step of bourgeois democratization, his concern
for the second step, for socialist democratization, could be held in
abeyance. In contrast to Safenwil, however, this position placed him
at a greater distance from the proletarian milieu and tended to
remove him from the severity of the class situation. He lost some of
the caution found in the Safenwil sermons against the traditional
individualism of ecclesiastical preaching. Hence his preaching at the
Basel prison, the sermons of which epitomize so impressively the
pastoral dimension to all Barth's theology, appears not to have
prompted Barth to reflect on the social context of the penal system[42]
in a way similar to his observations of the situation of industrial
workers in Geneva and Safenwil. In his personal life-decisions Barth
was exceptionally free from bourgeois motivations. But the antibourgeois elan of the Safenwil pastor lost its force when, upon his entering
the academic milieu, the previous praxis could no longer be continued. Our classes hold us all tenaciously fast. The counterweight of
our ideas cannot offset the influence of our social existence on our
consciousness, the bourgeois slant even to a theology antibourgeois
in tendency. This antibourgeois tendency would have needed a
stronger practical elucidation in order to withstand effectively the
"embourgeoisement" of Christianity within the church. How much
that tendency in Barth's theology could be overlooked is shown by
the surprise and denial which its exposition by Marquardt finds precisely in the circle of Barth's former students.

4. Barth was quite clearly a man of the church. It was the arena
of life and responsibility in which he placed himself, the milieu he
was never to leave behind—as the academic world was for Bultmann
and various kinds of intellectual circles were for Tillich. Barth's sharp
critique of the church and its social milieu evidently never brought
him to the temptation to abandon the empirical church, and the early
Tillich's assertion that the kairos had emigrated from the church to
the proletariat only left Barth shaking his head. The Reformed tradition into which he was born (by virtue of infant baptism!) was
something he took seriously, radicalized, corrected at many points,
and broadened ecumenically. His consciousness of tradition is apparent in every volume of the *Church Dogmatics*. Not only (understandably!) did he never feel any desire to switch over to one of the other

existing Christian confessions, but neither did he ever see himself called to turn his back on the empirical church in order to seek new ecclesiastical forms. In that he took his life in the church for granted, Barth may well be especially alien to many members of the younger generation for whom remaining in the church any longer is scarcely tolerable. Perhaps a closer study of the Safenwil materials will show that after the Safenwil period, during which a critical relation to the church presumably outweighed one that was affirmative, his way of taking life in the church for granted increased. Of course, for Barth the sequence: Jesus Christ—real community of Jesus Christ—empirical institutional church, is always one of extremely dialectical identities in which the following term is constantly called into radical question by the preceding term. In her empirical reality the church is always just "nominally a church"; indeed, whoever looks only at the empirical reality will see only a nominal church (CD IV/2, 617 f.). Barth took his life in the church for granted as part of the praxis of his faith. Because the gospel is entrusted to the empirical church, he believed it was also at work in her, and he used it critically against her empirical reality—always in the hope of faith that eventually the gospel will succeed in making the nominal church into a genuine church. Because of the presence of the Bible and the gospel, he placed hope in the church against appearances. Despairing of the embourgeoised, petit-bourgeois church, many young Christians today abandon the ecclesiastical institution. They seek and experience community in their own action groups, or they put their hope in socialist groups instead of church communities. The best among them do not want to separate themselves from the gospel, but to separate the gospel from its ongoing credibility crisis by virtue of its association with the ecclesiastical institution. In their own way they want to confess themselves to the gospel in groups that better correspond to the gospel's anticapitalist tendency. How would Barth have made clear to them, on the basis of his own ecclesiology, the priority of the relation of the institutional church to the gospel? The sequence—socialism of God's kingdom, real socialist groups, empirical socialist groups—is also a sequence of dialectical identities in which the preceding term always stands in critical relation to the one that follows it. Is it less adventurous to set one's hopes on the empirical

church than on socialist groups? Can't the latter be a praxis of the
same hope of faith—justified by the fact that it concerns the realization of a progressive movement toward the new humanity founded
in Jesus Christ? Do socialist groups have *a priori* no possibility of
being "a provisional representation" of "the salvation already taken
place in Jesus Christ for all persons," especially if "provisional" means
"in a broken form, imperfect, endangered and questionable" (CD
IV/2, 621 rev.)? Of course, the empirical church, the ecclesiastical
community, is that institution whose purpose is to proclaim the
gospel. But Christians in "worldly" groups bring the gospel into those
groups. Is it excluded at the outset that a "provisional representation"
of the gospel might occur in that way—that the gospel might be
witnessed more clearly to the world through those groups than
through a church so connected to definite social interests and structures contrary to the gospel that the gospel, to which she gives lip
service, is truncated and distorted and can no longer be recognized?
Ecclesia Romana habet baptismum, sed negat baptismum, said Luther. The fact that a church has the gospel does not protect her from
negating it. It seems to me more correct not to separate oneself from
such a church, but to wait, as Luther did, until she expels one (if at
all) on account of protest against her empirical reality. Hence it is no
more my decision to leave the institutional church than it was
Barth's. Yet it seems to me that the early Tillich's question cited
above is just as burning today as it was then, and that this question,
which apparently never really troubled Barth, needs to be posed here
as one that is very troubling for many today.

5. Barth set his hopes on the empirical church. But the transformation which he expected from her and for her would so revolutionize her essence that one may well question whether trust in the
effective power of the Holy Spirit active in the proclamation is and
can be a sufficient response to the problem. Undoubtedly this trust
always concerns the hope of faith for the miracle of the Holy Spirit,
yet surely that is to be distinguished from a faith in miracle which
makes things easy for oneself and takes refuge from reality in a
comfort which would be no more than self-deception. Suppose one
has a present-day state church or a parish community before one's
eyes and then recalls everything Barth says about the "real church,"

the "order of the community"—about the Christian community leading the way for the civil community. What matters for the community and her individual members is "that her life actually express the gospel" (CD IV/3, 845 rev.) "with her message as well as with her structure" (Barmen 3). Of course, that also means in terms of her "political worship," which Barth believed could by no means be left up to individual Christians according to the standards of their worldly reason, but must also be exercised collectively. If, as Barth argued in 1952,[43] that usually begins as groups and individuals within the church lead the way, then its goal is nonetheless to bring along the entire community, which in turn is to bring along the society. What possibility is there, however, that this idea will become a reality? Surely Barth cannot be satisfied that now and again it should consolingly take place in individual instances—that, for example, a World Council of Churches should undertake a program against racism or that North American church leaders should be far ahead of the mass of their constituency on the race question or in protest against the Vietnam war. Such individual occurrences are not to be minimized; they give courage again and again to hope in, and work with, the empirical church. Yet Barth intends something more: an ongoing social influence of the church that corresponds to the "direction and orientation" given by the gospel, an ongoing precedence of the church in overcoming the social *status quo*, the true community as a cadre of the avant-garde. It is no accident, however, that institutional church bodies, along with the bulk of their members, are just the opposite: conservative blocs that from time to time, with difficulty, are moved only by external groups and movements, to follow along more by force than by choice, usually as the tail end of a general development. They are capable of nothing else. Their rigid composition and their consciousness, along with the consequent abbreviations and distortions of the gospel, express their actual social existence. Yet as we read the broad ecclesiastical statements in the doctrine of reconciliation (CD IV/1–3), we seek in vain for a detailed consideration of such conditions. They are mentioned here and there, but only as a "temptation" of the community, as a temptation to accommodation—more as ties in which the church could become entangled if she is not careful than as ties in which she is already caught and from which she must extricate herself. The ties arise, according to Barth, for example, through the fact that the community understands the gospel under the specific influence of "philosophical, historical, national, cultural, political [and] economic factors" of her life at the time (CD IV/3, 821). Curiously, Barth discusses these "factors" as if they were optional and at the community's disposal, as if it were simply a matter of decision whether the community initiated something good or ill with them. What does Barth actually have in mind with all these splendid descriptions (which must be read and considered again and again) of the church as something "which is produced concretely and historically in this world" through the working of the Holy Spirit (CD IV/1, 652)? Where does he see this *ecclesia visibilis* which partakes of world events, but also transcends them (CD IV/3, 730 rev.), which—as "one human group among others"—exists *"totally dependent* upon her environment and *totally free* over against it" (p. 734 rev.)? Historically and materialistically, we know this "phenomenon" well as "totally dependent," but not at all as free, and Barth knows that. Nevertheless, a dualism pervades his presentations: here "the real community of Jesus Christ," "this alien colony living in tents" (CD IV/3, 744 rev.)—there the phenomenon of the church accessible to everyone. Mediation between these two poles occurs only through trust in the miracle of the Holy Spirit, in which, thanks to election, we may hope ever anew that precisely this phenomenon will become the people of God. Yet Barth never pushes forward to a more precise analysis of these discrepancies, and in view of his criticism of the church and his Safenwil background that is quite remarkable. It is right to trust in the promise of the Holy Spirit; only because of this promise can we believe in the church of Jesus Christ and even in the empirical church, and only on that basis do we recognize her again and again. But this trust does not allow us to make things easy, sparing us an analysis of the forms of dependence and deceiving us about their significance. The liberating Word of God is no magic formula which changes everything with one blow. What the Word of God changes consists in the fact that it creates the readiness for change, that it liberates to this readiness. The class-bound character of the church does not belong on the same plane as the other forms of dependence of the *ecclesia visibilis* in the linguistic, cultural, and national conditions of her environment. A class system is always a system of oppression. The church's class-bound character means complicity in and benefiting from a system of oppression. Witness to God can only be given by a church that stands in the class struggle against the class system, by a church that wants to eliminate the class system, not preserve it.

Barth always hoped that the church would be renewed and liberated through a renewed sermon, which his theological work was supposed to serve. In the following years he failed to emphasize that, along with the activity of preaching, comprehensive work for structural change in church and society was also necessary. Thus he was to content himself with a one-sided focus on the problem of the sermon and on the form of the traditional sermon-oriented worship service, as if on that basis alone the ecclesiastical world, and from there the rest of the world, could be lifted from the clutches of bourgeois entrapment. This consideration forces us to raise the question whether a vestige of idealism is not at work in Barth here, a vestige of the idealist faith in the power of ideas, namely, that on the basis of the right theology, the right praxis will be created. In Safenwil he knew that only if the church's proclamation were connected to socialist praxis could it be of service to the Word of God, and he knew that only if it were grounded in such a praxis could a theology develop which would again feed back into praxis in a purifying and indicative way. As his later statements and activities show, he also knew this later on, but he did not state it so persistently and powerfully. Nor did he bring it to bear in such a way that a relapse would be prevented into the idealist faith in the power of correct theory, into the idealist confusion between the self-authenticating power of God's Word, with which Barth was concerned, and the self-authenticating power of correct speaking about God. As he recalled in March 1966 to the assembly of the "No Other Gospel" movement in Dortmund: Without an accompanying political praxis, without staging a similar movement and rally against West German rearmament, against the Vietnam war, against the new anti-Semitism, and for the recognition of the East German government and the eastern borders, their *"correct confession"* would be only a "dead, cheap, pharisaical confession that strains out gnats and swallows camels," but not a *"genuine,* valuable, and fruitful confession." There, against such a confusion, he himself expressed once again in unmistakable terms his lifelong theological and Christian conviction of the unity not only between theory and praxis but also between ecclesiastical and political praxis.

V

We can no longer pose these questions to Barth. We can no longer ask him why the Safenwil clarity indeed continued through these admittedly clear signs, yet not with the same open participation in socialist praxis, so that a controversy about what he meant could then arise. We did not ask him when we were still able to ask him. We did not ask him then, because the same historical causes were at work in us which discredited the socialist movement and led it astray into resignation about the possibilities of socialist efforts and even into down-playing the present class structure. The questions of which we are conscious today are thus not condemnations, but rather an occasion to consider the historical conditions and limitations that affect us all, even a great and beloved teacher who was far ahead of his time and contemporaries, and who in his perception of the one thing necessary in order to proceed creatively rather than destructively in the work to transform the world is still always far ahead of us.

In 1931 Barth presented a book to his pupil and friend Fritz Lieb with the dedication: "To the representative of the 3d International from a representative of the 2½ International." At that time Fritz Lieb was already a disillusioned representative of the Third International, and he later broke with it completely in protest against Stalinism. As Marquardt has shown, in this dedication Barth was lightheartedly saying not that he indeed stood on the left, though somewhat less to the left than Lieb, but that at bottom he held an even "more leftist" position. In Switzerland there was a group under Robert Grimm which called itself the "2½ International" in order to express that it stood to the left of the Second International (the social democratic), but did not submit to the hegemony of Moscow. Barth subscribed to this position. When, during the same period, he joined the SPD—provoked by an account of the "Dehn affair" by

Gottfried Traub in *Eisernen Blätter*—I expressed my scorn to him about this lame gesture, but he asked in that case just where one could go, if one no longer wanted to remain merely a political spectator, since the Communist Party was out of the question for me as well. He then allied himself with a left-wing circle within the Bonn SPD. A year before that, he had once greeted me as I was stepping into the house with the praise: "Herr Gollwitzer, I was told that yesterday evening you stood in an assembly and sang the 'Internationale.' You are making great progress!"[44] During the severe depression of the first days of the 1933 summer semester, he contradicted every optimism that the Nazi government would soon be just as ruined by mismanagement as the previous governments. To him it was clear that we were facing the ominous result of a long German history. As we listened together at Karl Ludwig Schmidt's to the radio broadcast of Hitler's Tempelhof Field speech on the evening of May 1, 1933, some were of the opinion that the German workers would not tolerate the destruction of their unions and that before too long they would be forced to mobilize. Barth maintained the contrary: "You forget the enormous power of a totalitarian state—and you forget that they are German workers. They will gladly fall in line!"

In the next weeks we urged him to break his silence about political and church-political events. (Some freedom still existed; we were not yet accustomed to the oppression.) He procrastinated; he had no inclination. Then he wrote a long manuscript. One evening he read it to Charlotte von Kirschbaum and Hellmut Traub. H. Traub relates that it was a completely political and unprecedentedly sharp manifesto. The two listeners immediately responded that it would be impossible to publish; the next day he, the publisher, and the printer would all be sitting in prison. Angrily, he put the manuscript away. It no longer seems to exist. After a few days he began writing again and had soon completed a new essay, which he once again read to the two. It was the now well known first number of *Theologische Existenz heute*. The two were enthusiastic and besides that satisfied that it could be published. Barth, however, enraged, threw the pages at their feet and left the room with the words: "There you have your 'politically coordinated' *(gleichgeschaltete)* theological existence!"[45]

This incident from his life serves as a commentary on the convic-

tion, expressed in the Foreword to CD I/1, "that we cannot reach
the clarifications, especially in the broad field of politics, which are
necessary today and to which theology today might have a word to
say (as indeed it ought to have a word to say to them!), without having
previously reached those comprehensive clarifications in theology and
about theology itself with which we should be concerned here" (CD
I/1, xiii)[46]—and "that a better church dogmatics (even apart from
all ethical utility) might actually make a more important and weightier contribution, even to questions and tasks such as German liberation, than most of the well-intended material which so many, even
among theologians, think they can and should produce when they
dilettantishly take up such questions and tasks" (CD I/1, xiii rev.).
What is here to be understood along with the words "politics" and
"German liberation" is expressed by the path from Geneva and
Safenwil down to the letter to Eberhard Bethge, and in summary is
best expressed by that shopworn and much abused—as the fierce
reactions to it indicate—yet nonetheless useful word: *socialism.*

NOTES

1. "Jesus *is* the movement for social justice, and the movement for social
justice *is* Jesus in the present." This was how Barth put it in his lecture to
the organized workers at Safenwil on December 17, 1911 [reprinted in this
volume].

2. To what a great extent he, without changing his political views, pursued
his theological work without making visible the previous connection to his
political position is shown by his failure to react in any way negatively to
Bultmann's letter reporting the public appearance of F. Siegmund-Schultze
in Marburg, and to the thesis of the theological students there, which
Bultmann communicated favorably (Karl Barth and Rudolf Bultmann, *Briefwechsel 1922–1966,* ed. by B. Jaspert [Zurich: Theologischer Verlag, 1971],
pp. 24 f.). Even in 1933/34 he was to insist that his theological opposition
to the German Christians was not politically motivated (which is correct,
since indeed his political position was always evangelically, and thus theologically, motivated), and that—he appealed to the students who had heard him
as witnesses—his theological position implied no affinity at all to democracy
and socialism (which was a peculiar misunderstanding caused by that particu-

lar situation and which he corrected a few years later). Cf. Barth's article on leaving the associate editorship of "Between the Times": "Abschied," in *Zwischen den Zeiten* 11 (1933), pp. 536–554—now reprinted in J. Moltmann, *Anfänge der dialektischen Theologie,* Vol. II (1963), pp. 313–331. Cf. also Karl Barth, "Gottes Willen und unsere Wünsche," *Theologische Existenz heute,* Heft 5, 1933, pp. 7 ff.

3. Thus again and again in Barth's essays on the East-West conflict, 1945–1950.

4. As it was by W. Herrmann in a postcard to Barth that the latter liked to show. Cf. Herrmann's article, "Die Türken, die Engländer und wir deutschen Christen," *Christliche Welt* 29 (1915), cols. 218 ff., 231 ff.; see also W. Huber, *Evangelische Theologie und Kirche beim Ausbruch des Ersten Weltkriegs,* in *Studien zur Friedensforschung,* Vol. IV (1970), pp. 148 ff.

5. W. Huber, *loc. cit.,* p. 207; see the entire section on the early Barth, pp. 202–209.

6. Karl Barth, "The Christian Community and the Civil Community," (1946), in Barth, *Community, State, and Church: Three Essays,* ed. by Will Herberg (Doubleday & Company, Inc., 1960), pp. 149–189, especially section XIV. Cf. in this regard Barth's 1919 critique of Friedrich Naumann: "Blumhardt, however, readily recognized precisely in the radicalism and teleological thought of the socialists the analogy to the kingdom of God for our time." (Karl Barth, "Past and Future: Friedrich Naumann and Christoph Blumhardt," in *The Beginnings of Dialectic Theology,* ed. by James M. Robinson [John Knox Press, 1968], p. 44 rev.) And in the Tambach lecture from the same year: We must as a church demonstrate the "new orientation to God in terms of the *whole* of our life . . . not as irresponsible spectators and critics *over against,* but as comrades sharing in hope and guilt *within,* the *social democracy*—in which *our* time now places the problem of opposing the existing order, in which the analogy to God's kingdom is given, and in terms of which it must be proved whether *we* have understood this problem in its absolute and relative significance." (Karl Barth, "The Christian's Place in Society," in Robinson (ed.), *The Beginnings of Dialectic Theology,* pp. 318–319 rev.)

7. Karl Barth, *The Epistle to the Romans,* tr. by Edwyn C. Hoskyns (Oxford University Press, 1933, 1968), Preface to the Second Edition, p. 10.

8. So in Barth's Geneva "humanism" lecture of 1949 (*Theologische Studien,* Heft 28, p. 5): "The Christian message is the message of the humanism of God."

9. Karl Barth, *Der Römerbrief,* 1st ed. (Bern: G. A. Bäschlin, 1919), p. 392.

10. It is no accident, as Marquardt observes, that Barth's statements about

socialism are most reserved, and even denigrating, precisely at the time when he again returns to public political engagement, at the time around and after 1933—for example, in the excerpt from a letter to Paul Tillich published by Ernst Wolf. [EDITOR'S NOTE: On April 2, 1933, Barth wrote to Tillich: "Membership in the SPD does not mean for me a confession to the idea and world view of socialism. According to my understanding of the exclusivity of the Christian confession of faith, I can 'confess' myself neither to an idea nor to a world view in any serious sense. Hence I also have no necessary intrinsic relation to 'Marxism' as such. . . . As an idea and world view, I can bring to it neither fear nor love nor trust. Membership in the SPD means for me simply a practical political decision. Placed before the various options that confront a person in this regard, I consider it right *rebus sic stantibus* to espouse the party (1) of the working class, (2) of democracy, (3) of antimilitarism, and (4) of a conscious, but judicious, affirmation of the German people. I saw these requirements for a healthy politics fulfilled in, and only in, the SPD. Therefore, I choose this party. And because I do not want to abandon responsibility for the existence of this party to others, but want to assume and share this responsibility myself, I have become a member of it. I could also fundamentally manifest this decision in still more active forms. Up to now I supposed that I had neither the equipment nor the time nor the call for that, and I certainly presume that it will also remain that way in the future. I could not, of course, say for sure that it will necessarily remain that way. . . . A prohibition against the idea of socialism is something I could only come to terms with in all freedom at the place where even I must speak about it (in theological ethics). That means doing so without considering that the present government gives priority to the idea of nationalism, but rather drawing the idea of socialism into consideration and establishing its relatively critical significance strictly on theological grounds. If one should deny me this, then I would have to set myself in opposition and take the consequences upon myself. . . . Conversely, the freedom to adopt purely political decisions, positions, and possibly actions is precisely the point on which for me everything depends. The freedom, or the specific use I make of it, when I align myself with the SPD and become known as an SPD member by those who think the same and those who think differently, by my colleagues and students, by the men of the church and my theological readers, and by whomever it may happen to interest—that belongs (in contrast to the idea of socialism) to my existence, and whoever does not want to have me that way cannot have me at all. I would no longer be credible to myself and others as a theologian if I allowed myself in this civil relation to be pressured into a different decision than this, which corresponds to my convictions in political relations. You understand, this is the case precisely because in contrast to you I have no line of retreat into an esoteric socialism. My socialism is only exoteric; that is precisely why I cannot have my name removed from the party rolls. . . . In the face of mere advice and above all in the face of a demand by the present government, I will have to stand by my decision. . . . It can do a lot, this government; it can, for example, at its discretion dismiss and retire whomever it will. It cannot, however, do everything; it cannot, for example, compel a free man to become another for its own sake. I say this without heroic defiance and desire for martyrdom. It is simply out of the question. . . . I even want to confess to you that I wish that in Germany there might be still other free men of some reputation so deeply involved that they would have to keep their names listed in this poor little party roll book: To do otherwise is simply out of the question. Yet here everyone will have to act according to his own premises. And I quite understand that your premises must lead you to a different conclusion in this matter. I will rebuke you as usual only in this, that your premises do not exist in a proper theology (without an esoteric socialism)." Quoted, with permission, from Ernst Wolf, " 'Politischer Gottesdienst': Zum 80. Geburtstag des 'Politikers' Karl Barth," in *Blätter für deutsche und internationale Politik,* 11 (1966), Heft 4 (pp. 289–301), on pp. 290 f.] For another example, see Barth's "Abschied" from *Zwischen den Zeiten* (see note 2 to this essay).

11. Karl Barth, "The Word of God and the Task of the Ministry," in *The Word of God and the Word of Man,* tr. by Douglas Horton (Harper & Brothers, 1957), pp. 207 f. rev.

12. Barth, *The Epistle to the Romans,* 2d ed. (Hoskyns tr.), p. 478.

13. Barth's adjoining remark was overlooked that "it is most improbable that anyone will be won over to the cause of reaction—as a result of reading the Epistle to the Romans!" *(Ibid.)*

14. For affinity to democracy, see Karl Barth, "Church and State," in *Community, State, and Church,* ed. by Will Herberg (Doubleday & Company, Inc., 1960), pp. 144 f., n. 34. For resemblances to the natural law of the Enlightenment, on Jean Jacques Rousseau, see Karl Barth, "The Christian Community and the Civil Community," in Herberg (ed.), *Community, State, and Church,* pp. 163 f.

15. Barth, "The Christian Community and the Civil Community," *(loc. cit.),* section XIV.

16. Paul Tillich, "Critical and Positive Paradox" (1923), in Robinson (ed.), *The Beginnings of Dialectic Theology,* pp. 131–141; see also Tillich's essays on Barth from 1926 (Paul Tillich, *Gesammelte Werke,* Vol. XII, pp. 187–193) and 1935 (Paul Tillich, "What Is Wrong with the Dialectic Theology?"

Journal of Religion 15 [1935], pp. 127–145).

17. Karl Barth, *"No! Answer to Emil Brunner*, tr. by Peter Fraenkel (London: The Centenary Press, 1946), p. 93 rev.

18. *Ibid.*, p. 92 rev.

19. *Ibid.*, p. 87.

20. Barth, *Römerbrief* (1st ed.), p. 248 (on Rom. 8:19–22).

21. *Ibid.*, p. 247.

22. *Ibid.*, p. 245.

23. *Ibid.*, p. 246.

24. *Ibid.*, p. 247.

25. Thus CD IV/2, 721–725, and "The Christian Community and the Civil Community"—prepared through the analogy between heavenly and earthly *polis* in "Church and State."

26. Cf. E. Przywara, "Das katholische Kirchenprinzip," a lecture given at the University of Münster (February 5, 1929), at the invitation of the Protestant faculty of theology, in reply to Karl Barth's "Der Begriff der Kirche," *Zwischen den Zeiten* 7 (1929), pp. 277–302.

27. EDITOR'S NOTE: Previously in this essay the word *Gleichnis* has been rendered as "analogy." From this point it will be rendered as "parable" in order to maintain the contrast developed here to the *analogia fidei.*

28. Cf. Barth's essay, "Luther's Doctrine of the Eucharist: Its Basis and Purpose" (1928) in *Theology and Church*, tr. by Louise Pettibone Smith (London: SCM Press, Ltd., 1962), pp. 74–111.

29. This rejection of "anticipation" in "The Christian Community and the Civil Community" (section XIV) excludes, of course, neither the concept of anticipation in the political theology of J. Moltmann, J. B. Metz, and others nor the talk of "fragmentary" realizations of the kingdom of God in P. Tillich. Rather, with these the same is meant as in Barth's concept of "parable."

30. "The Christian Community and the Civil Community," section XIV.

31. EDITOR'S NOTE: In September 1919, Barth addressed a gathering of German religious socialists at Tambach in Thuringia. His lecture "The Christian's Place in Society" (in *The Word of God and the Word of Man*, pp. 272 ff.) is notable for signifying Barth's break with religious socialism (but not socialist politics) and his early attempt to place God's revelation in Jesus Christ at the center of his thought. (Cf. Karl Kupisch, *Karl Barth in Selbstzeugnissen und Bilddokumenten* [Hamburg: Rowohlt Taschenbuch Verlag, 1971], pp. 43 ff.)

32. Cf. Hromádka's letter to Barth in the Festschrift volume *Antwort: Karl*

Barth zum 70. Geburtstag am 10. Mai 1956 (Zurich: Evangelischer Verlag, 1956), pp. 3–13.

33. Friedrich-Wilhelm Marquardt, *Theologie und Sozialismus: Das Beispiel Karl Barths* (Munich: Chr. Kaiser Verlag, 1972), p. 312.

34. *Evangelische Theologie* 28 (1968), pp. 555 f.

35. Karl Barth and Rudolf Bultmann, *Briefwechsel 1922–1966*, pp. 24 f.

36. Paul Tillich, *Auf der Grenze* (1962), pp. 54, 46.

37. In Alfred Andersch's novel *Sansibar oder der letzte Grund* (Fischer-Taschenbücherei, Nr. 354, 1959), this still haunts Barth, who is portrayed as the "great churchman from Switzerland" who removed God to "unreachable distances" and consigned the world to the devil; for all that, it strikes Andersch at least as "remarkable" that the "most upright" among the pastors "were those who adhered to this comfortless doctrine" (p. 107).

38. How socialist praxis can open one's eyes can be seen in comparing two theologians of almost the same age, Barth and Friedrich Gogarten (Gogarten was a year younger), i.e., in comparing Barth's Safenwil writings to the nonsense that Gogarten wrote in 1915 in the *Protestantenblatt* on the occasion of the First World War. (Cited by W. Huber, *Evangelische Theologie und Kirche beim Ausbruch des Ersten Weltkriegs*, in *Studien zur Friedensforschung*, Vol. IV [1970], p. 143.) See also T. Strom, *Theologie im Schatten politischer Romantik* (Munich: Chr. Kaiser Verlag, 1970), pp. 69 ff. Like Barth, Gogarten was interested in a new order of society, but, confined within academic-bourgeois borders, he stumbled around in this respect with his head in the clouds.

39. Cf., in *Römerbrief* (1st ed., 1919), p. 332, the outlook toward "the other, the fulfilled historical hour when the now-dying embers of Marxist dogma will flare up anew as world truth, when the socialist church will rise from the dead in a world become socialist."

40. As was the theme of the open evening for students in his home at Bonn during the second semester of 1930/31: The programs of the political parties.

41. *Zwischen den Zeiten* 9 (1931), p. 453.

42. Cf. Barth's "Antworten auf Grundsatzfragen der Gefangenenseelsorge" (1960) and my commentary upon it in U. Kleinert, *Strafvollzug* (Munich, 1972), pp. 46–67.

43. Cf. "Political Decisions in the Unity of Faith," in Karl Barth, *Against the Stream: Shorter Post-War Writings: 1946–52*, ed. by Ronald Gregor Smith (London: SCM Press, Ltd., 1954), pp. 147–164.

44. See my article "Erinnerungen" in the issue of *Stimme der Gemeinde* on the 80th birthday of Karl Barth, May 1966, cols. 281–288.

45. EDITOR'S NOTE: The slogan *Gleichschaltung,* or "political coordination with the Nazi regime," expressed the governmental policy for all areas of German life.

46. Here, of course, the notion of a sequence, soon to be overcome, is still discernible.

4

Karl Barth as Socialist: Controversy Over a New Attempt to Understand Him

HERMANN DIEM

On the theological scene, Friedrich-Wilhelm Marquardt's book *Theologie und Sozialismus: Das Beispiel Karl Barths* (Munich: Chr. Kaiser Verlag, 1972) has recently appeared. In view of its contents one must ask whether what we have here is the *Karl Barth of tomorrow*.

What ought to be said about Karl Barth *today*, however, is a difficult question to answer. For the moment it may be left open. The veterans of the church struggle are dying out. To the extent that they entered Lutheran Church councils after 1945 through the Confessing Church's "half-seizure of power," they were unable to alter the ecclesiastical structure along the lines of Barth's "order of the community." Beyond that, a theology professor can only observe that after the "God is dead" theology ran its course, Barth's dogmatics was again studied seriously here and there. Whether that will lead to a rediscovery of the specific task of dogmatic theology, however, remains to be seen, and the situation will be very different from one university to the next.

We will have to start, therefore, from the Karl Barth of *yesterday:*

From "Der Sozialist in Karl Barth: Kontroverse um einen neuen Versuch, ihn zu verstehen," *Evangelische Kommentare* 5 (1972), pp. 292–296. Translated and reprinted with the kind permission of the author and the journal.

the Barth who placed the task of dogmatics at the center in a new way and who traced the whole misery of his time to the neglect of that task. Through such neglect, the practical disciplines of theology had lost their orientation to dogmatics and had thus discredited the whole enterprise of "theology as a science": "It is still not so very long since dogmatics was felt to be the great embarrassment of a scientific theology. But that was the time when theology in the precise sense had no scientific self-consciousness, but regarded it as necessary and possible laboriously to nourish itself by borrowing, first from philosophy, and then above all from history. . . . The bad conscience and dissatisfaction with which dogmatics was then pursued among other theological disciplines . . . was well founded." (CD I/2, 771 f. rev.) Over against this situation Barth asked "whether theology is still not perhaps the true and basic science from which the whole *universitas litterarum* has not only derived historically, but to which it can only return, in so far as scientific self-awareness has its true and original foundation there" (CD I/2, 772 rev.). And he added in warning: "Let there be no deception: Only on such a basis, only as theology assumes the power of its position midway between Bible and church [i.e., midway between exegesis and praxis] is all this possible" (CD I/2, 772 rev.).

At the time, this judgment about the state of contemporary theology was strongly contested. University theologians and church leaders considered it as the sharpest of provocations. Since then several decades of theological history have passed in which the dispute has been modified or even silenced. Nonetheless, Barth's prognosis at that time is today more contemporary than ever: "The time of theology's internal disintegration and external impotence and shame will inevitably recur the moment this position is again forgotten or abandoned, instead of being maintained still more strictly than has been possible in the short interval that separates us from the time of which we speak" (CD I/2, 772 rev.). We can only observe that this position has again in fact been abandoned and hence that the "impotence and shame" that Barth mentions has recurred in theology in such a way as to suggest that Karl Barth had never lived. The remarkable thing, moreover, is that those at fault here are precisely those who align themselves with Barth's theology, even if in very different ways. On the one hand, there are those who retreat in his name to a dogmatic fundamentalism that is incapable of perceiving the church's responsibility for the world. On the other hand, there are those who want to pursue the task of theology and church in the political realm, yet who threaten to lose the dogmatic ground under their feet.

As an example of the first group, we may take the "No Other Gospel" movement, which broadly dominates the German church situation, especially in the synods, and which compels the church leadership to take notice. Its theological basis is twofold: first, a reasserted orthodoxy, which has never been more scholastic, and which, as could have been learned from Barth, has already proved disastrous for theology; and second, a pietist theology of awakening. In combination, these two seem theologically invincible, because faith as trust *(fides qua)* and faith as assent *(fides quae)* are supposed to supplement and complement each other mutually. This well-known amalgam from the history of theology has been unmasked precisely in Karl Barth's dogmatics as a glossing over of all theological problems.

In 1966 when he was asked by a convener of the "No Other Gospel" movement's Dortmund assembly to comment on the "confession" made there, Barth in a very brusque letter understandably refused to get involved in the dogmatic problems of such a "confession" and instead posed a series of counterquestions. He asked whether the conveners were ready and willing "to start a similar 'movement' and 'great assembly' against the desire to arm the West German army with nuclear weapons, against the Vietnam war and the German government allied with the Americans who wage it, against the ever-recurring outbreaks of vulgar anti-Semitism (desecration of graves) in West Germany, and for a peace treaty between West Germany and the Eastern European governments that would recognize the borders existing since 1945." "If your *correct* confession," Barth wrote, "to Jesus Christ crucified and raised again for us according to the Holy Scriptures includes and expresses that in itself, then it is a *genuine*, valuable, and fruitful confession. If not, then for all its correctness, it is a dead, cheap, pharisaical confession which strains out gnats and swallows camels."

More indignant than grieved by Barth's reply, churchmen in that circle supposed that they could cite the Barmen declaration against him. What has changed since Barmen, 1934, however, is the political situation in which the church must bear witness that "Jesus Christ, as he is attested for us in Holy Scripture, is the one Word of God which we have to hear and which we have to trust and obey in life and in death" (Barmen 1).

At the same time it is well known that concrete directives for society cannot be adduced in a simple way from Scripture. Nevertheless, the church cannot simply abstain from taking a stand as long as she proclaims the coming of Jesus Christ as salvation for the world. Barth responded so contentiously to the Dortmund conveners because Christianity in West Germany (on which he was taking a stand)—for whatever reasons, whether from political lethargy, or from a supposedly ecclesiastically grounded abstinence from the tasks actually before it—was simply silent. At the same time it must constantly be remembered to whom Barth concretely turns. In his famous "Letter to an East German Pastor" from 1958, he had to speak differently than to those at Dortmund: "God above all things! He is also above the atheism and materialism by which your government indeed really goes too far. I am familiar with that large book of teachings and pictures which begins with planetary nebula and ends with portraits of Marx, Lenin and (in my copy) Stalin."

Meanwhile, the discussion of Karl Barth's theology has proceeded on several fronts. An especially comprehensive volume is Helmut Gollwitzer's *The Existence of God as Confessed by Faith* [The Westminster Press, 1965]. A further entry into the discussion is Eberhard Jüngel's *Gottes Sein ist im Werden* ("God's Being Is in Becoming") [Tübingen: J. C. B. Mohr, 1965]. According to Jüngel, all the objections to be raised against Gollwitzer's book may be traced back to the question of "why Gollwitzer neglected from the outset to specify the concept of God's being in a Trinitarian way and precisely in this specification to maintain the historicity of God's being" (Jüngel, p. 7). That is the basis on which the remark in Jüngel's Foreword must be understood: "This paraphrase is being published because in contemporary theological discussions, both on the part of Herbert Braun and also—*mirabile dictu*—on the part of Helmut Gollwitzer,[1] the following trains of thought initiated by Karl Barth for contemporary theology have remained unconsidered" (Jüngel, p. vi).

A response to this criticism on Gollwitzer's part is unknown. One will have to see it, however, in Gollwitzer's foreword to Marquardt's book *Theologie und Sozialismus*, even though Jüngel is not mentioned by name: "Here a Barth suddenly emerges who moves in on us in a very different way than had become evident to many who had known him. It is also a very different Barth from the one who becomes visible in the hitherto existing secondary literature about him with its richly scholastic features. Where it is so politically understood, the gospel once again challenges us very differently than where it is based simply on the relation between God and man such that our relationship to the world becomes a secondary, or even arbitrary, matter." (Marquardt, p. 8.)

What Gollwitzer means by his verdict about the "richly scholastic features" of Barth interpretation becomes even clearer in the preface by Marquardt himself: "Generally, it is resisted that theology must take seriously the political conditions of its possibility, i.e., that traditional historical and philosophical reflection on its ideas must be completed through a mode of reflection that is social" (Marquardt, p. 10). As the "germ cell" of his book he designates the "antiauthoritarian [left-wing] students," and the task of transmitting theology to those who are where the action is, but are "running away from theology without ever having rightly caught sight of it" (Marquardt, p. 11). To meet this challenge, "of course, a protest is needed against an involuted 'theology in itself' and now more than ever against a well-manicured 'Karl Barth in himself,' concocted especially in Germany to buttress the ecclesiastical and academic authority structure. This book is that protest." (Marquardt, p. 12.)

In the introduction Marquardt gives an account of his procedure: "Barth once said that the acceptance of Marxist elements still does not make one a Marxist. So we must guard ourselves against stamping him as such against his own self-testimony. Hence, this work is not entitled 'Theology and Marxism,' but 'Theology and Socialism.' Socialism with unmistakable 'Marxist elements' is the decisive characterization of Barth's political position as demonstrated here." (Marquardt, pp. 33 f.) Barth's concept of socialism and Marxism was basically nonideological. Because in materialism he saw hidden something of the resurrection of the flesh, he was able, according to Marquardt, to incorporate Marxist elements in a way that was not only ethical and practical, but also intimately theological—both Biblically and dogmatically. What is at stake is thus "an analysis of the socialist influence on Barth's theology" (Marquardt, p. 16).

Yet even Marquardt questions whether an explicitly practical political position can be shown to influence theology. "Aren't social action and Christian dogmatics generically irreconcilable modes of human self-expression and assertion? Isn't it the case that at most they can only be connected to each other externally, that they possess no demonstrable intrinsic connection, and certainly none that can be proven in a scientifically objectifiable way? Barth certainly created anything but a socialist or Marxist theology, and he allowed no Christian-socialist amalgamation of any kind to dominate his thought. The difference between Barth's explicitly political and his explicitly theological statements makes this clear: He neither theologizes politics nor politicizes theology." (Marquardt, p. 16.)

"A position must be taken from both sides of these questions" (Marquardt, p. 17). And that a position not only *can* but *must* be taken from both sides at once is precisely what Marquardt wants to demonstrate with this book. To Marxists it is self-evident, according to him, "that there is a direct connection, or at least one that is clearly visible in its manifestations, between social reality and every intellectual construction, including of course those of theology. . . . Here thinking as such is critically analyzed 'from below to above' on the basis of its connections to the economic 'substructure' and to social 'praxis.' " (Marquardt, p. 17.) "Until now no theological analogy to this procedure has been worked out methodologically, and it seems at first glance as if precisely the example of Karl Barth shows the *a priori* impossibility of inducing theology 'from below.' This procedure seems—not least under Barth's powerful influence—to be contrary to theology, for theology thinks under the primacy of something normative; the origin and goal of its thought transcend all conditions that in themselves are merely conditioned. Therefore, there can ultimately be no 'influences' that touch its essence." (Marquardt, p. 17.) Its historicity is simply a form of expression; its historical content is its connection to the uniqueness of God's Son, Jesus Christ. This notion of the essentially theological has created in the tradition a logic, an order of thinking, peculiar to itself, as well as a whole constellation of questions and problems designed to guarantee the integrity and identity of theology through every conceivable modification. (Marquardt, p. 17.)

Now certainly no one can say of Barth that he did his theology in a social and political vacuum. Marquardt is concerned to show, however, that Barth's public activity "also had—and here the analogy to Marxism arises—material and formal repercussions upon his theologizing as such" (Marquardt, p. 18). "If not theology in general, at any rate Barth's particular theology showed itself in a unique and unprecedented way to be open to a reception of the Marxist theory-praxis relation" (Marquardt, p. 18). Hence "with ever-increasing clarity, the 'human deed' in general was displaced by the exclusive deed of the incarnate Son of God which includes all men in itself" (Marquardt, p. 24).

Marquardt's entire book stands or falls on that which he sees developing in Barth "with ever-increasing clarity." "As in the case of the [earlier] concepts of the 'revolution' of God, the 'living' God, and 'resurrection,' so also eventually in the case of the political-ontological relation to praxis, Jesus Christ was placed in the political vacancy. More precisely, Jesus Christ became the Biblical and political concretion of those attributes formerly discerned in that which was living, revolutionary, resurrected, and practical. The question is this: Does this Christological focus imply a theological *break,* or is it to be linked up with the previous cluster of ideas? . . . The Biblical Jesus Christ as exposited in church dogma assumes the *function* that revolution, life, resurrection, and praxis had previously exercised in relation to God and human society, as well as to theological thinking; he is meant to be understood in this function." (Marquardt, p. 24.) Marquardt attempts to show that such an interpretation is fundamentally possible through an exposition of the *Extra Calvinisticum,* of the *anhypostasis* and *enhypostasis,* and of the *assumptio carnis.*

As a theologian one can only read with astonishment that the *Extra Calvinisticum,*[2] by which Barth rejected all attempts at a "mediating" or natural theology, was the doctrine that enabled him to ground the content of such theology. Marquardt's thesis here is this, that Barth's total negation of natural theology was a "polemical action waged from a peculiar theological basis that was not yet fully developed," and that "at the same time it was a means of confronting Nazism politically" (Marquardt, p. 263). In the politically quieter times beforehand and afterward, Barth supposedly not only affirmed, but with the help of the *Extra Calvinisticum* actually assimilated, the truth content of natural theology.[3]

Marquardt attempts to corroborate this thesis in his section entitled "The *assumptio carnis* and the 'Human Species' " (Marquardt, pp. 265–275), where he appeals especially to Barth's study *Christ and Adam: Man and Humanity in Romans 5*. He sees Barth setting a course "that expands and completes the Christological *anhypostasis* (the *anhypostasis* of the human nature of Jesus Christ) through an anthropological *enhypostasis:* the *enhypostasis* of the *humanitas*, of the collective 'human species' in the person of the incarnate Word" (Marquardt, p. 267).[4]

Barth worked his way to this position "only gradually." "He still finds himself within the Reformed tradition when he considers the collective meaning of the *assumptio carnis* in the connection between 'Christ and his own.' . . . The Son, 'because he never wants to be known without his assumed humanity,' never wants to be known 'without the mystical union of the elect with his person as the head of his kingdom.' . . . As we have seen already, the human nature . . . assumed into unity with his existence is implicitly that of all men. In his being as man God has implicitly assumed the humanity of all men. . . . Within humanity is the church, which exists 'anhypostatically and enhypostatically' in Jesus Christ as 'the second form of his one existence,' the 'second form of his body.' At the end of time Jesus Christ will be the *'totus Christus'*—'Christ with his Christendom.' " (Marquardt, p. 267; citations are from CD IV/2, 59 f. rev.)

Marquardt continues: "However, Barth always pressed beyond this collectivity as grasped merely *ecclesiologically*. The Adam-Christ typology in Romans 5 was for him from the outset the occasion for an interpretation in terms of the *history of the human species* which led beyond the ecclesiastical view" (Marquardt, p. 267). If Jüngel wants to explain the connection in the typology "ontologically," then he misunderstands "the completely different dimension and intention of Barth's argumentation" (Marquardt, p. 269).[5]

However, according to Barth in his study *Christ and Adam,* our starting point is "that we have to understand Adam from *Christ,* and ourselves from our unity with *him,* and not the reverse. . . . Jesus Christ is the secret and the truth even about sinful and mortal man and thus the secret and the truth about *human nature* as such. . . . The question is simply not raised here about what it is specifically that makes the Christian into a special human being. We hear only about what it means for the human being as such that his objective reality in Adam does not stand as final, but rather that it is surpassed and included and illuminated by his objective reality in Christ, and placed in its service. . . . Paul obviously had no intention of fathering an idle and arbitrary speculation when, in vs. 12–21, he proceeded to this further account of the same topic. . . . Our status as believers is based on our prior status as human beings; more concretely, it is based on our status as Adam's children and heirs—as persons who are weak, sinners, godless, and enemies. . . . That is why as believers we are not outside, but within the kingdom of Christ. We have come *to* Christ, thus becoming believers and Christians, because we had already come *from* Christ, so that there was nothing else for us to do but believe and become Christians." (*Christus und Adam,* pp. 51 ff.; cf. E.T., pp. 109–112.)[6]

From Barth's argument Marquardt then draws the following conclusion: "Not only Christians, but all persons are included in the realm of Christ's effectiveness. Dogmatically reversed, this means that the reality of Christ is the 'framework and realm in which human beings as such are included' (*Christus und Adam,* p. 50)." (Marquardt, p. 270.) As a consequence of this "dogmatic reversal," the nearness of salvation of Christians and non-Christians is supposedly also reversed. "Since as human beings they already exist in the domain of Christ's reality from the outset, as Christians they are then also able 'to consolidate' their relationship to Christ by belonging to the church. . . . The unity occurring in Adam between individual human beings and humanity in general obtains all the more for the individual human being taken up in Christ. Hence, when seen from the Christological standpoint, the existence of 'the individual person in humanity' and of 'humanity in the individual person' is a structural

factor of the *humanitas* which the Son of God has assumed into unity
with himself. *The human species exists enhypostatically in Christ.*"
(Marquardt, p. 271.) Just *who* has dogmatically reversed *what* here?[7]

By this time, at the very latest, Marquardt would have to have
noticed that the course which he imputes to Barth, but which he
actually develops on his own (that of expanding and completing the
Christological *anhypostasis* through an anthropological *enhypostasis*),
results in making the Christological categories of the *an-* and *enhypostasis* completely meaningless. The *anhypostasis* as the conceptual counterpart to the *enhypostasis* simply vanishes. Marquardt
seems not to have understood at all that the essential and primary
interest of the doctrine of the *anhypostasis* pertains to "the *imper-
sonalitas* of the human nature of Christ" (CD IV/2, 49).

As Barth writes: "By *hypostasis, persona,* was meant the independent existence (the *propria subsistentia*) of his humanity. Its *hypostasis* is, *longe eminentior,* that of the Logos, no other. Jesus Christ
exists as a man because and as the eternal Son exists, because and as
this Son makes human essence his own, adopting and exalting it into
unity with himself. Therefore, Jesus Christ as a man exists directly
in and with the one God in the existential mode of his eternal Son
and Logos—not otherwise or apart from this mode. He exists . . . in
the *one* form of human nature and human being, as elected and
prepared and actualized by God, yet not autonomously, as would be
the case if that with which God unites himself were a *homo* and not
humanitas." (CD IV/2, 49 rev.)

Theologians have often raised the objection against this theologoumenon that it indirectly affirms the *enhypostasis* as "the identity
of the existence of the man Jesus with that of the Son of God" (CD
IV/2, 49). The question is whether this identity involves "at an
important point a denial of his true humanity, a concealed or even
blatant docetism, since it must obviously belong to the true humanity
of Jesus Christ that he should have an independent existence as a
man like us." To this Barth replies: "It is true enough that the
humanum exists always in the form of actual men. This existence is
not denied to the man Jesus, but ascribed to him with the positive
concept of the *enhypostasis.* But it is hard to see how the full truth
of the humanity of Jesus Christ is qualified or even destroyed by the

fact that as distinct from us he is also a *real* man only as the Son of God, so that there can be no question of a peculiar and autonomous existence of his humanity." (CD IV/2, 49 rev.) This theologoumenon is not superfluous, according to Barth, for what depends on it is "no less than the fact that in Jesus Christ we do not have to do with a man into whom God has changed himself, but unchanged and indirectly with *God himself;* no less than the *unity* in which as man he is the Son of God, and as the Son of God man; and finally no less than the *universal* relevance and significance of his existence for all other men" (CD IV/2, 49 rev.).

However, this "universal relevance" is precisely what Marquardt is concerned about when he sees Barth pressing beyond a merely ecclesiastical view toward an interpretation in terms of the history of the human species. The way is thus prepared for Marquardt's own thesis: "The human species exists in Christ enhypostatically" (Marquardt, p. 271). With this thesis Marquardt has perverted Barth's teaching that the categories of the *an-* and *enhypostasis* are indispensable to describing the mystery of the incarnation, by imputing to Barth a direction which "expands and completes the Christological *anhypostasis* through an anthropological *enhypostasis:* the *enhypostasis* of the *humanitas,* of the collective human species in the person of the incarnate Word" (Marquardt, p. 267). It has apparently escaped Marquardt that at the same time he has had to abandon the decisive doctrine of the *anhypostasis,* since it can no longer have any meaning in his conception. In just that way he has undercut the Christian *sacramentum* and destroyed it or made it superfluous.[8]

Marquardt, however, finds his interpretation of the *enhypostasis* of Christ in the human species confirmed by Barth's discussion of the *assumptio carnis* in *Christ and Adam.* He says that for Barth the Adam-Christ typology "was from the outset an occasion for an interpretation leading beyond the ecclesiological view to one in terms of the history of the human species" (Marquardt, p. 267). He contends that "Barth added this structural factor of the history of the human species onto the traditional dogmatic specifications of the *humanitas*" (Marquardt, p. 271). Yet this is precisely what Barth has not done. At the conclusion of his study he writes: "This is especially what we have to learn from Rom. 5:12–21: What Adam was, we are also, and so is everyone who following him and with us is called a human being; what we and all human beings are, the one Adam already was and is. A human being is at once a distinct individual and only a distinct individual, here and now in the strictest particularity, yet as such, together with all others, in the fullest sense, a responsible representative of humanity. He is always for himself and always for all men. . . . If we base our thinking on this text, then we must depart from every collectivism to the left and every individualism to the right. The true human being, as here presented, allows neither the one interpretation nor the other." (*Christus und Adam*, pp. 53 f.; cf. E.T., pp. 112 ff.).[9]

Marquardt's attempt to impute the possibility of a "natural theology" to Barth, at least for "quieter times," does not only rest on a conceptual confusion in Christology. Rather, here is the key to the tendency of his entire work, which he openly presents, after having supposedly derived it from Barth: "For the historical structuring of humanity according to species there are of course precedents. They belong—in whatever form—to the foundation of theological thinking in the first half of the nineteenth century." (Marquardt, p. 271.) The fact that Barth once set out against this theology does not disturb Marquardt at all. Supposing that he has put this objection behind him, Marquardt audaciously asserts: "By differentiating between *homo* and *humanitas*, Barth joins with Feuerbach in his understanding of humanity. But that is precisely what brings him into an obvious affinity with Feuerbach's idea of the history of the human species, and toward a description of Jesus as the 'representative of the species.' For while Jesus is not the species in itself, he cannot possibly be conceived without it. . . . Via Feuerbach, theology as shaped by Barth finally emerges from its metaphysical, cosmological orientation into its sociopolitical phase. 'Reality' is no longer determined by nature and the human subject over against it, but by the social essence of the human species." (Marquardt, pp. 271 ff.)

From here the way then goes farther, to Karl Marx and his second thesis on Feuerbach: "The question whether objective truth can be attributed to human thinking is not a question of theory, but is a *practical* question. In practice man must prove the truth, that is, the reality and power, the this-worldliness of his thinking. The dispute over the reality or nonreality of thinking which is isolated from practice is a purely *scholastic* question." (Karl Marx, "Theses on Feuerbach," II, in *Marx and Engels, Basic Writings on Politics and Philosophy,* ed. by Lewis S. Feuer [Doubleday & Company, Inc., 1959], p. 243 rev.)

To be sure, Marquardt would not falsify the antispeculative thrust of Marx's thesis on Feuerbach "by using it speculatively and allowing something against its sense to be said about God which it says about man. It seems quite possible for us to establish, however, that this thesis (and the other Feuerbach theses in general) can develop its critical power even within theology, and by no means only in a critique of the concept of God initiated from without, but rather— much more interestingly—even in an intrinsic critique of theological talk about God." (Marquardt, p. 277.)

What here approaches us as *Karl Barth tomorrow* has now been made clear. When one recalls the reference in Marquardt's preface to the "antiauthoritarian students" as the "germ cell" of the book, then one will have to grant that the students could be running around with a theologian who is more secure in the saddle than Marquardt when it comes to Christology. Apart from that, however, the question whether the students will "rightly catch sight of" theology (a question that must be raised because of the book's claims for itself) is one that—in view of Karl Barth's theology as Marquardt presents it—can only be answered in the negative.

NOTES

1. EDITOR'S NOTE: Helmut Gollwitzer and Herbert Braun, *Post Bultmann locutum: Eine Discussion zwischen Helmut Gollwitzer und Herbert Braun, am 13. Februar 1964 in der Johannes-Gutenberg-Universität zu Mainz am Rhein* (Hamburg: H. Reich, 1965). Cf. John Godsey's interview with Karl Barth: "I asked Barth what he thought of Eberhard Jüngel. . . . Barth replied that he was very hopeful. . . . I asked his opinion of Jüngel's latest book, called *Gottes Sein ist im Werden . . .* which purports to be a paraphrase of Barth's doctrine of the Being of God. In it Jüngel calls in question Helmut Gollwit-

zer's understanding of Barth's doctrine, as Gollwitzer has represented it in his controversy with Herbert Braun over the question of how one speaks responsibly of God. Barth asserted that the book was excellent, and summed up the matter with, 'Gollwitzer is correct vis-à-vis Braun, but Jüngel is correct vis-à-vis Gollwitzer!' " (From John Godsey, "Barth's Life After 1958," in Karl Barth, *How I Changed My Mind* [John Knox Press, 1966], p. 82.)

2. EDITOR'S NOTE: The term under discussion here, the so-called *Extra Calvinisticum*, originated in the course of post-Reformation Lutheran-Calvinist debates about the doctrine of Christ's person. How are the two natures of Christ to be conceived? Does the human nature of Christ share in the majesty of his divine nature? Conversely, does his divine nature share in the passibility of his human nature? The Lutherans tended to adopt a fully dialectical view in which both questions are answered in the affirmative: Christ's human nature partakes directly in his divine majesty; his divinity partakes directly in his human suffering. This view was known as the *communicatio idiomatum*. The Reformed alternative to this view became known as the *Extra Calvinisticum*. In contrast to the Lutheran view, the Reformed conception was more nearly paradoxical than dialectical: Christ's human nature does not directly partake in his divine majesty; rather, it does so indirectly by remaining finite and creaturely even as it is joined hypostatically to his divinity. By the same token, Christ's divinity does not directly partake in his human suffering; rather, it does so indirectly by remaining infinite and eternal even as it is joined hypostatically to his humanity. Accepting the full consequences of their position, the Lutherans insisted that the human body of Christ was as ubiquitous as his divinity (by virtue of the *communicatio idiomatum*). This insistence was crucial to their affirmation of Christ's bodily presence in the elements of the Eucharist. To the Calvinists, these notions were unacceptable. In short, the force of their doctrine of the *Extra Calvinisticum* was to affirm that the eternal Son of God was united, but not restricted, to his humanity, and that his finite humanity was united to, but not subsumed by, his divinity. (Cf. E. David Willis, *Calvin's Catholic Christology: The Function of the So-called Extra Calvinisticum in Calvin's Theology* [Leiden: E. J. Brill, 1966]; and Ian D. Siggins, *Martin Luther's Doctrine of Christ,* [Yale University Press, 1970], pp. 230–239.)

3. EDITOR'S NOTE: In his book, Marquardt makes two basic points about the *Extra Calvinisticum*. Materially, he contends that Barth's understanding of the *Extra Calvinisticum* makes it possible for him to accept "natural theology" within a theology of revelation. Just as Christ's divinity makes possible a theology of revelation, so his humanity makes possible a place for the content of natural theology. The doctrine of the *Extra Calvinisticum*

supposedly intimates to Barth that the incarnation of the eternal Word is not simply restricted to the *man* Jesus as such, but includes the humanity of Jesus and thus by implication that of all men. Historically, he argues that Barth first glimpsed the inclusiveness of the incarnation through reflection on the doctrine of the *Extra Calvinisticum,* and that he then developed the meaning of this inclusiveness more fully in his later writings.

Diem is interested in challenging both of Marquardt's points. His argument as presented here is an abridged version from his longer article on the same topic. There he argues three points: (1) After 1924 Barth's view of natural theology remained more or less constant. It did not change in the 1930's during the heat of the Church Struggle, nor in 1959 when he published CD IV/3, nor in 1961 in a letter to the *Brüdergemeinde.* (2) Barth never indulged in a "total negation of natural theology," not even in 1934 in his famous assault on Emil Brunner. After 1924 Barth always placed natural theology in Christological perspective and thus always kept a place for it in his thought. (3) Barth did not modify his view of natural theology under political pressures or for political purposes. He did not use an attack on natural theology as "a means of confronting Nazism politically." His attack on natural theology was strictly for theological purposes. (See Hermann Diem, "Die Christologie Karl Barths in der Sicht von Friedrich-Wilhelm Marquardt," *Kerygma und Dogma* 20 [1974], pp. 138–157, on p. 143.)

4. EDITOR'S NOTE: The terms *anhypostasis* and *enhypostasis* need to be clarified, since neither Diem nor Marquardt pauses to define them directly. The terms were first used as a pair by Leontius of Byzantium, and are not to be attributed to Cyril of Alexandria, though it is true that Leontius used the terms to elucidate Chalcedonian Christology along the lines laid down by Cyril. The Chalcedonian Creed stated that the incarnate Word exists "in two natures," divine and human, each complete and each with its own distinctive properties and operations which the union did not impair. Cyril's emphasis, however, and that of the Alexandrian East, had been upon the unity of the person of Christ and upon the ontological priority of the Word. Alexandria feared that the affirmation of two natures in Christ would imply that Christ had two existences, independent and equal in status, the one divine, the other human.

The contribution of Leontius was to accept the Chalcedonian formulation, "in two natures," but to interpret it along lines that preserved Cyril's emphasis upon the priority of the Word and the unity of the Word made flesh. Leontius achieved this conceptual reconciliation in terms of the *anhypostasis* and *enhypostasis* of the human nature of Christ. The humanity of Christ has no independent existence of its own apart from Christ's divinity as the eternal Logos. The humanity of Christ always exists in unity with his divinity. The humanity of Christ exists in, and only in, the eternal Word. The positive side of this doctrine rules out "docetism": The humanity of Christ, which always exists in unity with the eternal Word, is real humanity. The negative side of the doctrine rules out "Ebionitism": The humanity of Christ, which is always real humanity, exists only in unity with the eternal Word; apart from this unity there is no such humanity. The positive side is what Leontius calls the *enhypostasis* ("existence in") and the negative side is what he calls the *anhypostasis* ("no other mode of existence"). Christ's real humanity always exists in his divinity and has no other mode of existence.

The effect of this teaching is to retain the unity of the incarnation, while allowing for the phrase "in two natures," by giving priority to Christ's divinity as the eternal Word. The divine nature of Christ gives rise to his human nature; his human nature gains its existence from having the divine nature as its subject. The incarnation is always the incarnation of the preexistent eternal Word. The incarnate Word is the eternal Son of God who became man *(enhypostasis)*. Jesus the man is always none other than the eternal Son of God *(anhypostasis)*. (Cf. J. N. D. Kelly, *Early Christian Doctrines* [Harper & Row, Publishers, Inc., 1960], pp. 238 ff.; Williston Walker, *A History of the Christian Church*, 3d ed. [Charles Scribner's Sons, 1970], p. 142; and Karl Barth, CD I/2, 163 ff.)

5. EDITOR'S NOTE: Diem thinks it is legitimate when Jüngel tries to work out the ontological implications of Barth's theology, but illegitimate when Marquardt tries to work out its political implications. Marquardt's point is that there is actually an anti-ontological thrust to Barth's thought. Barth tried to direct theology away from the abstract to the concrete. His theology, therefore, is much more open to left-wing Hegelian social thought than to abstract idealist ontologies. While Marquardt seems to be correct about where the emphasis lies in Barth's theology, it is difficult to see why political and ontological perspectives must be regarded as mutually exclusive.

6. EDITOR'S NOTE: Since the English version of Barth's *Christ and Adam* (tr. by T. A. Smail; Collier Books, 1955) is basically a paraphrase, the passages quoted here have been translated and cited according to the German text (*Christus und Adam nach Röm. 5* [Zürich: Evangelischer Verlag, 1952]). The corresponding passages in the English version are then also cited. The English version has been followed wherever possible.

7. EDITOR'S NOTE: Diem objects to the way Marquardt imputes "universalism" to Barth. Just as he will go on to argue that the *"enhypostasis* of humanity"* in Marquardt's interpretation seems to make the incarnation

superfluous, so here Diem argues that it seems to make the church superfluous. What place is there for a community justified by faith, if grace operates so completely objectively that faith and church are unnecessary for salvation? Diem's argument against Marquardt about ecclesiology and universalism is much stronger, in my opinion, than his argument about the incarnation. Marquardt's emphasis on an "anthropological *enhypostasis*" makes Barth seem like a universalist for whom the church is not really necessary. It is clear, however, that Barth is not a universalist in this sense. (Cf. Joseph D. Bettis, "Is Karl Barth a Universalist?" *Scottish Journal of Theology* 20 [1967], pp. 423–436.)

8. EDITOR'S NOTE: Diem's argument here is as follows: Marquardt, in the name of Karl Barth, proceeds to pervert and destroy the mystery of the incarnation. Marquardt speaks of the *enhypostasis* of the human species. This use of the term *enhypostasis* can only mean that in the human species itself, the eternal Word of God becomes incarnate. Jesus becomes a mere symbol for the incarnation of God in humanity. The *anhypostasis* of Christ's humanity simply vanishes. What sense does it make to say that Christ's humanity has no other mode of existence than in unity with his divinity, if his humanity merely symbolizes the *enhypostasis* of the entire human species, if the entire human species exists in hypostatic union with the eternal Son of God? In the *enhypostasis* of the human species, by which the human race would be deified or made capable of deification, the mystery of the incarnation, the central Christian mystery, is distorted beyond recognition. Such an *enhypostasis* makes the incarnation of the Word in Jesus superfluous. In this way Marquardt arrives at his supposedly desired goal of a natural theology without Jesus Christ.

If Diem seems to have misunderstood Marquardt at this point, it can be traced to Marquardt's loose, at times even muddled, use of the terms *anhypostasis* and *enhypostasis*. Marquardt's main point is this: When Barth speaks of "humanity," he uses the term in a sense that is realist rather than idealist, social rather than individual, political rather than ontological. In other words, Barth uses the term as concretely as possible. When he speaks of the "humanity of Jesus Christ," he is thinking of that humanity in the concrete, realist sense so that by implication the significance of Christ's humanity is equally realist and concrete: political, social, and historical. At this point, it seems to me, Marquardt has interpreted Barth correctly.

Diem seems to be right, however, when he charges that Marquardt has failed to grasp the meaning of the term *anhypostasis*. The term means, as we have seen, that Christ's humanity actually has no other mode of existence apart from its unity with his divinity. Marquardt, however, associates the

term *anhypostasis* with the *Extra Calvinisticum,* that is, with the eternal
Word as it exists apart from, but in relation to, the act of incarnation.
Marquardt thus uses *anhypostasis* not in the sense of a nonactuality, but in
the sense of a potentiality. In other words, he seems to think that the term
anhypostasis can refer to the human nature of Christ existing as a potentiality
in the divine nature apart from the act of incarnation, that *anhypostasis*
refers to something like the eternal Son of God's concrete possibility of
assuming the humanity prepared for him for the purpose of incarnation.
Hence, Marquardt can speak of Barth "expanding and completing" the
Christological *anhypostasis*—as if it pertained to a potentiality and not to a
nonactuality (and an impossibility). Barth indeed conceived of Christ's
humanity as existing as a potentiality within the eternal Son of God (e.g.,
see CD IV/2, 50), but he never designated this potentiality by the term
anhypostasis. So Diem seems to be right that Marquardt's use of *anhypostasis*
is confused, but what about Marquardt's apparent intention? Did Barth
"expand and complete" the divine potentiality for incarnation "through an
anthropological *enhypostasis:* the *enhypostasis* of the *humanitas* . . . in the
person of the incarnate Word"? (Marquardt, p. 267.)

Once again Marquardt's use of terms seems confused and misleading. In
his critique of Marquardt, Diem construes the term *enhypostasis* in its
conventional, literal sense, by which an "*enhypostasis* of the human race"
could only mean an unmediated hypostatic union of the human race with
the Son of God. But is this really what Marquardt means? In a Christian
context this notion would be so absurd, especially when attributed to Barth,
that Diem might well have attempted to penetrate beyond this confused and
confusing use of terms. What Marquardt is really getting at is simply that
Barth construed the humanity of Christ's *enhypostasis* in realist and concrete
terms, as discussed above, so that it might be said that Barth "expanded and
completed" the divine potentiality for incarnation by implicitly attributing
social, political, and historical significance to Christ's humanity. Moreover,
the mystery of the incarnation does not become superfluous for Marquardt,
because he *never* suggests that the relation of sociohistorical humanity to
God exists apart from the mediation of the incarnate Word. Rather, he
suggests that by extension all humanity can be conceived as existing anhypostatically and enhypostatically in Christ, just as the church can be so
conceived (cf. CD IV/2, 60).

9. EDITOR'S NOTE: See note 6 to this essay. Cf. Karl Barth, *God Here and
Now,* tr. by Paul M. van Buren (Harper & Row, Publishers, Inc., 1964), pp.
6 f.

5

On Reading Karl Barth from the Left

DIETER SCHELLONG

It is unusual when a volume of technical theology—especially one of such scope and difficulty—goes into its second edition after only half a year. Evidently, it takes up a timely topic to which there had previously been no proper access. This book, Marquardt's *Theologie und Sozialismus*,[1] concentrates on two questions which, it seems to me, have remained uncomfortably open. The first concerns the wide-spread embarrassment about the theology of Karl Barth, which is historically intelligible, but difficult to come to terms with. The second concerns a certain theological deficit in social and political engagement and in reflection about the church's newly important social dimension. By discussing both questions at once, Marquardt has been able to bring unresolved issues back onto the agenda and to rearrange issues under active consideration so that the attention aroused by his book is completely justified.

It would indeed be interesting to examine not only Marquardt's book but also the reactions to it, because in some ways they are quite extraordinary, and something could be learned from them about the contemporary theological situation. However, I must limit myself

From "Barth von links gelesen—ein Beitrag zum Thema: 'Theologie und Sozialismus,'" *Zeitschrift für evangelische Ethik* 17 (1973), pp. 238–250. Translated and reprinted with the kind permission of the author and the journal.

here and can only cast side glances at judgments from other quarters. It remains completely outside my purview that Marquardt's work was rejected as a *Habilitationsschrift* by the *Kirchliche Hochschule* in Berlin. In order for one to be able to comment on that, the scholarly evaluations *(Gutachten)* would have to be made public in unrevised form, but even then I am not sure a discussion would serve any purpose. By contrast, it is certain that Marquardt's book has already created new interest in Barth on the part of many who could previously find no access to him and who thus neglected his work. As a result, Barth's contribution can once again become fruitful for theological discussion. I have just come from a seminar on Marquardt's book, which I discuss here with gratitude toward all who participated.

The intention of this book can be described as follows: Marquardt wants to show that socialism and theology have something to do with each other and that Barth's theology provides a specific example that can be instructive for a meaningful new relationship between theology and socialism today. The salient point here is that socialism is not simply assigned to a slot in social ethics (as *one* theme among many), but is presented as relevant to the foundations of theology. Accordingly, Marquardt's deliberations focus on the central topic of dogmatics, the doctrine of God and Christology. At that very point he establishes a relation between theology and socialism in Barth which is made explicit and thus presented for further reflection. According to Marquardt, Barth does not develop his doctrine of God "purely" from the requirements of the theological subject matter, but also from socialist praxis and socialist interests. Thus his doctrine of God bears in itself the marks of this experience and this intention.

With this thesis it seems as if Marquardt has nullified everything Barth said and demanded about the freedom of theology from alien influences. Barth appears as a theologian of culture—now as a theologian of socialist culture. Marquardt's critics recall to the contrary that Barth set out precisely to overcome the theology of culture: Is he now supposed to appear as its continuer? At any rate, it is difficult to make out whether Marquardt's critics are more concerned about Barth's freedom from cultural-theological influences in general or whether their antipathy is kindled particularly by the claim that this cultural theology is socialist in character. Thus, for example, one critic (Michael Jacob), who presents himself as "antibarbarian" and who places great value on thinking, perceives "contemporary and cultural analogies" between Karl Barth and Thomas Mann: It is no accident that both pursued their major works during dark years (Barth, the *Church Dogmatics;* Mann, *Joseph and His Brothers*) and "in that very way wanted to make a *conscious* contribution to the humanization of their times."[2] In principle, however, such analogies admit the validity of Marquardt's approach; and, if one takes the above remark in full seriousness, all the questions that Marquardt poses are justified. Nonetheless, the above critic violently rejects Marquardt's starting point from all sides. Something seems to be amiss here.

Marquardt saw himself as prompted by the nature of Barth's concepts to ask about their background and origins. At the same time he began to read Barth "from the left"—in a double sense: First of all, "to read from the left" means simply to read in the customary sequence: Marquardt went back to the historical beginnings of Barth's theological work in order to pursue its development and thus to glimpse the motive forces and tendencies at work within it. This procedure corresponds to an inner necessity and has long since been applied to other thinkers (Luther, Hegel, Marx). Barth himself realized this, and, as the foreword to the re-edition of the first-edition *Romans* shows, he was concerned that his early works be taken into account. Anyone who has become accustomed to viewing Barth's theology as a self-contained system will be forced by this presentation of his living involvement in the sociopolitical developments and decisions of our century to regard the supposed purity of his thought as tainted. Yet anyone who was cut off from Barth's thought by its apparently self-contained character will now, upon seeing how connected it is to reality, be able to take an interest in it. And since at the same time Marquardt reads Barth "from the left" in the political sense, Barth's thought is once again situated in the midst of contemporary political conflicts—just as it always was during his lifetime!

Marquardt's methodological question is simply about the life setting *(Sitz im Leben)* of Barth's theology. Here, however, the term "life setting" is not limited to that of worship—as is often the case in form-critical study of the Bible and in that interpretation of Barth's theology which sees it arising simply from, and in relation to, the sermon. Rather, the term "life setting" here refers to theology's social context. From his writings it is already known that Barth was involved—and even extremely active—in the social conditions and events of his time and that his theology developed in the midst of this involvement. In the same way it is also known that, at least during the period of his theological beginnings, Barth was socially and politically committed to a socialist perspective. That he held the task of preaching to be central does not conflict with the fact that—for Barth as for everyone else—preaching is connected to the experience and activity of the preacher and the community, in concrete social relationships. Barth's correspondence with Thurneysen while at Safenwil makes it clear that his study of the Bible took place in view of the urgent issues and tasks of the day, not as a theological procedure "in itself" (cf. Marquardt, pp. 95 f.). This approach cannot have been irrelevant to the results that his Bible study produced.

To that extent it is difficult to understand what is inappropriate about Marquardt's way of posing questions; nor can it be disputed that socialist matters were important to Barth. Rather, what we finally have before us is an interpretation that raises the sociological question about context—to which everything today must be exposed —even about the theology of Karl Barth, and yet which still takes his theology seriously as theology. This sociological, political, yet nonreductionist approach is what gives Marquardt's book its significance. Even the weaknesses which naturally accrue to such an initial, trailblazing effort do not detract from its achievements. The weaknesses are discernible if one goes into the details and wants to clarify the exact nature of the specific relationship between theology and socialism in Barth. In consequence I must proceed in somewhat more detail—not in order to place the fundamental significance of this book in question, but rather to take up the conversation which Marquardt has begun. For even at those points where he remains unsatisfactory or falls into contradiction, something correct has been claimed, it seems to me, which should not be allowed to fall away, and which, if modified and made more precise, can be fruitful for further work.

A first difficulty arises through the fact that Barth's understanding of himself was ambivalent. On the one hand, Barth saw his theological beginnings completely in connection to the social conditions and political events from 1911 to the First World War. At the same time he saw them in the perspective of the exploited working class, which (according to Barth's own view) he really confronted for the first time in Safenwil. Barth's autobiographical sketch from 1927, which has meanwhile become available as an appendix to the volume of his correspondence with Bultmann[3] shows this clearly. On the other hand, Barth no longer saw his matured theology in such a context; rather, he saw it as demanded strictly by the subject matter and developed solely on the basis of the Biblical witness. Therefore, Barth is associated with the strictly self-contained objectivity of theology, which appears to disallow Marquardt's way of posing questions as something alien.

Whether Marquardt has seen the contradiction between this latter component of Barth's self-understanding and his own interpretative starting point, I do not know. There are passages where he would apparently like to see the contradiction removed (cf. p. 258)—above all, in relation to the task of Biblical exegesis. He holds that Barth recognized and accepted the time-bound character of all exegesis, and thereby affirmed the socially conditioned nature of Biblical exegesis, so that for him the only question was which side the exegete took up in society. It is striking, however, that Marquardt adduces no evidence for this contention. The one passage (CD IV/3, 821) cited by Marquardt (pp. 105 f.) signifies exactly the opposite in its context: Barth indeed sees the time-bound and socially conditioned influences upon Scripture exegesis, yet considers them illegitimate; he believes they can be overcome. Such influences must in his opinion be eliminated so that the text can speak freely. Similarly, Barth's objection to cultural Protestantism *(Kulturprotestantismus)*—that it lives in captivity to the bourgeoisie—is not counteracted by a connection to the proletariat. Instead, Barth posits the *freedom* of theology and church from *all* philosophical and social influences—a freedom which is supposed to consist in the fact that these influences (which are certainly always present) can be seen through, relativized, and corrected. Hence, what corresponds to Barth's rejection of bourgeois theology is not the affirmation of a proletarian theology, but rather the demand for a free theology. As a rule, the counterconcept of the proletariat is absent from Barth's critique of the bourgeoisie and of theology's bourgeois captivity. Indicative of this position is the way Barth speaks of the free theologian[4] and the way he could describe himself as a free man.[5]

Marquardt thus interprets Barth against this prominent side of his understanding of himself and his theology. Barth was not sociologically oriented. He did not know the method which questions the contents of dogmatics about sociopolitical origins, influences, and tendencies; he would hardly have considered it to be appropriate theologically. This does not mean, however, that therefore this method must not be applied to Barth. It must rather be asked whether the sociological way of posing questions can remain ignored as Barth ignored it and whether Marquardt does not here proceed necessarily and helpfully beyond the way questions were posed by Barth.

Yet as already noted, these observations concern only one side of Barth's self-understanding. On the other side Barth could and did orient, and even derive, at least his theological beginnings—but not only those—from their social and political context. And since Marquardt starts from those beginnings, he certainly has the right, if not the duty, to pursue this line of inquiry into Barth's later theology. In this way Marquardt discovered that Barth carried over the leading concepts of his early social engagement into the most intimately dogmatic areas of his thought. If, for example, in 1922 Barth develops the social vision of a kingdom of love in freedom and of freedom in love, and goes on in CD II/1 to describe God as he who loves in freedom, then it can only be wondered at that a connection between the two has only now been seen and thematized by Marquardt. The same turns out to be the case for the concept of revolution (and transformation), which Barth utilized in the doctrine of God and in Christology—not exclusively and extravagantly, but certainly emphatically and with purpose. That this use of language is finally taken seriously and questioned as to its origin and meaning should not be astonishing. It is astonishing only that it was allowed to pass unnoticed for so long. Here Marquardt has performed pioneer work. Michael Jacob, however, the critic previously mentioned, would continue to consider Barth's way of talking about revolution as little as possible. Supposedly, in the first-edition *Romans*, such talk is only homiletically conditioned. Hence, Jacob defuses the first-edition *Romans* together with Jülicher by confining it to homiletics, against Barth's own objection.[6] For the fact that the notion of revolution reemerges in the *Church Dogmatics*, this critic can only give the explanation that it occurs "in the heat of the battle,"[7] and he then interprets the concept of revolution in the sense that "it may be a turn of phrase." One notes the intention and ponders for his part such a barbaric lack of seriousness toward Barth's thought, for example, in the face of the careful and considered way Barth takes up the concept of revolution into Christology (CD IV/2, 171 f.).

By contrast, Marquardt takes Barth at his word. There should no longer be any reason to want to go behind it. The task will rather be to press Marquardt to go farther and to make his thesis more precise. For it seems to me that there are still many points in need of clarification. Here one may agree with Jacob that it is not sufficient to interpret the significance of the concept of revolution for the early Barth's concept of God primarily from the exegesis of Romans 13 instead of from the exegesis of other passages that are more decisive not only for the Pauline Romans but also for Barth's commentary.

Above all, it must be worked out more clearly why Barth's socialist interests fell within *theology* and what that was supposed to mean. According to Barth, it did not mean what religious socialism attempted—a theological interpretation of socialist movements. Barth sharply differentiated his theology from religious socialism. One might have hoped that Marquardt would have presented this differentiation more precisely, for only on that basis can the relation of theology and socialism in Barth be determined. At the same time, it must also be realized (Marquardt describes, but does not make full use of this in Ch. 3, section 1) that whereas the religious socialists judged the socialist movement positively, for Barth and Thurneysen a negative experience was decisive. Barth's autobiographical sketch, mentioned earlier, describes the negative experience of 1914 unequivocally, as does Thurneysen's discussion from the same period.[8]

Afterward Barth transplanted into theology the socialist hopes forfeited in reality; yet, according to Barth, that of which theology speaks is indeed the true reality. "Revolution" as a real transformation he was now to connect with God and was thus able to preserve it and the hope for it. Political reality was thereby exonerated, and Barth's theological concept of revolution could no longer be directly located in a political way (as Marquardt wants to do when he places Barth "to the left of Lenin" and describes his position as anarchism). Political action is henceforth a parabolic witness, but as such it is not "anarchist," but rather, as Marquardt can also see (cf. pp. 33, 151, 165 ff.), "reformist"—at any rate elastic and pragmatic, even if on no account indeterminate. When grounded in God, the sociopolitical revolution is relativized. It thus needs to be brought out more clearly than Marquardt does that in the first-edition *Romans* Barth defined not only the state but also *revolution* in terms of "statutes and machine guns."[9] The mistrust toward every "existing order" (including those to come), which the second-edition *Romans* expresses, is already in evidence here. In kind, however, the mistrust is not political (and hence not anarchist), but rather theological. It goes hand in hand with a devaluation of all human attempts at revolution, since these only produce existing orders once again, and hand in hand with a "passive conservatism," as Barth says about Jesus as God's revolution (CD IV/2, 173 ff.). That is Barth's persistent orientation from the first-edition *Romans* on. Hence the interpreter's task is not to describe this theologized socialism as "socialism." That enterprise is hopeless—as is evident from the vacillation and lack of unity in Marquardt's concept of socialism. Rather, the task is to elucidate the meaning of this theologizing of socialism (in sharp differentiation to religious socialism) and thus to understand the political elements raised up into the theological sphere.

The reason Marquardt remains so unsatisfactory at this point may lie in the fact that, unlike Barth, he does not come from a negative experience. Rather, he wrote his book out of a positive experience, the hearty affirmation of the left-oriented student movement in Berlin. He thus finds himself in a situation that is different from Barth's, but similar to that of religious socialism. The acuity which allows Marquardt at last to grasp the socialist implications of Barth for the first time is thus rooted in the very situation which tends to blur particular details in the analysis.

Nevertheless, that is not everything which must be said here. For even if one would have liked Marquardt to distinguish more precisely at this point, one must still see that he has basically called attention to something correct and important. Even if Barth's theology is not to be described in directly sociopolitical terms, it must still be translated and pursued back to its sociopolitical and intellectual roots. And in this regard Marquardt correctly points (p. 305) to the peculiarly colorful socialism of many critical intellectuals in the period before, during, and immediately after the First World War, which is also found, for example, in expressionist literature. Among others, these intellectuals include George Lukács (the later prominent critic of expressionism), Ernst Bloch, and Antonio Gramsci. Like Barth, they were all born around the middle 1880's; prior to the First World War, they had already beheld the imminence of collapse and the vision of something new—first a new man, and from there a new society.

The early works of these critical intellectuals were all published at around the same time, between 1910 and the early 1920's: Lukács' *History and Class Consciousness* (1922), Bloch's *Geist der Utopie* (1918), Barth's "twilight of humanity" in the two Romans commentaries (1919, 1922), and finally Karl Korsch's *Marxismus und Philosophie* (1923). T. W. Adorno has stressed that it was not the famous decade of the '20s which brought the intellectual (and artistic) turning point, but rather the earlier period up to the beginning of the '20s. Martin Heidegger was already a secondary appearance: *Being and Time* first came out in 1927 and was able to reach back to the original impulses of the previous works in order to generalize and neutralize them. Meanwhile, the instigators of genuinely creative unrest had already gone farther (in completely different directions— Barth, for example, into strict dogmatics) in order to come out of the unrest into a new formation.

These very thinkers were suppressed from view among us, however, and were allowed to lapse into obscurity, so that in retrospect the '20s were able to slip into the foreground. And it was disastrous that during the period when Nazism was finally in ruins and better stimuli might have been sought for consideration, the writings that Nazism had suppressed still continued to remain invisible so that the intellectual climate came to be renewed precisely under the influence of Heidegger. What did those who studied after 1945, for example, know of *History and Class Consciousness* and of its author's existence; what did they know of Korsch or Gramsci, of Rubiner or Hiller?—to mention only a few. Even historical research was to focus on the period around the First World War in only a very hesitant and restrained way. How was one supposed to be able to understand Barth under these circumstances? Marquardt finally situates Barth once again among his contemporaries in their intellectually formative years from approximately 1910 to 1920. Much in Marquardt's polemic can be explained from the fact that he wants to get free from the shadow of a theology under Heidegger's influence in order to be able to catch sight of the impulses of the years prior to *Being and Time*. In this way it seems to me on purely historical grounds that Marquardt has set upon the right course for a correct understanding of Barth.

It is difficult to generalize about the restless young left-wing intellectuals of the period prior to the '20s; the lack of clarity in Marquardt's attempt to define the socialism of Barth and his generation stems largely from this objective difficulty. That generation was grasped by an indeterminate historical consciousness that the bourgeoisie was coming to an end, that bourgeois society was on the brink of collapse—a rather general kind of contemporary mood, nourished more by Dostoevsky than by specific experiences and precise analyses. Thus Barth knew, for example, before he became a pastor and before he had reached his theological turning point and critical insight, that the pastorate was at bottom impossible.[10] Perhaps following the young Lukács (and Thomas Mann was immediately to adopt this from him), one can characterize the central contents of this generation's experience as *Sehnsucht* ["a profound longing"]—*Sehnsucht* in the face of a world dissociated from the bourgeoisie. The tendency toward socialism was an expression of this *Sehnsucht* and was in that regard rather vague. Above all, this *Sehnsucht* could not be satisfied with the realization of socialism as it occurred in Russia. That was not it. That was not what one had dreamed about and wanted in view of the demise of the bourgeoisie and the horror of the war. Marquardt is right: Something anarchistic, something syndicalistic, something in search of spontaneity characterized the intellectual socialism of that period, in Barth as in Lukács, in Korsch as in Gramsci, and, in a completely different way, in many literary expressionists. Nevertheless, in many cases work with the party was not shunned, but at the same time it was not uncommon for Lenin's theory of the party to take on a completely different appearance and a completely different sense: One sought a vanguard that would inwardly permeate the whole, whether this vanguard was now a band of poets or intellectuals, or whether it was—as in Barth's case—the church.

The fact that *Sehnsucht* was the dominant element for Barth and Thurneysen is discussed by Marquardt under the apt heading, "Theology of the Question." He attempts to interpret this element as a thinking "toward God" which, between the second-edition *Romans* and the Anselm book, Barth was then to resolve in terms of a thinking "from God" (which was actually nothing more than a *reference* to God under the eschatological reservation, pp. 195 f.). Whether the distinction between "toward God" and "from God" *("auf Gott hin"/ "von Gott her")* is illuminating or not seems, to me, questionable. It stems from a characterization proposed by A. Rich to distinguish between the theologies of L. Ragaz and H. Kutter, yet it can hardly be transferred to Barth, and it will not suffice to describe the theological turn from the second-edition *Romans* to the Anselm book, in my opinion. However, it is clear what Marquardt is getting at. He would like to show that at the heart of Barth's theology there is a questioning, a seeking, a *Sehnsucht*—a theology which even as a theology of revelation does not proceed from a possessing of God, but rather always stands in an Old Testament, waiting, "reformed" situation. To that extent it could be said—if one wanted to use this terminology at all—that Barth's theology, since it took itself to be a Biblically grounded theology, is always a thinking both "toward God" and "from God" at the same time (with various emphases). Even the later volumes of the *Church Dogmatics* with their copiously developed Christology simply produce what the early Barth considered to be the only thing possible: a prolegomena to Christology, that is, a reconsideration of the conditions of the possibility of speaking about Christ as the one who is the object of *Sehnsucht* and hope. If certain of Marquardt's critics—such as Diem and Jacob—now treat Barth's Christology as if it were a solid block that can be used to beat others over the head, then that no longer has much to do with Barth. Barth distinguished quite sharply between Christ and Christology in order to guard against the supposition that proceeds as if Christology were an answer or a method to open all locks, as if it were more than a clarification of the conditions under which we who wait upon Christ can speak about the One who is awaited and strain toward him in expectation. Precisely this intention is what Marquardt has grasped. As Marquardt sees, however, this also means that at the same time that Barth's theology is historicized, it must be investigated with regard to the *Sehnsucht* of its contemporary context, and that otherwise it cannot be apprehended.

In this respect a certain narrowness in Marquardt's presentation must be noted, namely, the restriction to the biographical. The point is not only that Barth's biography provides too little to go on to assert in any precise sense of the term that "Karl Barth was a socialist" (p. 39). Rather, as a biographical description, the assertion that "Karl Barth was a socialist"—even if made more precise—contains too little value as a judgment, for the biographical is not so important and illuminating as Marquardt thinks. It would have to be shown why, to what end, and how Barth's theology is formed and situated among the social conditions, developments, and tasks of its time. Indeed, at the outset Marquardt announces that he wants to try to grasp Barth's theology in historical and materialist perspective. For that, however, Barth's biography and subjective convictions are of less consequence than the economic and political history of the period in question. If the accent were shifted accordingly, the presentation would become more objective, since it now carries the slightly offensive tone of a biographical revelation ("Karl Barth was a socialist"). From a historical and materialist perspective, this will not do. Nevertheless, one will still have to take into account the nearness of all this to Barth's general profile as well as the novelty with which Marquardt advances the discussion.

Above all, then, further clarification is required about how to pose historical and materialist questions from within theology. Here Marquardt tends programmatically to go beyond the application of sociological methods. He acknowledges that his approach is new and that it requires further cooperative work (pp. 25 f.). Here he strikes upon a theme previously known to the criticism of religion only as a total rejection of theology. To take up the historical and materialist method into theology itself is a bold new advance whose consequences can still not be foreseen. In any case the class-bound character of theology will have to be consciously adopted as a theme of theological work, and it is at this point that Marquardt finds the methods of the social sciences to be clearly insufficient.

Yet in my opinion it needs to be asked once again what Marquardt means by "historical and materialist" (p. 17), for at this point I see in him a rather vague and hasty treatment of the concept of praxis. He speaks of praxis as determinative of consciousness, whereas the historical and materialist interpretation of history says that social structure is what determines consciousness. Why does Marquardt replace "structure" with "praxis"? To consider this question I must digress briefly. According to the historical-materialist perspective, "structure" (by which consciousness is determined) encompasses not only the conditions of the productive forces and the activity within them but also the division of labor and the various relationships of possession that thus arise— hence the division of, and adhesion to, the classes. To reduce all this to "praxis" is proper and customary at the point where one wants to turn away from a treatment of class divisions and from the class-bound character of consciousness. "Praxis," to which the historical-materialist aspects are then reduced, comes simply to mean "work." There are certainly enough Marx interpretations of this sort. They go astray not by stressing work, but by isolating it. At the same time, of course, Marx meant something else by "praxis," namely, the revolutionary activity, transformation, and upheaval of social relationships. At present it is evident that even the revolutionary understanding of praxis can be isolated and hence overdrawn. This happened in the student movement at the end of the 1960's and prompted Adorno (in my opinion rightly) to speak of the praxis fetishism of the student left. Adorno did not appreciate, however, that this praxis fetishism has objective grounds: When bourgeois persons try to align themselves with the working class, this in itself requires an act—a decision and a deed—and hence "praxis," even if nothing further takes place or comes out of it. When a bourgeois person wants to define himself as proletarian, unremitting efforts at creating a new self-identity are necessary, whereas a worker *eo ipso* belongs to the exploited class and for him socialist praxis thus begins at the point where he begins to work for a real overthrow of relationships. Applying this to the fundamental historical-materialist outlook: If *structure* determines consciousness, then only a proletarian can actually have a proletarian consciousness, whereas bourgeois students are never quite able to abandon the bourgeois level of consciousness. If, however, *praxis* were capable of determining consciousness, then bourgeois persons could attain proletarian consciousness through the corresponding praxis—and often enough their praxis will then actually be a development of their own consciousness without regard to "practical" needs and results. When that happens, however, the praxis is not proletarian and thus their consciousness cannot become proletarian. The result is a vicious circle; "praxis" must be invoked all the more doggedly.

Yet back to Marquardt: I do not say that Marquardt is caught up in this circle, but it seems to me that in the book his distance from the "revolutionary" phase of the student movement is not yet so great that he is able to see through and rectify the two elements which arise from different interests, yet mutually reinforce each other—namely, the isolation and the highly stylized presentation of "praxis." In consequence, the reference to the "category of praxis" frequently seems to be a clarifying and purifying alternative to the "category of theory." Yet even "praxis" is a theoretical category: It cannot be directly contrasted to a "theoretical" starting point and attempted solution. In addition, Marquardt applies "praxis" to so many perplexingly different things in Barth that even the concrete contents of the concept do not achieve clarity. He makes "praxis" include everything from Barth's labor union activity through his membership in the Social Democratic Party to his preaching activity, his academic instruction, and finally even his thinking itself (p. 280). The theory-praxis relation that Marquardt wants to elucidate thus dissolves.

It is probable that the more precisely Barth's differences from religious socialism were analyzed, the better his practical sociopolitical involvement would be understood. Much like the contemporary student movement, religious socialism devoted completely bourgeois efforts to attain identity with the proletariat (hence the theological interpretation of socialist movements). Barth's theological skepticism toward all "existing orders," on the other hand, freed him for social praxis as something profane—at any rate his praxis became modest and *ad hoc* within the scope of what was possible and close at hand for him. It is no accident that Barth joined the Swiss Social Democracy at precisely the same time that he broke theologically with the religious socialists. The example of Karl Barth in Safenwil seems to me to show that the pastor's situation is not necessarily so entangled in the bourgeois class that no solidarity with the exploited would be possible. Barth would certainly not have claimed to be proletarian and to have divested himself of bourgeois consciousness. Rather, he would have understood himself as belonging to the bourgeoisie "as if he were not" bourgeois—in other words, as relativized, corrected, and liberated to solidarity in an *ad hoc* way by the Biblical message.

Yet all these considerations are not intended to dispute the fact that Marquardt is basically right when he emphasizes praxis and that he has thereby advanced our understanding of Barth's theology decisively. There are three aspects of significance here: First, it basically corresponds to Barth's attention to reality that thinking ought not to obscure human praxis in the comprehensive sense, but rather must serve it. Second, Barth's theology was never a closed system of thought, but rather was open to human praxis in the sense that only human activity could demonstrate whether, and to what extent, that which theology says is true. That is connected to the third point, that Barth speaks about God's praxis as something which can only meaningfully be witnessed to by human praxis. This point must be sharpened in terms of Barth's separation from religious socialism. A religious interpretation of human movements means that existing praxis is taken as God's praxis. By contrast, Barth places God's action against that which exists (negative experience; *Sehnsucht!*). What God does supersedes everything in existence and thereby everything revolutionary. It creates a transformation which can only be expressed in the Word and for which one can only hope. When this Word is accepted in hope, however, then human activity must necessarily follow which corresponds and witnesses to God's activity.

In Marquardt's investigation the stress lies on the third of these points, on Barth's talk about the revolutionary God. In a review of

Marquardt's book, W. Schlichting has underscored the importance and correctness of this interpretation of Barth, which recognizes that the main contents and impetus of Barth's theology is the God who acts in a revolutionary way and who thus entails a real transformation.[11] Yet against Marquardt, Schlichting disputes that this theology can be derived from socialist tendencies; one supposedly understands Barth more correctly if one recognizes that Barth's way of speaking about God follows Biblical thought exactly. However, there can be no alternative at this point, in my opinion. Even Barth did not read the Bible in a germ-free cell, and the organization of his thought, which certainly accentuates certain contents of the Bible and materially criticizes others, cannot be severed from his sociopolitical situation and activity. The fact that Barth did not give a historical account of his situation or of his use of the Bible is one of the reasons why Marquardt's book is so important, without being in the least intended to detract from Barth's Biblical foundations.

Worthy of particular attention is the way Marquardt exhibits the revolutionary contents of Barth's doctrine of God in the area of Christology, especially in Barth's interpretation of the incarnation and the resurrection. In both cases Marquardt sees Christ related to the world and its transformation. In the exposition of Barth's theology of the resurrection (pp. 243–248), Marquardt shows above all that Barth viewed the situation of the world as really transformed through the resurrection of the crucified Christ and held that the Christian message derived first of all from this transformation. When M. Jacob notes that Barth designates Christ's resurrection as the (living, reality-transforming, verdict-passing) Word of God,[12] then that serves only to confirm Marquardt, for it underscores that Barth denies the transformation of reality to the Christian word of witness and claims it instead for the history of Christ. Marquardt wants to preserve this view whereas Jacob appears to want to correct it by interpreting the category "Word" in Bultmann's sense of the term. There is a difference here, but it is a question of adding to or subtracting from Barth; it does not touch Marquardt's interpretation. Yet it seems less helpful to me when Marquardt designates Barth's Christology of the real transformation of the world as "theology of history" *(Geschichtstheologie).* (P. 245.) And it needs to be specified in future work just how the transformation is conceived *extra nos* (in Christ) and how Barth employs the term "ontological"—this in order to emphasize that the *extra nos* transformation concerns us and thus is really an *actual* transformation and not merely a "possibility."

Marquardt's interpretation of Barth's doctrine of the incarnation engenders further questions, since Marquardt wants to argue that, according to Barth, when the Son of God became flesh, he assumed the human *species* unto himself (pp. 265–275). I must here omit the very difficult details in order to inquire about Marquardt's intention. Marquardt would like to supplant Christ's relation to the soul of the individual and to nature through a relation of Christ to the human species understood in materialist and human terms. In this way Christ is understood such that the materialist and human context of humanity is constituted through him and can be presented in terms of co-human "collectives." It cannot be contested that once again Marquardt has grasped Barth's intention. Yet whether this can be demonstrated in direct connection to the doctrine of the incarnation seems questionable to me; that, however, is secondary and remains a matter for specialists. What concerns Marquardt is that the universality of Christ does not remain abstract, that it is not to be believed in as something which bypasses the reality of human interrelationships. The assertion of Christ's universality is a sociopolitical assertion. In that respect one should not want to contradict Marquardt either in Barth's name or in any other way.

With this observation we are up against the salient point which Marquardt makes with all the various courses of his interpretation; to have brought this point into view remains the contribution of his book, namely, that a theological assertion is implicitly a sociopolitical assertion, that this is no different even in Barth, and that this for Barth and in Barth's sense is no disgrace. Moreover, if one asks what social politics Barth's dogmatics implies (in the sense of origins and consequences), then the term "socialism" is not badly chosen. That is a point that cannot be talked away even in the face of all the details in need of clarification that we have discussed.

I will therefore go into no further detail. In view of the richness and the sometimes confusing, but always stimulating, loose ends of the book, and in view of the depth of Barth's theology, there would otherwise be no immediate end in sight. I would like only to call attention to some things in Marquardt that have not yet been mentioned: *(a)* the particularly instructive and fruitful sections on Barth's concept of "origin" (pp. 207 ff.) and on the relativizing of consciousness as transcending the bourgeois perspective (pp. 248 ff.); *(b)* the section which—despite all correct intentions—is thoroughly in need of discussion, namely, "The *Extra Calvinisticum* and the Structure of Natural Theology" (pp. 257 ff.); *(c)* the illuminating discussion of Barth's attitude toward Germany and of his understanding of political preaching (pp. 55 ff.); as well as *(d)* the review of Marxist Barth-interpretations (pp. 340 ff.), which essentially demonstrates how little Barth has there been understood and appreciated—and which thus stimulates further thought.

In conclusion, I would like to raise a question that necessarily arises from Marquardt's starting point. How is dogmatics (with political implications) related to political ethics? Marquardt does not pursue this question any further. Only once does he place Barth's preaching in relation to ethics: "The gospel speaks to the human and political question of *meaning;* the ethicist under the presupposition of the gospel speaks to the political questions of specifics, to the questions of how, when, and in what connection" (p. 63). My question is whether it is really appropriate to set up the question of *meaning* as a clarification and specification of relationships for ethics, whether the question of meaning itself isn't still quite bourgeois, a product of the late bourgeoisie's uncertainty. On this matter I know of no distinction between dogmatics and political ethics which is really satisfactory. Yet even here one would do well to attend to the example of Karl Barth, because as Marquardt ascertains, but does not explicitly work out in terms of this distinction, Barth expected no answer about meaning from the gospel; rather he heard it speaking of the *powers* that *transform* the world.

NOTES

1. Friedrich-Wilhelm Marquardt, *Theologie und Sozialismus: Das Beispiel Karl Barths* (Munich: Chr. Kaiser Verlag, 1972; 2 Aufl., 1972).

2. Michael Jacob, ". . . noch einmal mit dem Anfang anfangen . . . ," *Evangelische Theologie* 32 (1972), pp. 615 f., n. 35.

3. Karl Barth and Rudolf Bultmann, *Briefwechsel 1922–1966,* ed. by B. Jaspert (Zurich: Theologischer Verlag, 1971), pp. 301 ff.; above all, see p. 306.

4. Karl Barth, "Das Geschenk der Freiheit," *Theologische Studien* 39 (1953), pp. 21–28.

5. Karl Barth, *Letzte Zeugnisse* (1969), pp. 37 f.

6. Jacob, *loc. cit.,* p. 612.

7. *Ibid.,* p. 620, n. 61.

8. Eduard Thurneysen, "Zum religiös-sozialen Problem," *Zwischen den Zeiten* 5 (1927), pp. 513 ff.

9. Karl Barth, *Römerbrief,* 1st ed. (Bern: G. A. Bäschlin, 1919), p. 377.

10. Karl Barth, "Moderne Theologie und Reichsgottesarbeit," *Zeitschrift für Theologie und Kirche* 19 (1909), pp. 317–321.

11. W. Schlichting, "Sozialismus und biblische Denkform," *Evangelische Theologie* 32 (1972), pp. 595 ff.

12. Jacob, *loc. cit.,* p. 619.

6

Political Theology and Social Ethics: The Socialist Humanism of Karl Barth

JOSEPH BETTIS

Thirteen years ago Will Herberg described the work and influence of Karl Barth in the following way:

> Karl Barth is, beyond all doubt, the master theologian of our age. Wherever, in the past generation, men have reflected deeply on the ultimate problems of life and faith, they have done so in a way that bears the unmistakable mark of the intellectual revolution let loose by this Swiss thinker in the years immediately following the first world war. . . . If any man has ever put his sign on the thinking of his time, it is Karl Barth, the father of the "dialectical theology."[1]

Herberg was right. Nevertheless, American theologians continue to ignore Barth. His influence, if even acknowledged at all, is viewed with suspicion. At best his thought is accorded only historical interest; one phase in the evolving theology of the modern period. There are a few who continue to read Barth and write about him as if his thought should be taken seriously within the contemporary debate, but we appear to most American theologians to be a little peculiar, if not perverse.

I believe there is one explanation for both these facts: the fact that

From *The Scottish Journal of Theology* 27 (1974), pp. 287–305. Reprinted with the kind permission of the author, the journal, and the publisher, Scottish Academic Press Ltd.

Barth is the theologian par excellence of the twentieth century and the fact that he is ignored in America. The explanation is that Barth's theology necessarily implies a radical socialistic and humanistic ethic that is a direct threat to the liberal capitalist ethic that dominates the American mentality.

Of course, liberals have known for a long time that Barth considered them anathema. And they usually returned the favor. Liberals assumed that since Barth disagreed with them, he must represent a conservative, confessionalistic, authoritarian, dogmatic, preliberal position. On the contrary, and this is the thesis of this paper, Barth represents a radical, dialectical, socialist, humanistic, postliberal theology and social philosophy.

Perhaps unfortunately, much of Barth's language has contributed to the judgment that his thought is a return to preliberal dogmatism or fideism. But his choice of language forms was deliberate. Barth judged the real threat to humanity in the first half of the twentieth century to be liberalism, and he chose forms of expression that made it unmistakably clear that he did not share the liberal perspective. Rather than being a return to the language forms of some assumed dogmatism, Barth's use of language serves notice that he breaks cleanly and definitely with the presuppositions of liberalism. The significance of this understanding of Barth's use of language should not be underestimated. It points to the fact that Barth, perhaps more than any other contemporary theologian, was conscious of the historical *Sitz im Leben* of his thought. When he said that theology must be continually done over again and that his own thought was merely a gloss on the history of theology, he was indicating that he considered the primary significance of his theology—and of all theology—to be its historical function.

Of course everyone knows that Barth was interested from time to time in politics. There was the time as a pastor in Safenwil when he was involved in the labor unions, the Religious-Socialist movement, and the Social Democratic Party. There was the profound conflict with Nazism and with the German Christians. There was the Barmen Declaration. There was his service in the Swiss army, his preaching to prisoners in the Basel jail, his trip to Hungary, and the famous letter to the East German Pastor, to which I will return later. All these events are well known. The question is, are these political activities integral to Barth's theology, or are they incidental activities of the man who, during the period when most of them occurred, was also writing the *Church Dogmatics?*

I believe most American theologians would answer that these political activities are incidental to Barth's theological work. Most people would say that Barth's theology has no direct political content. Or, they would say that Barth's social ethic is an absolutistic ethic, an eschatological ethic, suited for "between the times," but unsuited for providing any help in the hard political decisions of everyday life.

There are other interpretations. Perhaps the most important is contained in a book which appeared in 1972, *Theologie und Sozialismus*, by Friedrich-Wilhelm Marquardt. I learned of the book through Markus Barth, at the Toronto meeting of the North American Karl Barth Society. Professor Barth's address,[2] which contains a penetrating and provocative summary of Marquardt's work, as well as an intriguing description of the waves it has made in European theological seas, will appear soon in the *Canadian Journal of Theology*.

Marquardt argues that Barth is a socialist and that his theology is a product of his study of Marx.[3] The sources of Barth's theological socialism lie in the frustrations he experienced as a pastor in Safenwil. Barth was frustrated by the ineffectiveness of the liberal efforts at social reform. He was also frustrated by the liberal theology which did not do justice to God. So he saw liberalism as a mediocre and ineffective middle way—true neither to the world nor to God. His dialectical theology was developed as a way of expressing a radical, socialist position which would be true both to the transcendence of God and to the demands of historical struggles for justice.[4]

I believe Marquardt overstates the case. But I also believe that he points to an essential dimension that most American theologians overlook. I believe that Barth's mature theology, as it is expressed in the *Church Dogmatics,* leads directly, inevitably and necessarily to radical political ethics. And I believe that this necessary interrelation of theology and politics is essential for any theology which would be true to its responsibility to speak honestly and truly about the living God.

Obviously, it would be impossible to prove such a sweeping evaluation of Barth. We could quote texts from the *Church Dogmatics* alone almost ad infinitum on either side, to say nothing of the other published and unpublished literature. I am more interested in presenting an option and suggesting a new way of looking at Barth. I believe we have been handicapped in our evaluation of his theology because our politics have been essentially the politics of liberalism. We have accepted the liberal presumption that nothing of significance occurs to the left of the classical liberal position. If we widen our politics to include radical socialistic humanism as a valid political position, then Barth's theology takes on an entirely new and politically significant dimension. In other words, I believe people have said Barth was nonpolitical and didn't have a social ethic when what they really mean was that they didn't like his socialist politics or radical ethics.

The Relocation of the Ethical Question

Barth is accused of propounding an eschatological and absolutistic ethic that ignores the ambiguities of history and is of no help in dealing with particular moral issues. It is true that Barth refuses to engage in moralism or casuistry. But his alternative is not some transcendental ethic with no actual or political consequences. On the contrary, Barth's ethic leads directly to radical political consequences. But Barth wants to relocate the ethical question. This is the thrust of II/2, §36, Section I, where he discusses the relationship between general ethics and theological ethics.

Liberalism sought to avoid the dogmatism and authoritarianism of earlier theology by substituting an ethic rooted in pragmatic humanism. The liberals thought that they were substituting an intrinsically valid ethic, derived directly from categorical humanistic imperatives, for the older extrinsic, moralistic authority. Liberalism did not escape the problem. It merely substituted the arbitrary authority of pragmatic humanism for the arbitrary authority of the older moralism. Barth seeks to redefine the ethical question in such a way that the ethical imperative carries its own intrinsic validation. Theologically this means understanding the authority of God as different from all kinds of worldly authority and understanding obedience to God as different from all other kinds of obedience. The intrinsic law functions in an entirely different way from other laws.

When we take up this problem from our starting-point in a knowledge of the God who elects man, it is inevitable that right at the outset it should undergo a change of form by which it is immediately differentiated from what is usually regarded elsewhere as the ethical problem, and in such a way as to exclude in practice any return to the ethical questions and answers that arise from other starting-points. As compared with all ethical enquiry and reply which is differently orientated that which has its source in God's predestination must always be and become something distinctive both as a whole and in detail. Certainly, the question taken up is still that of human action, of human existence as such. But for us this question is at once the question of human obedience. Starting out from the knowledge of the divine election of man, we can know of no human action which does not stand under God's command, of no human existence which does not respond in one way or another to God's command, which has not the character of obedience or disobedience to God's command. We do not know any human action which is free, i.e., exempted from decision in relation to God's command, or neutral in regard to it. And for just the same reason we do not know any free investigation of good and evil.[5]

In IV/1, Barth presents a long interpretation of Genesis 3 supporting this position. The question of the serpent about the tree of the knowledge of good and evil is the question of whether the essential nature of human beings is to be obedient to the law of God or whether their essential nature is to be lawmakers and lawgivers. Now the essence of lawmaking and lawgiving is not that one dispenses law, but that he or she acknowledges that the only laws that exist are the laws which one may or may not choose to obey. That is the difference between Barth and the liberals. Liberalism refuses to recognize the existence of intrinsic law. Barth agrees with liberalism's rejection of the older orthodoxy's definition of law which merely took human law and attempted to hang a divine imperative around its neck. But he does not come to the conclusion that there is no intrinsic law. The older orthodoxy accepted the heteronomy of divine law, but made its authority extrinsic. Liberalism saw the need for an intrinsic authority, but could attain it only through autonomy. Barth wants to define divine law as both heteronomous and as possessing intrinsic authority.

> It is true, of course, that this command also says: Do this and do not do that. But in the mouth of God this means something different. Do this —not because an outer or inner voice now requires this of you, not because it must be so in virtue of any necessity rooted in the nature and structure of the cosmos of man, but: Do this, because in so doing you may and will again live of and by My grace.[6]

If people refuse to acknowledge the existence of intrinsic law, they have already committed themselves to their superiority over everything else. They refuse to admit that anything outside themselves can have an inalienable claim on them.[7] This transition from heteronomy to autonomy is the source and the effect of human pride. It is, therefore, according to Barth, one of the basic components of sin.

When he rejects human autonomy, does Barth reject the significance of human existence and retreat to a pre-humane authoritarian heteronomy? This judgment would certainly be true were it not for the difference between God's law and human law. Everything hangs on his understanding of heteronomy. Any other law outside human beings would be an enslaving heteronomy, but God's law is *totaliter aliter* and submission to it is not dehumanizing but fully humanizing because it involves submission not to extrinsic heteronomy, but to intrinsic heteronomy; to the way things are.

This distinction between intrinsic law and arbitrary law is not, of course, for Barth a restatement of natural law. There are two problems with natural-law theory: it denies the newness and openness of human nature, and it implies a spurious distinction between the laws of nature and the laws of God. It reverses the relationship between command and creation. When Barth speaks of command and obedience he wants to emphasize his distance from natural-law ethics. I have used the inadequate word "intrinsic" to emphasize the fact that the divine command is not arbitrary, but is, rather, the explication of what it means to be a free and open human being. Barth wants to show that this human freedom is found neither in submission to natural or arbitrary law, nor in liberal "autonomy," but in radical openness. Barth's problematic is to avoid the basically antinomian liberal ethic which makes man the measure on one side and natural-law moralism on the other. He uses "divine command" as a way of showing that there is a third kind of ethic, rooted in the grace of God and the freedom and openness of man.

The problem with autonomy is that men and women are simply not autonomous, and the attempt to be so is an effort in futile self-contradiction.

> Here, too, we must first say that this is a futile and impotent and useless undertaking which is foredoomed to failure. . . . A sharp distinction has been made between good and evil in all their spheres both high and low. All men in both their public and private being and activity are set in the light of this distinction. All created time, all human history and every individual history, is seen by God in its right and wrong, and moves forward to the manifestation of the judgment fulfilled in Him. As against that, man only wants to judge. He thinks he sits on a high throne, but in reality he sits only on a child's stool, blowing his little trumpet, cracking his little whip, pointing with frightful seriousness his little finger, while all the time nothing happens that really matters. He can only play the judge. He is only a dilettante, a blunderer, in his attempt to distinguish between good and evil, right and wrong, acting as though he really had the capacity to do it. He can only pretend to himself and others that he has this capacity and that there is any real significance in his judging. There is no necessity for all this. He can unquestioningly and unreservedly allow that God is in the right and accept and acquiesce in his decisions concerning him. He can then be at peace with God, knowing his own case, doing right in freedom and avoiding wrong in the same freedom. But instead he moves against God and sets up and defends and maintains his own right. In so doing he puts himself in the wrong. His own judging and deciding lead him into a constant fog and error. Neither in his own cause nor in that of others can he be a wise and righteous judge. He wants that which is therefore impossible, and he cannot attain it.[8]

What all this means is that the choice between good and evil is not the ethical question. The choice between good and evil is a fabrication to hide us from the ethical question. The choice between good and evil implies that we know what is good and what is evil and also implies that we are capable of distinguishing between them and choosing between them.

The effort to build an ethics based on the choosing between good and evil is, therefore, as Barth sees it, characteristic of human inauthenticity and immorality. The truly ethical thing to do does not involve in any way an attempt to judge between good and evil.

> The concealment is particularly strong at this point. It is surprising that in the Christian Church more offense is not taken at the fact—or have we simply read it away?—that in Gen. 3 the desire of man for a knowledge of good and evil is represented as an evil desire, indeed the one evil desire which is so characteristic and fatal for the whole race. The consequences for the theory and practice of Christian ethics—and not only that—would be incalculable if only we were to see this and accept it instead of regarding this very questionable knowledge—whether sought in the Bible or the rational nature of man or conscience—as the most basic of all the gifts of God. The armour behind which the real evil of the pride of man conceals itself is obviously thicker and more impenetrable at this point than at any other.[9]

Moreoever, the moment a person attempts to make a judgment between good and evil he or she is already trapped in an evil and self-defeating endeavor.

> The truth is that when man thinks that he can hold the front against the devil in his own strength and by his own invention and intention, the devil has already gained his point. And he looks triumphantly over his shoulder from behind, for man has now become a great fighter in his cause. I am already choosing wrong when I think that I know and ought to decide what is right, and I am doing wrong when I try to accomplish that which I have chosen as right. I am already putting myself in the wrong with others, and doing them wrong, when—it makes no odds how gently or vigorously I do it—I confront them as the one who is right, wanting to break over them as the great crisis. For when I do this I divide myself and I break the fellowship between myself and others. I can only live at unity with myself, and we can only live in fellowship with one another, when I and we subject ourselves to the right which does not dwell in us and is not manifested by us, but which is over me and us as the right of God above, and manifested to me and us only from God, the right of His Word and commandment alone, the sentence and judgment of His Spirit. To use the words of the serpent in Gen. 3, when our eyes are opened to the possibility of our own exaltation in judgment, we become truly blind to what is right and wrong. There then begins the long misery of my moral existence, in which I pardon myself today in respect

of that for which I am incontrovertibly judged by my true Judge, only to judge myself tomorrow for that in respect of which I am incontrovertibly pardoned, in which I am most confident where everything has gone astray, and tremble and hesitate and doubt and despair where I might have a sure hold and advance with the greatest certainty. And there begins the whole misery of the moral battle of everyone against everyone else, in which, whatever position we take up or line we adopt or banner we follow, we are always deceived about our friends as well as our enemies, wronging the former just as much by our affirmation as the latter by our negation, sowing and reaping discord as the children of discord. This being the case, the dreadful pagan saying is true that war is the father of all things—the war which is always holy and righteous and necessary, war under the sign of the promising crescent or the natural sickle or the useful hammer or the sacred cross, the war of blood or the (in God's sight probably no less infamous and terrible) cold war. When man thinks that his eyes are opened, and therefore that he knows what is good and evil, when man sets himself on the seat of judgment, or even imagines that he can do so, war cannot be prevented but comes irresistibly. When the Law and its commandments and prohibitions and promises and threatenings is taken out of the hands of God and put in those of man, when it is enforced and expounded and applied by man, then it can only bring wrath (Rom. 4).[10]

There can be no adequate analogy to God's authority and to the obedience required by it, since grace and faith are unique events. Nevertheless, some analogies are more useful than others. We usually understand being ethical to mean something like obeying more or less arbitrary traffic regulations. To be ethical means to discover God's laws and to obey them, just as we obey traffic laws.

This is a very poor analogy for obedience and for God's command, because God is not something which we may or may not obey, and obedience is not a response that occurs after the fact of grace. Faith or obedience is the other side of the event of grace or command. Obedience is the product of command and not a response to it.

A better analogy for the divine law and the obedience it requires would be the law of gravity. The law of gravity is also a law that requires obedience. We usually assume that it is impossible to violate the law of gravity and therefore it is not very useful as an analogy for ethical consideration. But we can violate the law of gravity, or at least we can try to do so. We can make judgments and live our life as if there were no law of gravity. The result, of course, would be catastrophic. And that is exactly the same result that comes from violating the laws of God: catastrophe.

The law of gravity is also an inadequate analogy. It is too close to natural law. The command of God is not static as is the law of gravity. It is always out of and into the unknown future and always new. It is always a challenge and not a limitation. Nevertheless, it is not arbitrary, and that is the important thing to grasp, especially in the context of ethics.

This is what Barth means when he calls disobedience the "impossible possibility."[11] He is trying to say that although disobedience is a possibility for men and women, and that they can choose to be disobedient, the result is catastrophic. In this choosing they are choosing an option without a future, an option that doesn't lead anywhere. Moreover, Barth wants to say that God's command is not an extraneous command like a traffic law. It is, rather, an intrinsic command, rooted in the way things are, or, rather, rooted in the free grace of God. It is the basis of creation and not the other way around. Ethical action (obedience) and unethical action (disobedience) are not two comparable ways of responding to the divine command. Obedience and disobedience are disproportional. One is the way to life, the other is the way to death. And these are intrinsic directions. They are built into the fabric of the decision. In fact, the divine command is the command that forces us to that position. If we are not forced to that position, we are not in the presence of the divine command.

The relocation of the ethical question means that the ethical question is not the choice between good and evil but the search for the heteronomous and intrinsic law with which we must come into harmony if we are to live authentically and creatively. To be faced with a choice between good and evil—i.e., to be faced with an "ethical" decision—is not to be faced with the command of God— i.e., with the real ethical situation. Authenticity and creativity are not things people can choose out of their autonomy, but are the product of submission to the real structure of their environment, the product of radical openness to the future—to grace. The choice between good and evil implies that people are already in touch with reality and their only task is its administration. Barth's relocation of the ethical question acknowledges the fact that men and women are not already in touch with reality, but that that search is the human task and it is possible only on the basis of grace. The choice between good and evil calls elements within our environment into question: the real ethical question calls us into question.

The Criteria for Ethical Action

Barth rejects the moralistic tendency to ground ethics in some kind of authority; he rejects confessionalism; he rejects any effort to ground ethics in an extrinsic source. But he also rejects the humanistic and pragmatic grounding of ethics that is advocated by liberalism.

What, then, are the criteria for ethical action? The essential thing to see in this regard is that Barth does not merely substitute one set of criteria for another. That is what liberal humanism did and that is what contextual ethics does. What Barth does is to suggest generically different kind of criteria.

In II/2, pp. 654 ff., Barth develops four criteria of ethical action. These criteria are elaborated in terms of the four words in the question, "What ought we to do?" "What" means that ethical action is open. "Ought" means that it is self-validating. "We" means that it is communal. And "to do" means that it is concrete. Action which is really ethical will exhibit these characteristics.

1. Ethical action is open. This means that it is always subject to change, reversal, redirection. Any action which is assumed to be absolutely and universally true or right is by definition unethical. Being ethical means recognizing that we are human and that all our actions are human actions and therefore subject to fallibility and to change. This does not mean that one must not commit himself. On the contrary, what is demanded is that one commit himself while at the same time recognizing that he is human and contingent and that his commitment might be a mistake. To be open means to acknowledge that we are not already in possession of the truth. We do not yet know what is the ethical thing to do. We are searching for the ethical and not possessors of it.

2. The second criterion of ethical activity is that it is self-validating. Barth is trying to say that the ethical question is not the question of trying to apply some criteria of the good and the true and the beautiful to some particular event or decision. It is not an effort to apply a universal to a particular. On the contrary, it is the attempt to find the universal. It is not a secondary question which assumes that the good is already known. It is a search for the good. It is only when we are in this frame of mind and working toward that end that we are within the ethical sphere.

3. The third criterion is that ethical activity is communal. It is a question of what "we" ought to do. This means in the first instance that it is not a generalized question about what "one" ought to do. It is direct and immediate. It has to do with what I am about right at this particular time. Second, it does not refer to me in isolation, but to the community. It must be activity that is open to the community and in which the community can engage. It cannot be privileged. It must be capable of open expression within the community. Any activity that we must keep hidden is not ethical.

4. Finally, ethical activity is concrete. It is not abstract. The ethical task is to come to the point at which I am asking the question about what I am to do in the actual situation I find myself and given the real options which lie before me. The greatest way to escape the ethical situation is to fly off into abstract moral questions so that I do not come to confront the reality that I am acting in a concrete particular situation right now. The words "to do" serve to remind me that the only ethical question is the one which actually does have potentials within the world I live in—and that means the sociopolitical world.

At this point Barth is very clear. Ethics is not abstract speculation. It deals with real options in the real sociopolitical world. It is concerned with changing that world. Moreover, there is no such thing as ethically neutral action. All activity is potentially ethical. And since a person is what his actions are, there is no dimension of human being that is not essentially ethical.

These four criteria constitute Barth's definition of ethical behavior. They may seem incomplete or lacking to someone who is looking for an ethic constructed in terms of means and ends, but it is exactly that extrinsic understanding of ethics that Barth wants to avoid. The criteria he has suggested do not permit an evaluation of action in terms of intended goals or results. They constitute, therefore, an effort to define intrinsic norms for ethical action.

Who Is the Enemy?

I began this paper with a quotation from Will Herberg about the significance of Barth as a theologian. Here is another passage from the same work of Herberg's, showing his evaluation of Barth as a political thinker.

> We need not agree with his particular way of understanding politics and war in a Christian perspective to recognize in his political theologizing during these stormy years the thinking of a great Christian theologian who has learned to take politics and culture with the utmost seriousness without for a moment abandoning his ultimate standpoint of faith, which infinitely transcends all political and cultural structures.[12]

Herberg's evaluation is especially important because he then goes on to criticize Barth's attitude toward communism. Herberg finds it inconsistent that Barth would attack the totalitarianism of Nazism, but refuse to attack the totalitarianism of communism. Barth's reply, which Herberg and many other American theologians find difficult either to understand or to accept, was that the real threat facing the church and the world today is not communism, but American capitalistic liberalism.

This does not mean that communism is good. Barth said that. But it does mean that Barth was always involved in evaluating the realistic options available in the light of his understanding of the Bible and making his judgments. And his judgment in this situation was that American anticommunism was a greater threat than communism.

Many American theologians criticized Barth for this position. Perhaps the sharpest criticism came from Reinhold Niebuhr, at least until 1969 when he revised his position.[13] Niebuhr's earlier criticism, however, remains a clear expression of a widespread criticism of Barth. In 1958 Barth wrote a Christmas letter to a pastor in East Germany, answering some of the pastor's questions about how to witness to Christ in a totalitarian state. Barth's response has since become famous. In it, among other things, he warns against confusing Christianity with any political position, even antitotalitarianism and especially anticommunism.

Niebuhr chooses Barth's letter as a basis for criticism. He points to Barth's "eschatological note" and agrees that from the perspective of God's justice, all men are equally guilty.

> Barth is quite right: East and West alike are in equal condemnation both by the real gospel and for finding his interpretation of the gospel irrelevant to all the anxious decisions which we must make in trying to avoid the spread of despotism on the one hand and to avert a nuclear holocaust on the other.

But then Niebuhr goes on to raise an objection:

> It is only at this point of our Christian witness, as we try to persuade the West that it must become conscious of being involved in a common fate of the nuclear dilemma with the communists, that Barth's above-the-battle Christian witness becomes faintly relevant to those of us who take our moral responsibilities in this world seriously and find no way of fulfilling them without engaging in hazardous political judgments. . . . He is certainly neither a "primitive anti-communist" nor a "secret pro-communist." He is merely a very eminent theologian, trying desperately to be impartial in his judgments. The price of this desperation is of course moral irrelevance.[14]

Just over a year later Niebuhr wrote, ". . . Barth has long since ceased to have any effect on my thought; indeed he has become irrelevant to all Christians in the Western world who believe in accepting common and collective responsibilities without illusion and without despair."[15]

There are two points in Niebuhr's analysis that deserve comment. First, it is not true that Barth's "eschatological note" points to the irrelevance of the gospel in political decisions. Barth is not "above the battle." That is Niebuhr's own problem and he has no business ascribing it to Barth! On the contrary, there is, for Barth, no sphere of life for which the gospel is not immediately relevant. Or, rather, if the gospel and the situation appear incompatible, Barth suggests that it may well be the situation, rather than the gospel, which is irrelevant. But this suggestion is not apolitical; it is radically political.

Niebuhr seems somehow to want to protect the gospel from direct involvement in political decisions and to leave these up to autonomous individuals. Barth, on the other hand, insists that the gospel is directly relevant to every political act. For Niebuhr politics involves decisions which are ambiguous and unclear. It is an area, therefore, in which the absoluteness of the gospel is not directly applicable. Christians must make "hazardous political judgments" in which the message of the gospel is uncertain or not applicable. It is ironic that Niebuhr turns out to be the one who cannot relate the gospel to political action, whereas Barth, on the other hand, does so consistently.

Second, it is significant that Niebuhr is blind to the real threat from the West. He does not talk about imperialism, nor about colonialism, nor about racism, nor about the militarism of the West which threatens the entire world. The only danger he can see for the West is that it might become involved in a tragic and mistaken nuclear holocaust with the East. Niebuhr is unwilling to entertain the possibility that the West may be as great or greater a threat to Christians and to humanity than the East. He is unwilling even to acknowledge Barth's judgment that the basic and fundamental direction of Western thought and politics is at least as destructive and probably more destructive than the fundamental direction of politics in the East.

In 1969, Niebuhr retracted his criticism of Barth.[16] It is characteristic of Niebuhr's greatness that his reversal is clear and unambiguous. The American involvement in Vietnam, as well as other political developments had enabled Niebuhr to see dangers and problems in American society that Barth had seen earlier. While Niebuhr concedes this point, however, it is not clear that he even sees the relationship Barth develops between the gospel and radical politics.

Niebuhr's early position is a classic example of what Herbert Marcuse calls one-dimensional thought.[17] The problem is not that Niebuhr disagrees with Barth. That would be healthy and constructive. The problem is that Barth represents an option which does not fit Niebuhr's liberal universe of discourse, so he assumes that it is no position. Rather than accept the responsibility of arguing with Barth, Niebuhr chooses to harangue him for "irresponsibility."

Niebuhr, like most liberals, sees the threats to humanity to come from the extreme right and the extreme left. He is unable to see that the greatest threat to humanity may well come from the middle. Certainly the dangers from the right are bad enough. One cannot have watched Alabama during the past ten years without seeing the poison that right-wing fascism can inject into the collective body of the human community. But it is not self-evident that the real threat in the United States today is from the extreme right. One of the favorite tricks of the devil is to establish an apparent enemy as a decoy while he quietly destroys us from an unsuspecting flank. And, in fact, today it is more likely that the real threat is from the anonymous administrators, the technocracy, what Noam Chomsky has called the new mandarins. The real enemy is not the extreme right, but the administrative establishment.

The extremists are bad enough, that is true. But the war in Vietnam was not fought by them. It was fought by the elected government of the United States. The invasion of Laos was not by the radical right. The coup in Cambodia was not instigated by the right. The continued bombing in Southeast Asia is not the work of the right wing. The domination of the Dominican Republic and the invasion of Cuba were not the work of the reactionaries. The Chicago police riots were not engineered by the extremists. John Sinclair and Huey Newton were not jailed by the right-wingers. The Panthers were not murdered and jailed by the reactionaries. Pacifists who are in jail because they refused to fight in an unlawful and genocidal war are not imprisoned by the radicals. The whole network of political arrests and trials in connection with demonstrations against the war was not the work of a right-wing fringe. The various illegal operations referred to as "Watergate" are not the work of extremists. The Native Americans at Wounded Knee were not under siege from the extreme right. The no-knock laws and the gun-control laws are not the products of the right wing.

In every case, it is the elected establishment, the new mandarins, the technocracy, the anonymous administrators who deny human rights and destroy the human community in the name of security and efficiency. Of course, that is not a new thesis at all. It is the linchpin of contemporary radical thought. Marcuse, Laing, Fanon, Chomsky, Oglesby, Cleaver, Roszak, Colin Morris, N. O. Brown, Erikson, Friedenberg, Ginsberg, Leroi Jones, Kesey, Hoffman, Rubin, Dellinger, and many others have made the point.

One does not have to accept the validity of the radical analysis to recognize its importance. The point is that the liberals and the liberal press refuse to discuss it. May one speak again of the treason of the intellectuals in this context?

This is what Marcuse calls the one-dimensional world view. Advanced technological society inevitably identifies the *status quo* with the way things ought to be. It is unable, therefore, to recognize the established order as a threat to humanity. This is why it appears that the only acceptable change must come through transformation and not revolution. When we submit to this hallucination, it prevents our joining those who have gone to jail rather than fight, it prevents our joining those who refuse to capitulate to the injustice and brutality of our government. It prevents our speaking plainly and bluntly and prevents our joining the struggle in the streets. It immobilizes us in confusion.

A careful reading of Barth's East German Letter reveals exactly how deeply he probes these political realities. His problem is to assess exactly what it is about a government that is oppressive or totalitarian and to point out that those are the elements that must be resisted.

Barth refers to I Peter 5:9 in which the congregation is encouraged to resist "your adversary the devil." Then he continues:

> It goes without saying that communism as such has something, even a great deal, to do with that "adversary"; but strictly speaking only in so far as it takes on the shape and power of a tempter who is capable of seducing and misleading people (and especially Christian people) into wrong attitudes and reactions toward himself—into anxiety, into blind hatred, into indecision and double-talk, into a serpentine wisdom severed from dove-like simplicity, into howling with the wolves or fear of being devoured by them, into collaboration or obstructionism, into desolateness and so to the use of all the false means and weapons that care-ridden mortals are wont to take up everywhere; in short, into that godlessness in action which is truly atheism. Where and in so far as communism thus misleads and seduces men—and only there and only so far—is it to be identified with the lion that prowls the East today. And the communism that would bring about this devastation must be resisted.[18]

Barth points out that the West also has aspects of the adversary, and because it does, the East German has companions throughout the world who share his struggle. This is considerably different from Niebuhr's summary of Barth's position. Niebuhr criticized Barth for counseling patience on the part of the East German Pastor. He wanted the East Germans to join the West in the struggle. But Niebuhr quotes only the first half of the paragraph. He misses Barth's crucial point which is that men all over the world are already together in their struggle against "the adversary."

> For this power too, with all that makes it foreign, is undoubtedly only a tool of God, inescapably fulfilling a function in God's plan. The judicial function of a rod of punishment? That too of course. After all, this power would not have overwhelmed you if leaders and people, in society, state, and church, had not sinned so grievously in the past. Certainly your part of the world is undergoing a painful purgation such as the West, sooner or later and in one form or other, will likewise be subjected to (perhaps at the hands of Asia or Africa).[19]

Barth's Socialist Humanism

I have argued that rather than hiding in an eschatological and irrelevant ethics of absolutism, Barth develops a radical social ethic that calls into question not only the presuppositions of dogmatism and moralism but also the unquestioned assumptions of liberalism. He rejects the casuistry of pragmatic humanism and substitutes an ethic which derives its validity from the intrinsic criteria of openness, self-validation, communality and concreteness. This is, in fact, an ethic that takes history seriously and sees it as an open process which is not so much to be directed as to be lived.

Barth's identification of the real threat to human life as the forces of totalitarianism and oppression that are inherent in the political systems of both East and West is not a counsel of indifference, but, on the contrary, a counsel for a radical and revolutionary struggle against the dominant orientation of advanced technological society. Because Barth refuses to identify the existing order as the political arena he has been accused of political irrelevance. But to recognize the bankrupcy of both capitalistic and communistic versions of advanced technological civilization is not necessarily resignation. It is also the basis for a radical and revolutionary politics that believes that this sociopolitical world is the world in which the struggle for human dignity and integrity is waged and won. Barth does not avoid political responsibility; he merely questions options defined acceptable by liberalism.

Barth finds evidence of "the adversary" in both communism and capitalism. But he does not attribute that to the inherent evil in politics and retreat into eschatological irrelevance. On the contrary, he attributes it to historical process which may and must be challenged. Barth looks forward to and expects a better world for men and women to live in. This is not eschatological; it is utopian. And he expects that world to come through a radical and revolutionary change in the present, dehumanizing sociopolitical structures. That combination of utopian vision and revolutionary method qualify him as a major force in the struggle for socialist humanism.

NOTES

1. Will Herberg, "The Social Philosophy of Karl Barth," preface to Karl Barth, *Community, State, and Church: Three Essays* (Doubleday & Company, Inc., 1960), p. 11.

2. EDITOR'S NOTE: See Markus Barth, "Current Discussion on the Political Character of Karl Barth's Theology," in *Footnotes to a Theology: The Karl Barth Colloquium of 1972,* ed. by Martin Rumscheidt; supplement to *Studies in Religion / Sciences Religieuses,* 1974, p. 91.

3. Friedrich-Wilhelm Marquardt, *Theologie und Sozialismus* (Munich: Chr. Kaiser Verlag, 1972). There are other commentators who have recognized the political character of Barth's thought.

4. Where does one look for confirmation of the political import of Barth's theology, to say nothing of its socialist thrust? The explicit political writings are too often written off as "occasional." And within the *Church Dogmatics* it is mainly a question of perspective rather than specific statement. There are, however, places to begin: Paul Lehmann has compiled a "little list" of basic sources for Barth's "theology of permanent revolution."

"1. The analysis of the role of revolution in a Christ-centered history under 'the great negative possibility' of submission in the commentary on Romans 12:21–13:7;

"2. The freedom of God for man and of man for God in an experienced movement from reality to possibility, centered in God's human presence in Jesus Christ and forming and transforming history as a predicate of revelation (KD, I/2, 14);

"3. The priority of election over creation, of people over things, of a chosen people over a random people, whose vocation among all peoples is the overcoming of history within history (KD, II/2, 33–34);

"4. Co-humanity is the basic form of humanity and people are being formed and fulfilled in their humanity in the reality and power of Jesus' relation to God and to man. In this reality and power, people are able to be *for* one another as well as *with* one another in a shared and fulfilled humanity (KD, III/2, 45);

"5. God is more certain than anything in creation and all things are instrumental to his human and humanizing presence in the world (KD, III/1, 41);

"6. The principalities and powers of this world have no ultimacy. They are radically instrumental to God's human and humanizing presence and activity in the world (KD, III/3, 49, 50);

"7. The claim of God is the operational reality of his presence and activity in the world. The Law is the form of the Gospel which means that patterns and structures of human relatedness in the world are never established in themselves and never self-justifying but instrumental to human reality and human fulfillment (KD, III/4);

"8. The inhumanity of man to man has been shattered and reconciliation, exposed as the humanizing style of human life in the humiliation and exaltation of one human being whose living, dying, and living again is the prototype and prospect of what humanity is to be. He makes the struggle to be human that doing of the will of God on earth as it is in heaven (KD, IV/1);

"9. There is an experimental community in the world, called and sent as the spearhead of that shaping of all men into the human reality, fulfillment and joy which God in Christ has begun and is carrying through towards that new heaven and new earth in which difference is a thing of beauty and a joy forever, the humanity of humanity is real and complete and God is everything to everyone (KD, IV/2, IV/3)."

(From Paul Lehmann, "Karl Barth, Theologian of Permanent Revolution," *Union Seminary Quarterly Review 28* [Fall 1972], p. 79.) Cf. also: Gabriel Vahanian, "Karl Barth as Theologian of Culture" *(ibid.);* John Deschner, "Karl Barth as Political Activist" *(ibid.);* Helmut Gollwitzer, *The Christian Faith and the Marxist Criticism of Religion,* tr. by David Cairns (Charles Scribner's Sons, 1962); and Helmut Gollwitzer, "Reich Gottes und Sozialismus bei Karl Barth," *Theologische Existenz heute,* Nr. 169 (Munich: Chr. Kaiser Verlag, 1972) [reprinted in this volume]. Each of the above contains additional bibliographical information.

5. CD II/2, 535.

6. *Ibid.,* p. 587.

7. CD IV/1, 434 ff.

8. *Ibid.,* p. 446.

9. *Ibid.,* p. 449.

10. *Ibid.,* p. 451.

11. CD II/1, 503–506.

12. Herberg, "The Social Philosophy of Karl Barth," *loc. cit.,* pp. 54 f.

13. *The Christian Century* 86 (Dec. 31, 1969), pp. 1662–1667.

14. Reinhold Niebuhr, "Barth's East German Letter," *The Christian Century* 76 (Feb. 11, 1959), pp. 167–168.

15. *The Christian Century* 77 (May 11, 1960), p. 571.

16. See note 13 to this essay.

17. Herbert Marcuse, *One-Dimensional Man* (Beacon Press, 1964).

18. "Karl Barth's Own Words: Excerpts from the Swiss theologian's letter to an East German pastor, with translation, subtitles and introduction by Rose Marie Oswald Barth," *The Christian Century* 76 (March 25, 1959), pp. 352–355.

19. *Ibid.*

Conclusion:
Toward a Radical Barth

GEORGE HUNSINGER

"Don't forget to say that I have always been interested in politics," remarked Karl Barth toward the end of his career, "and consider that it belongs to the life of a theologian. My whole cellar is full of political literature. I read it all the time. I am also an ardent reader of the newspaper."[1] This lifelong political interest, pursued with such evident ardor, led Barth to devote much of his career to relating theology and politics. A viable relationship, in his view, must be one of mutual clarification in which neither discipline is reduced to the terms of the other. Only if the two are not confused—with each retaining its own integrity—can either have anything to say. Theology must not be politicized, nor politics theologized. Theology can make its contribution to politics only by remaining theology, and vice versa.

Despite this rather simple-sounding and self-evident platform, Barth's view has been sharply challenged. Before we pursue his ideas in more detail, a glance at certain reactions of his critics will provide a useful backdrop. There have been basically three objections to the relationship of theology and politics in Barth's thought.

The first objection concerns Barth's theology itself. Some critics have charged that it is inherently inadequate to the political realm; it lays such an excessive stress on transcendence that it loses touch with the realities of immanence. Thus, Reinhold Niebuhr argues that Barth's theology is relevant only to moments of great crisis, not to

the more relative decisions of responsible political life. Niebuhr sees
Barth as having constructed a theology for the catacombs which "can
fight the devil if he shows both horns and both cloven feet," but not
if he shows "only one horn or the half of a cloven foot."[2]

Wielding a different metaphor, Niebuhr proposes that Barth regards the political terrain from "an eschatological airplane," soaring
at such a "very high altitude" that his theology is "too transcendent
to offer any guidance for the discriminating choices that political
responsibility challenges us to."[3] From such azure heights, Barth's
theology "disavows political responsibility in principle."[4] It is a form
of "religious absolutism which begins by making conscience sensitive
to all human weakness" and "ends in complacency toward social
injustice."[5]

This line of criticism has been echoed by others: Barth "has no
great conception of the social task of the church. . . . The real task
of the church for him is not to reform or improve society, but to
proclaim the Word of God, whose very import negates man and his
life in this world, and assures man of a truly new heaven and earth."[6]
According to this sort of criticism, then, Barth's theology tends
toward political complacency.[7]

The second objection concerns the character of Barth's political
judgments. Here it is stressed that Barth neglects the necessary task
of empirical analysis. Thus, Charles West, in his cold-war volume on
Communism and the Theologians, contends that Barth fails to concentrate "on the facts of human experience." "Barth seems, because
of his doctrine of all-embracing grace, to neglect his responsibility for
that difficult empirical analysis of real human relations, most especially in politics, which the Christian, just because of his faith, should
take more seriously than all others."[8] "We see throughout," West
writes, "the mind of a theologian at work whose direct interest in
. . . the ethical problems of the economic world as illuminated
. . . by the science of economics is slight indeed, and borrowed from
years ago."[9] Barth's neglect of empirical analysis, as charged here,
would thus correspond to the "complacent" drift of his theology.

The third objection focuses on the manner in which Barth actually
proceeds when moving from theological reflection to political decision. For Barth, according to this criticism, the distance separating

theology and politics proves to be so enormous (as between transcendence and immanence generally) that he can only bring them together in a way that is nonsystematic, ad hoc, and finally arbitrary.

Here the test case is the supposed inconsistency that arose when Barth did not reject communism and Nazism with equal vehemence. When only a sympathetic reprimand of communism followed his total condemnation of Nazism, many critics concluded that Barth's political judgments were not only ill-considered but actually capricious.[10] Among the chief exponents of this view were Emil Brunner, Reinhold Niebuhr, and Charles West.

Brunner numbered himself among those who could see "no fundamental difference" between communist and Nazi totalitarianism.[11] He censured Barth for not condemning every "semblance of collaborationism" with the communists as he had with the Nazis.[12] Niebuhr, issuing a similar censure,[13] went on to draw the systematic consequence: Barth's resistance to Nazism was "dictated by personal experiences with tyranny and not by the frame of his theology."[14] Likewise, Barth's critical sympathy for communism sprang from convictions residing "in his subconscious but not in his conscious approach to things."[15] In short, Barth's movement from theological reflection to political decision had no systematic grounding; "he did not relate these decisions with the content of the gospel."[16]

It remained for Charles West to provide the larger context. Barth's political outlook "seems to be only externally related to his theology."[17] Though never absent in principle, "the whole area of social questions *per se* . . . lies only on the periphery of his interest."[18] Barth's failure to integrate his practical politics with his formal theology results in an "arbitrary selection from different theological emphases for different political situations."[19] This leads one to ask "whether in politics, Barth does not select from his theology to ground opinions reached by other means."[20] If the ground for Barth's politics is not conceptual, then West, like Niebuhr, čoncludes that it must be broadly psychological. It is "one side of Barth's personality" to "delight in an irresponsible and arbitrary kind of freedom" and to be unhappy "unless he is going 'against the stream.' "[21] Not his theological convictions, but merely his personal experiences with labor unions, Nazism, and Swiss democracy suffice to account for his political outlook.[22] Finally, Barth's theoretical rather than practical bent helps to explain the dichotomy between his politics and his theology: "The encounter of his whole life has been primarily not with concrete persons and their problems, but with philosophical systems and movements of culture."[23]

If these objections, regardless of the obvious extravagance in some of them, are correct as a whole, then we are left with a genuine anomaly: One of the most fundamental Christian thinkers of modern times, with a deep personal interest in politics, proved conceptually incapable of integrating his political decisions with his formal thought. He could achieve no intrinsic relationship between them; his politics stayed fundamentally cut off from his theology. Barth the "politician" and Barth the theologian remain unreconciled in thought. Their otherwise capricious relationship can ultimately be explained only on the basis of Barth's personal psychology.

Those who remain dissatisfied with such *ad hominem* or psychological solutions are left with a string of questions. If politics is peripheral to his theology, then why did Barth so often insist that there is a political thrust to his formal thought? If his theology actually leads to such complacency, then what accounts for Barth's leadership in the resistance to Nazism? If his theology is incapable of discriminate political choices, then what explains his subtle, if controversial, discrimination between communism and Nazism? Are these questions simply to be answered by an appeal to Barth's individual psychology—as if his "personal experiences" left no imprint on his formal theological thought?

It is at this point that the work of Friedrich-Wilhelm Marquardt begins to assume its real importance. In his book *Theologie und Sozialismus,* Marquardt takes direct issue with such critical dismissals of Barth as those just cited. The "hiatus" so often alleged between Barth's theology and his politics is, according to Marquardt, "really a hiatus in the knowledge of Barth's interpreters which corresponds neither to Barth's understanding of himself nor to the direct wording of his theology."[24] Marquardt's work makes it possible to see for the first time the intimate connection in Barth's thought not simply between theology and ethics or between theology and politics, but precisely between theology and socialism.

A few detailed examples will serve to illustrate not only this point but also the merits and the shortcomings of Marquardt's work. Marquardt's frequent designation of Barth as an "anarchist" has caused unnecessary alarm among certain unsympathetic critics, probably because they associate anarchism with lawlessness and terror. For reasons of his own, which remain obscure, Marquardt chooses to highlight the anarchist element in Barth's thought while at the same time noting that Barth's socialism was thoroughly eclectic. Yet it is clear precisely from Marquardt's analysis that while Barth shared certain tendencies with anarchist theory, he shared none with anarchist praxis. When it came to praxis, Barth's socialism was thoroughly pragmatic, with affinities to both the more conservative "social democrats" and the more radical "left-wing socialists," depending on the situation. Hence a few definitions are in order to help sort out just where Barth stood on the political spectrum.

The definitions provided by Hans Gerth and C. Wright Mills in their book *Character and Social Structure* are as convenient as any. "Socialism" they define, generally, "as the demand for a planned economic order, producing for use rather than profit, and subject to central administration and budgetary accounting. This involves a fusion of economic and political orders by the extension of democratic practices to the economic order, which, in turn, makes for the elimination of property and income class privileges in favor of economic equality."[25] When Barth wrote that the political task of the Christian community was to "espouse various forms of social progress or even of socialism" (CD III/4, 545), depending, apparently, on how much was possible, he certainly had nothing else in mind. It was within a broadly socialist context of this kind that Barth shared certain tendencies with anarchists, social democrats, and left-wing socialists.

Anarchism, with its radical denial of the legitimacy of any existing order, stands to the left of all other socialist visions of society (whether social democratic, left-wing socialist, or bolshevist). For the anarchists, as Gerth and Mills point out, "all history has been full of evil power, for all power is evil, the existing state being an incarnation of sinful exploitation, and civilization a great progress toward the hubris of the powerful. In the course of history, the state is doomed."[26]

When Marquardt writes that "Barth thinks and argues with the radicality of the anarchists,"[27] his point is far from wrong, but he fails to secure it against possible misunderstanding. He analyzes the similarities between Barth's position and anarchism incisively, but fails adequately to specify the differences.

By the time he wrote his comments on Romans 13 in the second edition of *Romans*, Barth, like the anarchists, considered every existing order to be evil in itself. Although in the first edition he had greeted revolution with enthusiasm, he now regarded even an existing order established by revolution as merely the evil residue left over once social upheaval had subsided. Barth's attitude toward the state has often been labeled as conservative. In fact, Barth's intention was not that of legitimizing the existing order, but that of radically de-absolutizing it. Even his critique of the revolutionary—largely a critique of his earlier stance—was directed against bolshevist socialism from the standpoint of anarchist socialism. His political perspective was thus "anarchist" in the sense that he sought to criticize revolution from the left, to de-mystify the existing order, and to revolutionize the individual before changing conditions. Contrary to the way this section has customarily been read, the theology that Barth advances here has nothing to do with complacency. While recognizing the necessary limits of all political action, he wants to ensure that within any existing order, conditions will really be changed along socialist lines. Revolutionary hubris is no answer to this challenge.[28]

Barth was unlike the anarchists, however, in that his grounding for this position was fundamentally theological. The radical standard of his critique was derived, not from history, but from the kingdom of God. "It is only in relation to God that the evil of the existing order is really evil."[29] Whereas the anarchists had argued that historically the state was a necessary evil whose complete extinction would sooner or later be equally necessary, Barth argued instead that both its necessity and its eventual extinction were eschatological: The existing order must not be destroyed, but must be allowed to exist, as a negative parable to God's kingdom. In this negative way, the evil existing order "reveals that we have a hope—the hope of the coming world where revolution and order are one."[30] "The real revolution comes from God and not from human revolt."[31]

In relation to this real revolution, political praxis can always be only a witness, never a realization. Hence Barth did not subscribe to anarchist tactics. Despite his occasional appeals to direct action,[32] he did not indulge in the practical nihilism that repudiated parliamentary democracy while glorifying general strikes, spontaneous uprisings, and individual terror. His radical eschatology led logically to pragmatist political ethics. Like the social democrats, he was sometimes willing to support coalitions with nonsocialist or "bourgeois" parties—as in the case of the Weimar Republic. Like the left-wing socialists, he was at other times ready to cooperate with bolshevist parties—as in the case of the Committee for a Free Germany[33]—and also to resort to the use of violence, if necessary, in order to achieve or defend a democratic order—as in the case of resistance to Nazism.[34]

But in all cases Barth insisted on a harsh theological realism and a sober lack of illusions: All political activity stands under the wrath of God, who meets "the encroachments of government . . . with the sword of revolution" and "the encroachments of revolution with the sword of government." "Whether we attempt to build up some positive thing or demolish what others have accomplished, all our endeavors to justify ourselves are in one way or another shattered in pieces."[35] It is God who inspires revolutionary discontent, yet God alone who will bring about the true revolution of his kingdom.

Only within the context of this shattering recognition can there be responsible socialist action, and only within this context is Marquardt correct when he writes that *"nothing* is here 'abandoned' to the future, but rather, out of expectation of the future, the drive is released for responsible action in the present."[36] Barth clearly held that decisive aspects of the kingdom remain irreducibly future. It is Marquardt's inadequate attention to the eschatological context—with its elements of divine wrath and irreducible futurity—that detracts from his otherwise penetrating and original treatment of Barth's eclectic position in the socialist camp.

One of Marquardt's most effective interpretations concerns the socialist context of Barth's doctrine of God. Marquardt proposes that a somewhat inconspicuous phrase from Barth's dogmatics be elevated as the caption for his entire theological doctrine, namely, that God is "the fact which not only newly illuminates, but materially transforms, all things and everything in all things." (CD II/1, 258 rev.) This caption has the virture of emphasizing certain distinctive elements in Barth's thought: that "God" means the transformation not only of some things, but of all things; the renewal of the entire world, not simply the interior world of religiosity.[37] In other words, Barth conceives of God in strongly realist rather than idealist terms. God's sovereignty is not restricted to the realm of inward experience, nor to that of "historical consciousness," nor even to that of interpersonal relationships, but rather encompasses the concreteness of the world in all its dimensions, including both nature and politics.

This view of God's sovereignty, according to Marquardt, arises directly from Barth's early socialist activity. That is why Barth could write that "in the materialism of Marxism something lies hidden of the message of the resurrection of the flesh."[38] That is also why Marquardt stresses that Barth's famous description of God as the "Wholly Other" is of social rather than metaphysical import: The God who materially transforms all things is "wholly other" in his sovereignty over the evils of history and the injustices of society.[39] Again, that is why Marquardt contends that Barth's reversal of the scholastic dictum that "act is a consequence of being" to read that "being is a consequence of act" had an originally socialist rather than existentialist setting in Barth's thought.[40]

The evidence with which Marquardt substantiates this perspective is impressive. To take only the best example: With the affirmation that God is "he who loves in freedom," Barth's theological doctrine reaches its apex. Barth structures his entire mature discussion around this point.[41] In reference to this discussion, Marquardt notes first of all that God's love is communal in scope rather than simply personal,[42] and that God's freedom, because grounded in God himself, is a freedom to enter into a real relationship with the world, not merely with the individual.[43] Marquardt then points out that, at an earlier stage in his theological development, Barth had conceived of "freedom in love" and "love in freedom" as eschatological realities which constituted the essence of God's kingdom for the world.

In an early essay, "The Problem of Ethics Today," written in 1923, Barth describes God's kingdom "in this sense: as a task, not an object of desire; as a goal, not a termination of moral struggle; as that which enthusiast, idealist, communist, anarchist, and (despite all genuinely Lutheran teaching)—note it well—even Christian hope envisions as a reality here on earth: freedom in love and love in freedom as the pure and direct motive of social action, with a community constituted in justice as its direct objective." Love in freedom, Barth continues, means "putting an end to tutelage, or, rather, to the exploitation and oppression of man by man, putting an end to class differences and to national boundaries, to war, to coercion and violence in general. It means a culture of the spirit instead of a culture of things, humanization instead of reification, brotherhood instead of universal hostility."[44] A more programmatic appeal for socialist action could hardly be envisioned.

This paradigmatic example, along with many others, confirms Marquardt's thesis that Barth's concept of God arose from an originally socialist context of reflection. "Love in freedom"—once described as the direct goal of socialist action—ultimately becomes constitutive of God's being and grace. "Love in freedom"—which we ourselves can neither grasp nor realize concretely as an ideal social goal—Barth ultimately sees as given to us in and through the being of God. "Love in freedom"—while retaining its political context— henceforth becomes the object of parabolic witness rather than direct realization. Barth's thought thus developed from the socialist task to the gift of God's being, from eschatology and ethics to theology; yet eschatology and ethics remained as a structural moment in his doctrine of God. The socialist task and the eschatological goal received their ultimate grounding as God's gift. In this way religious socialism became evangelical theology.[45]

Despite this impressive point, Marquardt's interpretation runs into serious difficulties. Not content with this insight into Barth's theology and its development, Marquardt proceeds elsewhere not only to overstate his case but actually to reduce Barth's doctrine of God to its political function. Unfortunately, the examples that follow typify the spirit of Marquardt's work.

When he writes that Barth "conceives of God as praxis, power, this-worldliness and in this sense as reality,"[46] Marquardt formulates God's being *as* his act, not *in* his act—a reduction unknown in Barth. Again, when he claims that for Barth the message of the resurrection "is one and the same with the question of verifying our life in a moral, social, and political overcoming of death through victory,"[47] Marquardt, in a way alien to Barth, identifies Christ's resurrection with the object of political realization rather than political witness. Again, when he stresses that for Barth "the question of God is not only explicated, but also answered, in sociopolitical terms,"[48] Marquardt makes theology subservient to politics—something Barth explicitly set out to avoid.

In this interpretative mode Barth dwindles to a kind of socialist Ritschl. The shape of Barth's theology becomes Ritschlian, except that where Ritschl was a bourgeois moralist, Barth becomes a socialist theorist. Although there are two foci to the Ritschlian ellipse—the religious gift and the moral task—"activity in God's kingdom" ultimately receives greater stress than "redemption through Jesus." For Marquardt as for Ritschl, the kingdom becomes a reality to be actualized in and through human action, not a reality to be actualized by God alone. God's "religious function" is ultimately subordinate to his "moral function"; justification by faith is subordinate to reconciliation in the world; God, to the kingdom of God; theology, to anthropology. Religion becomes a sort of annex to morality. That is why Barth could castigate Ritschl for making Christianity subservient to a practical ideal of life.[49] For Ritschl, justification conceived as effective was identical with reconciliation (and ultimately with bourgeois ideals). For Marquardt, God conceived as effective is identical with socialism. This theological contour has little to do with Barth.

What takes place in this mode of Marquardt's interpretation is not only a religious-socialist reduction of Barth's mature theology but also an unconscionable narrowing of it. Marquardt is not wrong to stress that there is a lasting socialist dimension to Barth's thought. He is wrong, rather, in stressing this dimension to the exclusion of all else, and at times subordinating all else to this dimension. "The one perfection of God," writes Barth, "His loving in freedom, is lived out by Him, and therefore identical with a multitude of various and distinct types of perfection." (CD II/1, 322.) Marquardt's narrow politicism loses touch with the sheer multiplicity and polyphony of God's perfection in Barth's thought. "The real God is the one God who loves in freedom, and as such is eternally rich. To know Him means to know Him again and again in ever new ways . . . in the abundance, distinctness and variety of His perfections." *(Ibid.)* Yet in Marquardt's defense it must again be urged that for Barth one of the "ever new ways" in which God's perfection is known is indeed, in a political context, called "socialism."

No doubt the most notable—and most disputed—aspect of Marquardt's work is his overall view of the development of Barth's thought. Once again, though not without its difficulties, the socialist perspective which Marquardt opens up may well be one of his most lasting achievements. In what follows I will not pause to criticize Marquardt's work any further. Rather, as a supplement and guide to the readings collected in this volume, I will attempt to provide a brief chronological grasp of the various stages in Barth's early theological development. Without intending to be comprehensive, I will correlate Marquardt's political perspective with the more nearly theological perspective of Hans Frei in his largely unpublished opus[50] on the nature of Barth's break with liberalism. Thus, I will restate the early development of Barth's theology in a political context.

Barth started publishing in 1909. His break with liberalism dates from 1915. Yet most interpreters of Barth have paid little attention, if any, to his earliest writings. As the real beginning of his theology, they usually take the second (thoroughly revised) edition of Barth's commentary on *Romans,* which did not appear until 1921. This interpretative tack has led to innumerable false impressions of Barth's work. (For example, it lies behind the misplaced critical blasts of Reinhold Niebuhr and others presented at the outset of this essay.) The interpretations of Marquardt and Frei, on the other hand, both have the merit not only of starting with the earliest Barth but also of devoting considerable attention to the widely neglected first edition of Barth's *Romans,* published in 1919.

Marquardt's thesis, in its defensible form, is that Barth's concept of God was built, in part, on the basis of practical socialist experiences, and thus constantly retained an intrinsic relationship to society and politics.[51] The picture which emerges from Marquardt's work is that Barth, from his earliest essays to his final volumes of dogmatics, desired above all else to work out a viable theological solution to the problem of theory and praxis—including political praxis. It was, in fact, the *political* question of theory and praxis which ultimately precipitated Barth's break with liberalism—not merely the theoretical inconsistencies of liberal theology which disturbed him so much in themselves. A look at the chronology of Barth's development in its political context will substantiate this claim.

In our study of this chronology, three questions will be of importance: First, what was Barth's theological position? Second, what was his political position? Finally, how did he relate the two?

I. The Liberal Becomes a Radical (1909–1919)

A. Barth's Early Liberalism (1909–1915)

During this period Barth published three major essays. Each reveals a deep concern about the question of theory and praxis. The first, "Modern Theology and Work for the Kingdom of God,"[52] written during his student days in 1909, conveys the theory-praxis distinction in its title. Modern liberal theology was the "theory" that Barth then espoused, and work for God's kingdom was the "praxis" he was personally anticipating in the form of the pastorate. His dilemma was that liberal theology seemed to stand in direct contradiction to the praxis of God's kingdom.

Liberal theology, Barth proposed, consisted of two decisive elements—religious individualism and historical investigation—and both were problematic when it came to praxis. Religious individualism was problematic, because it attempted to ground revealed truth in the mere subjectivity of religious experience. Likewise, historical investigation was problematic, because, as a scientific procedure, it demanded a universal validity for truth claims which it could not provide with its relativistic results. The relativism of experience and the relativism of history both served to undermine the claim to universal validity implicit in the revelation that grounded the praxis of God's kingdom.

If this was the dilemma of modern theology, then what theoretical content remained for praxis? Barth's answer was meager: "the more or less precise knowledge of the Christian past, whose scientific relativity is quite clear to us, and our own religious life—if indeed we have one."[53] This historical and experiential content, Barth added, was both the strength and the weakness of liberal theology. The dilemma, however, was unresolved: Subjectivism and historicism both relativized the claim to revealed truth, whereas the concept of God's kingdom and its praxis implied, by definition, a validity that was universal. Barth remained at a loss when he sought to connect modern theology to the practice of the Christian life, yet he saw no alternative to the modern perspective. With this theology as his credo, he entered the pastorate.

In the second essay, "The Christian Faith and History,"[54] written from the pastorate in 1910 but not published until 1912,[55] Barth continued his search for a theoretical framework adequate to justify, interpret, and communicate the praxis of God's kingdom. The relationship of faith to history, he noted, forms "the indispensable presupposition and theoretical basis" of pastoral praxis.[56] The issue, as Barth defined it, was twofold: Faith presupposes that God has revealed himself in history, yet historical investigation can countenance no historical interventions by God; consequently, "God has disappeared from history."[57] Furthermore, faith is subjective and internal, whereas history is factual and external; how can an external event of the past become the basis for an internal and immediate experience such as faith?

Both sides of the issue receive the same solution—revelation as history becomes effective through faith. Revelation is "historical" in that faith arises only within the historically continuous Christian community. On the other hand, revelation is transhistorical and "immediate," in that faith is the direct, inward experience of Christ's communal presence. The "history" that concerns faith, therefore, is external in the historic community and internal to the individual believer. Only through faith, and not through historical investigation, can divine revelation in history be known. Only through faith, moreover, can the historical event of revelation be experienced in the present. "The Christ external to us is the Christ within us."[58]

The basis for praxis which Barth proposed was thus the "coinherence" *(Ineinanderstellung)* of history and faith. Revelation as history was a subjective event in the ongoing faithful community. Faith and history were merged in religious experience. Once again, Barth had failed to secure a basis for praxis which could support the claim to a universally valid revealed truth. Relativism remained in conflict with the meaning of the revelation which formed the basis for praxis.

During this phase of his theology, Barth's political outlook began to undergo a profound transformation. His political views during his student days are unknown, but, given his Marburg background, they were probably anything but socialist. Yet when Barth took up his pastorate in Geneva in 1909, he soon encountered at first hand the misery of the industrial working class. What is known is that by the time he moved to Safenwil in 1911, he had already developed profound socialist sympathies—as seen in the address (reprinted in this volume) that he delivered to Safenwil workers shortly after his arrival. His active involvement in the most radical organized political movement of the day—the Social Democratic Party (Lenin's party when he was exiled in Switzerland)—is recounted in this book in the essays by Marquardt and Gollwitzer. What is important here is that a latent tension between Barth's liberal theology and his socialist praxis began to mount. When this tension was added to the conflict he already felt between modern theology and pastoral praxis, the breaking point was imminent. The unity he saw between his pastoral and socialist praxis demanded a new theoretical framework.

Barth made one last attempt to reconcile himself with liberal theology. The third essay from this period, "Faith in a Personal God,"[59] published in the spring of 1914, focused on the question that would continue to preoccupy him once he had left liberal theology behind: the meaning and the basis for language about God. The bearing of this question on praxis was again foremost in his mind, as we shall see, but the burden of his article was primarily conceptual: What does it mean to speak about God, and on what basis can we do so?

Barth first takes up the question of meaning. Two basic elements constitute the concept of God, a personal element and an absolute element. God's presence is personal; his transcendence is absolute. Yet when these two elements are conceived together, the result seems to be an irresolvable contradiction: If God is personal, he is anthropomorphically limited, and therefore not absolute. Conversely, if God is absolute, he is a complex of abstract qualities, and therefore not personal. The concept of a "personal God" seems therefore to be a contradiction in terms: Either God is anthropomorphic and not absolute or else he is abstract and not personal.

To untangle this conceptual dilemma, Barth turns to the question of the basis for theological language. That basis is not abstract but concrete. Theology speaks of God on the basis of concrete religious experience. Religious experience is preconceptual. Religious conceptualization is secondary to religious experience. It is not experience which must be harmonized with concepts, but concepts which must be harmonized with experience. If abstract concepts come into conflict with concrete experience, then it is the abstractions which must yield. The concepts of theology are merely formal; the material of theology is experiential. Abstract form must be in harmony, not in conflict, with material content. Theoretical reflection must be grounded in concrete reality: "Experience, praxis, or whatever one wants to call it, is the obvious presupposition, the source of all religious utterances."[60]

On the basis of concrete reality (experiential and practical), God's absoluteness and personality must simply be reconsidered. The absoluteness of God is not a complex of abstract qualities. Rather, conceived concretely as the sovereignty of his love, it takes shape in his kingdom for the world. Nor is the personality of God an anthropomorphic projection of ideal human qualities. That would again be an abstraction. Rather, conceived concretely, God's personality is his love as it takes shape in the immediate experience of faith. Thus God's love in both its personal and its absolute dimensions is not an abstract quality of reflection but a concrete reality of experience. When God's love is conceived concretely in this way, the previous dilemma disappears: "The absolute is a personality, a personality is the absolute."[61]

This solution, however, contained the seeds of dissolution for Barth's theology. At the outset of his essay he had outlined two approaches to the question of theory and praxis, one of which he considered valid and the other invalid. The approach he considered valid has already been indicated: Theory is a secondary reflection on the concepts implicit in praxis. Abstract concepts must be grounded in concrete reality. This approach rules out the other: Theory may not introduce concepts of its own that correct or supersede praxis. If that happens, theological assertions are formed on a false basis. Furthermore, concepts derived from experience cannot, in the face of inconsistency, appeal back to experience for a second time. Conceptual problems are conceptual, and must be resolved on conceptual grounds.

In a subtle yet fateful way, Barth's conclusions about God's love depended on the approach he considered invalid. He had successfully removed the previous conceptual inconsistency—God's personality and absoluteness no longer clashed—but two fundamental difficulties remained. The first was anthropomorphism. Feuerbach had argued that if theological assertions are grounded exclusively on the basis of human experience, then they are reducible to human experience without remainder. Barth, for his part, had argued that conceptual inconsistencies could not be removed by a second appeal to religious experience. Yet this was virtually the tack he was forced to take when he entertained Feuerbach's objection.

In applying the notion of personality to the concept of God, Barth insisted on a literal rather than merely symbolic sense for God's personal dimension: God's personal love was a concrete reality, not a secondary concept. If God's personal love is concrete and real rather than secondary and derivative, then it becomes impossible to analogize from human love to divine and back again, as Feuerbach had done. However, it would still be impossible to avoid the force of Feuerbach's objection, if the assertion of God's personal love were grounded in nothing more than an assertion about religious experience. For if God is a concrete reality apart from religious experience, then assertions about God's love must be logically independent of assertions about religious experience—otherwise "God" could be explained as wholly derivative from experience. In other words, "God's real personal love" would appear to be nothing more than a secondary concept derived from human experience, and would look very much like an objectified self-delusion. Yet having already asserted God's real, personal love on the basis of human experience alone, Barth had no recourse but to appeal back to this experience for a second time when confronted with Feuerbach's objection.[62] Before long, Barth would come to regard this line of reasoning to be as unsatisfactory in fact as he had virtually acknowledged it to be in principle.

The second difficulty was similar. It concerned the basis for asserting God's absoluteness as the sovereignty of his love. Once again Barth had no recourse but to ground this assertion in immediate religious experience, and once again he would come to regard this grounding as conceptually inadequate. Barth had argued that God's absoluteness was a concrete reality which took shape in his kingdom for the world. The scope of God's kingdom was social and universal, not merely individual and personal. Through the worldly shape of his kingdom, God's absoluteness was immanent as his universal sovereignty over all finite reality.

From Barth's later standpoint, the difficulty here was twofold. First, how could a reality that was to take shape externally in "the culture of objective social values"[63] be grounded merely in the realm of internal religious experience? Isn't it a contradiction to ground God's universal sovereignty in inward experience alone? Doesn't this grounding virtually reduce God's sovereignty to the realm of inward experience? Second, if God's sovereignty is universal, then how can this be reconciled with the persistence of evil in the external realities of politics and nature? How can God's universal sovereignty be grounded in human experience if human experience is manifestly one of bondage and oppression in the external world? Through this twofold line of questioning, Barth would soon find himself forced to conclude that the idea of God's universal sovereignty as a concrete reality could not be sustained in the theoretical framework of liberal theology.

Barth's 1914 essay can be read as an attempt to reconcile the liberal theology of his student days with the religious-socialist concepts he had gradually acquired in the course of his pastoral praxis. He was seeking to reconcile a theology of immediate experience, derived mainly from Schleiermacher, with a radically realistic eschatology, derived mainly from Hermann Kutter. (The direct influence of Christoph Blumhardt did not come until later.) Under the influence of religious socialism (and perhaps to some extent of John Calvin, whom Barth had begun reading as a pastor in Geneva), Barth had already departed from the tendency of liberal theology to explain away the realistic-historical elements in Scripture.[64] The future belonged to the sovereignty of God, who would bring his will to light, and to pass, not only inwardly in religious experience but outwardly in "the culture of objective social values." God's sovereignty entailed a realistic, external reference—including a political reference—and a hope for the external world.

It was Kutter, not Schleiermacher, who originally enabled Barth to achieve some connection, however tenuous, between his theology and his radical politics. The religious-socialist concepts which Barth at first employed will become much better known once the volume of his early socialist writings (which Marquardt is presently editing) appears in the series of Barth's hitherto unpublished manuscripts, now in the process of publication.[65] However, a review article[66] written on the eve of the First World War, in which he attacks the views of Friedrich Naumann (an eminent political and religious liberal), provides a good example of how Barth related theology and politics at the time. He already sensed a strong affinity not only between a viable Christian theology and socialist politics but also between liberal theology and liberal politics.

The connection between a viable, realist theology and socialist politics is explicit in Barth's presentation, whereas his association of liberal theology with liberal politics remains latent. Yet the latter is discernible in retrospect, given Barth's imminent disillusionment about liberal theology's political endorsements. In the article on Naumann, Barth conceives of the relationship between theology and politics as a relationship between "the absolute" and "the relative." For Naumann, "the absolute" is consigned in principle to the moral realm and has no political bearing. For Barth, this can only mean in effect that Naumann pursues politics "under the presupposition that there is no God."[67] Barth acknowledges that politics is the art of the possible, that it transpires in the realm of "relativity" with all its attendant compromises and concessions. But it is one thing to idealize compromises and concessions and quite another to recognize that they are provisional and imperfect realizations of something greater. "It is one thing to live in the world of relativities and to become completely satisfied with aesthetic good pleasure at how wonderful it all is, and quite another to live in the world of relativities with a constant disquiet and longing *(Sehnsucht)* for something better which is to come, for the absolute goal of a humane social life beyond all temporal necessities."[68] To adopt Naumann's liberal politics would be to forgo a deeper understanding of the causes of social evil and to accommodate oneself to a world of wars and capitalism.[69]

"The gospel of the absolute and living God,"[70] wrote Barth, opens up a very different perspective. There is only one contemporary political direction "which distinguishes itself from all other types of politics by taking the absolute, God, with political seriousness"[71]— the international movement of socialism. This movement alone has finished with "the realities of the present aeon—with capitalism, nationalism, and militarism."[72] This movement's revolutionary, not merely reformist, attitude commends itself, because "we expect more from God"[73] than capitulation before present political possibilities.[74] Only a revolutionary movement such as socialism can correspond to the revolutionary theological content of the gospel.

Before long, Barth would come to conclude that the relativism of liberal politics was endemic to liberal theology. The unmitigated relativism of liberal "theory" led logically to that of liberal "praxis." By totally accommodating itself to modern culture, liberal theology had forfeited a standpoint of its own and had rendered itself virtually pointless. It had no adequate basis to speak about the proper subject matter of theology—the sovereignty of God—and no adequate basis to avoid the force of Feuerbach's objection. It had, moreover, no adequate basis to criticize and counteract the evils of contemporary society, and no adequate basis to hope and work for a really better world, despite the experience of a worse one. By the eve of the First World War, the fault lines of Barth's break with liberalism had become manifest.

B. *Away from Liberalism (1915)*

"One day in early August 1914," wrote Barth more than thirty years later, "stands out in my memory as a black day. Ninety-three German intellectuals impressed public opinion by their proclamation in support of the war policy of Wilhelm II and his counsellors. Among these intellectuals I discovered to my horror almost all of my theological teachers whom I had greatly venerated."[75] For Barth, this shocking event signaled nothing less than the end of nineteenth-century liberal theology. "In despair over what this indicated about the signs of the time I suddenly realized that I could not any longer follow either their ethics and dogmatics or their understanding of the Bible and history."[76]

Despite this dramatic moment of recognition, Barth's disillusionment with liberal theology not only had been nascent for many years but would take months really to sink in. It would be difficult to overestimate the sense of moral commitment with which Barth (and generations of theologians before him) had adhered to the "scientific method" of modern theology. As Barth had written in his student essay from 1909, this method had become for the modern theologian "nothing other than a test of his moral uprightness—with it his personality stands or falls."[77] This total moral commitment to the canons of modernity was largely why such a cataclysmic event—the theological and political "sellout" of his venerated teachers—was necessary finally to dislodge Barth from his Marburg theology, forcing him to reexamine the logic of his position.

Even so, the break came in stages. It was apparently not until the spring of 1915, for example, that the immediate implications first became clear. Eduard Thurneysen tells of a trip in April of that year when he accompanied Barth to Marburg to take part in the wedding of Barth's brother. The companions found to their dismay that a kind of prowar hysteria was hanging in the air in Marburg's ecclesiastical and theological circles. One evening, while sitting with none other than Friedrich Naumann, the uncle of the bride, they heard him remark that one now sees how well "religion can be used for purposes of conducting the war." Barth flared up: "What do you mean 'use religion'? Is that permissible? Can one do that?" On the return trip home, Barth and Thurneysen stopped off in Bad Boll to see Christoph Blumhardt, whom Thurneysen knew personally but whom Barth had never met. In the course of discussing the current situation, Blumhardt commented that "world is world, but God is God." This affirmation impressed Barth deeply. It coincided with his growing sense that God, not the world, is the primary reality and that it is God who calls the world into question, not vice versa. Barth departed from Bad Boll confirmed not only in his dismay at liberal theology but also in his recognition that a radically new theological beginning was needed. Soon he would resolve to make that beginning himself.[78]

Several years later Thurneysen wrote to Barth: "What kind of earthquake region is this into which we have stumbled quite unconsciously in the very moment that we decided we had to read the New Testament a little differently and more exactly than our teachers who were men worthy of honor, or the moment when we could no longer be deaf to Blumhardt and could *no longer* share the faith of Schleiermacher (do you remember the evening rendezvous in Leutwil when we first said that aloud?) . . ."[79] The sequence of these lines, apparently chronological, confirms that the great disruption in Barth's thought which began in August 1914 was not consummated until some time after April 1915. It was Barth's direct encounters with Naumann and Blumhardt which finally drove him from Schleiermacher and into theological work. It was and remained intolerable for Barth that the sovereign God and his Word should be so misused by the contemporary church as to support the political horror of the war. The decadence which that represented compelled him to break with the dominant tradition of academic theology and—starting in the spring of 1915—to search for a new foundation on which ecclesiastical and political work could rest.

In pursuit of a new theological foundation, Barth first pored intensively over the writings of the elder and the younger Blumhardt. Barth seized upon the Biblical realism of the former ("Jesus is victor!") and combined it with the realistic eschatology of the latter. This was the first step toward a realistic reconsideration of the promises of God which Barth was seeking for church and society. A renewal of all things in the world, he believed, could occur only through a renewal of theology and faith.[80]

It is widely believed, on the basis of certain statements by Barth himself, that his break with liberalism took place strictly on theological grounds. In view of these statements, Marquardt has been roundly criticized for stressing that Barth's disillusionment with liberal theology cannot really be appreciated apart from its socialist context. The relevant statements by Barth are as follows: "For twelve years I was a minister. . . . I *had* my theology. It was not really mine but that of my unforgotten teacher, Wilhelm Herrmann. . . . Once in the ministry, I found myself growing away from these theological habits of thought and being forced back at every point more and more to the specific *minister's* problem, the *sermon.*"[81]

These statements do nothing to rule out Marquardt's insistence that they include a socialist context, even though Barth does not choose to mention it here. The problem of the sermon was for Barth a problem of praxis, and praxis for him included socialist politics. It must be remembered that Barth had broken with liberalism politically long before he did so theologically. Years before the outbreak of the First World War, he had become active in the socialist movement and acquired a socialist perspective. During those years, his growing sense of God's sovereignty had served to ground his socialist praxis at the same time that it was pulling him away from his earlier "theological habits of thought." In this sense, Barth's *political* rejection of liberalism not only preceded, but actually facilitated, his theological rejection of liberalism. His political break with liberalism had led him to a new sense of God's sovereignty, and his new sense of God's sovereignty was at stake in his revulsion at the events of August 1914.

Barth's revulsion at those events—the outbreak of the war and its political endorsement by both liberal theology and the German socialist party—was not simply theological. It was also a socialist revulsion. The liberal betrayal of theology had been compounded by the socialist betrayal of socialism. Neither theology nor socialism, as it turned out, would regain the status it had held prior to the war. It was as a socialist as well as a pastor that Barth responded to these shattering failures.

The political failure of his venerated professors had revealed a much deeper theological failure. Barth saw no course but to break with liberal theology in principle. At the same time, he broke with the socialist movement, but he did so over tactics, not in principle. Barth's socialism had always been (and always remained) practical rather than theoretical. The theoretical grounding for his socialist praxis was strictly theological. For that reason he had refrained from joining the socialist party despite his active involvement in the movement. But when his public scorn at the party's war policy began to mount, he decided to make his affirmation of socialism clear by joining the party for the first time in 1915. On February 5 of that year Barth wrote to Thurneysen:

I have now become a member of the Social Democratic Party. Just because I set such emphasis Sunday by Sunday upon the last things, it was no longer possible for me personally to remain suspended in the clouds above the present evil world, but rather it had to be demonstrated here and now that faith in the Greatest does not exclude, but rather includes within it, work and suffering in the realm of the imperfect. The socialists in my congregation will now, I hope, have a right understanding of my public criticisms of the party.[82]

During his early ministry, Barth made no separation in principle between socialist praxis and preaching. "In about one of every four sermons of that period," according to his son, Markus Barth, "he mentioned current political, social and economic issues . . ."[83] When in 1915 Barth set out to find a new theological basis for preaching —for "the specific minister's problem, the sermon"—he was seeking a new basis for his socialist praxis at the same time. By insisting on a specifically socialist context for Barth's break with liberalism, Marquardt, far from misrepresenting the facts, has said no more of Barth than Barth toward the end of his career was prepared to say of himself: "I decided for theology," he remarked, "because I felt a need to find a better basis for my social action."[84]

C. Toward a Radical Theology (1916–1919)

Barth had become convinced that his radical politics demanded a radical theology. The "embourgeoisement" of theology through liberalism had flattened the eschatological horizon. Having vitiated the concept of God from within, liberal theology could no longer imagine a concrete transcendence of the conditions of social existence. Consequently, this theology had succumbed in the face of political crisis. "The unconditional truths of the gospel," wrote Barth, "are simply suspended for the time being, and in the meantime a German war-theology is put to work, its Christian trimming consisting of a lot of talk about sacrifice and the like."[85]

A radical theology would have a definite political function: It would be conceptually impossible to suspend "the unconditional truths of the gospel" for the sake of political convenience. Christianity is not a "religion" which can be "used" to support the righteousness of demonic political adventures. Christian theology has a standpoint of its own, based on the sovereignty of God, which counteracts all religious attempts at self-justification, whether political or otherwise. This theology has nothing to do with a "religion" which can justify "the greatest atrocities of life—I think of the capitalistic order and of the war—"[86] but rather with "the establishment and growth of a new world, the world in which God and *his* morality reign."[87] This, in barest outline, was Barth's standpoint in 1916.

Barth's problem as he set out to ground this standpoint conceptually, was how to break with liberal theology without lapsing into the pitfalls of eighteenth-century orthodoxy. The path to such a new conceptual framework would be tortuous, with many twists and turns along the way. It would not, in fact, be consummated until around 1931. But from 1916 on, Barth's basic intention was clear: He sought a radically new theological relationship between "theory" and "praxis" such that the sole foundation of both would be the concrete sovereignty of God. God's sovereignty alone becomes the concrete ground, limit, and orientation of all human thought and action.

To ground "theory" and "praxis" in this way, Barth had to search for a new conceptual objectivity which would overcome liberal theology at the crucial point—its conceptual subjectivism and relativism. If God's sovereignty were conceived as concrete, objective, and real (as it had to be to make any sense), then Christian theology would have unconditional norms for thought and action—norms which were not subject to the capriciousness of the times and could not be suspended for the sake of convenience. Just as he had previously sought to derive theological concepts from the concrete reality of *human* praxis, so he would now seek to do so from the concrete reality of *God's* praxis. Concepts derived from the concrete praxis of God would provide the universally valid norms for human thought and action so necessary both to honor God with the mind and to prevent disaster in the world.

Although he sought a new objectivity in theology, Barth had no intention of repeating the errors of eighteenth-century theology. God was not a "supreme being" whose objective relation to the world was basically mechanical. Faith was not a kind of passive cognition of divine data in revelation and nature. Nor was theology a series of formal propositions deduced from Scripture and conditioned by general truths. When faced with the critical strictures of Kant and Hume about the limits to human cognition, the genius of liberal theology had consisted in overcoming this mechanical externality in the relationship between God and man. The genius of this move had depended largely on three factors, which, as Frei points out,[88] Barth had inherited from liberal theology and which he was never to repudiate: the dialectical form of theological thought, the primacy of God in revelation, and the centrality of Jesus Christ as the content of theological knowledge. Each of these inherited factors was instrumental as Barth set out to avoid the contours of eighteenth-century theology.

The dialectical thought form was instrumental in preventing theology from reducing God to an object. For Barth, God is not an object, but an abiding subject, who is objective in the sense of being over against man, but who can never be encompassed by (or identified with) human thought and action. The primacy of God as subject, secondly, was instrumental in preventing theology from reducing man to a passive receptacle for revelation. For Barth, God as subject does not destroy human self-determination, but rather determines human spontaneity *through* human self-determination so that in relation to God it becomes free for the first time. The centrality of Jesus Christ, finally, was instrumental in preventing theology from degenerating to a mechanical use of Scripture. For Barth, Jesus Christ as the content of Scripture is not identical with its "propositions," but is a concrete reality in his own right, who is disclosed by Scripture, and who through Scripture becomes the direct object of theological reflection. These differences between Barth and eighteenth-century theology were at least latent from 1916 on and would come to be expressed with ever-increasing clarity.

Despite this creative use of his inheritance from liberal theology, Barth's break with liberalism was, of course, fundamental. Apart from the factors already mentioned at length, two require special mention here. First, Barth rejected the immediacy of the divine-human relationship in revelation. Theology does not start from religious experience as the form whose content is revelation. Religious experience is not the object of theological reflection. It is not the concrete reality from which theological concepts are derived. The object of theological reflection is not the relationship of man to God in religious experience, but that of God to man in Jesus Christ. As a concrete reality in Jesus Christ, the relationship of God to man is objective and irreversible. The concrete reality from which theological concepts are derived is God's objective and irreversible act in Jesus Christ.[89]

Second, Barth rejected the "relational" thought form of liberal theology. Just as religious experience was not the object of theological reflection, so "relationalism" was not its formal structure. "Relationalism" describes the formal or conceptual nexus between the content of revelation and direct human experience. As Frei points out, Barth's rejection of relationalism apparently came in two stages.[90] The first stage came in 1915 when he rejected the relational nexus of revelation and religious experience. The second stage, however, did not come until after the first edition of *Romans*. In the 1919 edition, Barth had succeeded only in transferring the relational nexus from the internal experience of the individual to the external experience of history. This was the conceptual reason why Barth revised his commentary on *Romans*, as we shall see, though once again his change of course came from a specifically political impetus as well.

In the first-edition *Romans*, Barth's quest of a radical theology meant a complete rethinking of the concept of revelation. In contrast to liberalism, Barth now conceived of revelation as eschatology, not as religious experience. As he strove to formulate this concept consistently, Barth operated with three criteria which were to persist through every phase of his theology after the break with liberalism: Theological concepts, he held, must be exegetically consistent with Scripture, logically consistent with each other, and functionally consistent with praxis. These criteria were closely related. Barth believed that his radical political praxis was demanded and sustained by the realistic eschatology of Scripture. A more faithful exegesis of Scripture than that of liberal theology would lead to a more viable and more radical politics than had issued from liberal decadence. But the task of theology was not simply exegetical. It was also conceptual. Theology's proper task was conceptually to clarify the revelational content of Scriptural exegesis. In this way, the task of theology would be carried out in the service of human praxis, which demanded a firm conceptual and exegetical foundation. A new theology grounded in the praxis of God would supply the unconditional norms of human thought and action.

In the first edition of *Romans*, Barth's problem was to find the objective ground of God's irreversible relationship to man. His solution was to find this ground within the doctrine of God itself. God's irreversible relation to man is a concrete reality in Jesus Christ. In Jesus Christ, the God who is identical with himself (the Word of God is God) becomes the God who is related to man (the Word of God is "God with us"). The incarnation of God's Word is not grounded in temporal human experience, but solely in God's free act of election from eternity. The mystery of predestination is the objective ground of God's relationship to man. Through his eternal act of election, God, in freedom and grace, relates himself to man with an irreversible primacy and an irreducible objectivity.[91]

In his concrete act of election in Jesus Christ, God becomes the agent of something wholly new for the world. This new reality is the kingdom of God. God's kingdom is not confined to an abstract, internal experience. It is "the world as such and not some specially sacred region . . . in which the kingdom of God is to come."[92] Inaugurated by Christ's resurrection, God's kingdom is a present reality, not just a future possibility. Through the presence of his kingdom, God brings something concretely and socially new out of that which is passing away. He is at large in the world through radical change, bringing life from death, justice from oppression, and permanence from decay. As established by Jesus Christ, God's kingdom is this drastic and organic process, the process which discloses God's sovereignty by overcoming the corruption of the world. The organic unity of God, man, and the world, which was lost through sin and death, has been restored, and is being restored, through Jesus Christ in history.[93]

The political implications of God's kingdom are as radical as the theology from which they are drawn. "That Christians have nothing to do with monarchy, capitalism, militarism, patriotism, free-thinking, is so self-evident that I do not even need to mention it."[94] It is to be taken for granted that Christians will stand "on the extreme left."[95] The shape of Barth's politics here is, as Marquardt points out, already basically anarchist.[96] Barth explicitly places himself to the left of Lenin.[97] The state as such is evil and stands under the wrath of God. Christians should have nothing to do with it. "Thou shalt starve the state of religion. Thou shalt deny it the elevation, seriousness, and significance of the divine. Thou shalt not have your heart in your politics. Your souls are and remain alien to the ideals of the state."[98] Christians have only one concern—not the corrupt goals of the state, but the coming of God's kingdom, "the *absolute* revolution that comes from God so that he leaves the whole realm of the penultimate to the process of dissolution." Yet this means not complacency, but a radical attitude toward politics: The Christian must let "the healing unrest that is set in his heart by God deepen, grow stronger, and augment the generally rising flood of the divine which will one day itself break through the dams." Let there be "strike, general strike, and street fighting if there must be, but no religious justification or glorification of it . . . ; military service as soldier or officer, if it must be, but on *no* condition as military chaplain . . . ; social democratic but not religious socialist."[99] Political goals can receive no direct religious sanction. Nonetheless, Barth can look with hope toward the day "when the now-dying ember of Marxist dogma will blaze forth anew as the world's truth, when the socialist church will be raised from the dead in a world become socialist."[100]

Before long, Barth would come to see a serious conceptual problem with this radical eschatology and its implications. His theology had broken with liberalism in principle, but not yet fully in fact. Having begun as a break with subjectivism, his departure from liberalism had not yet led to a more fundamental break with relationalism. In the 1919 edition of *Romans*, Barth had conceived of God's kingdom as an organic, yet dialectical, process within the world. This conception had implied a relational nexus between God's kingdom and external historical experience. God had been conflated with revolution; Jesus Christ, with eschatology; eschatology, with an immanent historical process; the praxis of God in Christ, with that of man in the world.

The problem here was twofold. First, on these terms, the relationship of God to man in Jesus Christ was still reversible with that of man to God in an area of human experience. The concept of God had not yet been formulated objectively enough on its own terms. Its conceptual integrity was still threatened with collapse. Conceptually, it could still be interchanged with (and, in principle, reduced to) the experience of radical political change. "God" seemed to be a secondary derivation from the concrete reality of revolution. The force of Feuerbach's objection had still not been met.

Furthermore, the conflations in the first edition of *Romans* meant that socialist politics still had the kind of directly "religious" sanction which Barth had set out to avoid. The merging of God with revolution meant that Barth's theology still retained a distinctly religious-socialist cast. In contrast to religious socialism, however, Barth had intended to show that the relationship between theology and politics, while definite and unmistakable, was nonetheless indirect. Properly conceived, the doctrine of God led, on its own terms, to socialist politics, but without the relational conflations of religious socialism. Therefore, to break more fully with liberalism and to provide socialist politics with its proper theological ground, Barth resolved to root out the vestiges of religious socialism from his theology.

D. Away from Religious Socialism (1919)

"Once I was a religious socialist," wrote Barth. "I discarded it because I believed I saw that religious socialism failed to take as serious and profound a view of man's misery, and of the help for him, as do the Holy Scriptures."[101] Barth's attitude toward religious socialism had always been independent and complex. Prior to the war he had sought to combine Kutter's basically theological approach with Ragaz's concern to put principles into practice.[102] After 1915 Barth had then begun to draw heavily upon the theological insights of Christoph Blumhardt, the main inspiration of Swiss religious socialism, who profoundly influenced Kutter, Ragaz, and Thurneysen before eventually reaching Barth. The outbreak of the war, however, had disillusioned Barth not only with theological liberalism and the socialist "international," but also with the shape of religious-socialist theology.[103] Here, too, a fundamental break seemed necessary.

The persistence of religious-socialist elements into the first edition of *Romans*, which came to disturb Barth deeply, has generally obscured the fact that this phase of Barth's theology shared certain parallels with Ritschlianism. Certainly, Ritschl's direct influence here was remote. The fundamental difference, of course, was that Ritschl's outlook had been simply bourgeois whereas Barth's was specifically socialist. Yet Barth's stress on God's kingdom as a goal to be realized through human action, his activist view of faith, and his relentless attack on pietism and other forms of inwardness, all gave his theology a distinctly Ritschlian flavor. Barth's determination to root out the vestiges of "relationalism" from his theology after the first edition of *Romans* was basically a decision to rid his thought of this "Ritschlian" element.

While the dissatisfaction Barth felt with his theology was conceptual, the impetus to revise it was largely political. As Marquardt points out, Barth was writing the first edition of *Romans* before and during the bolshevist revolution in Russia. He came to Romans 13 toward the end of 1918, at approximately the same time as the revolution in Germany and the national strike in Switzerland.[104] Barth had welcomed these events as instances of the revolutionary process of God's kingdom. Of the state, he wrote: "We fight it fundamentally, radically. . . ."[105] The evil existing order is "not to be improved, but replaced. The forces of injustice above and below" must be "eliminated through the forces of justice."[106] By the end of 1920, however, when he first decided that his Romans commentary needed a thorough revision,[107] the political situation had changed drastically, having brought far less than he had hoped: The Weimar Republic was already showing signs of slipping into a parliamentary quagmire, and the Russian revolution had long since assumed the grotesque physiognomy of a police state. As Marquardt suggests, having started from an "anarchist" vision of total and absolute revolution, it was a chastened Barth who turned to the revising of *Romans*. Barth now had so much to object to in the existing order that he could object to nothing more.[108] The tenacity of evil had outstripped the power of revolution.

The first sign that Barth was conceptually separating his theology from religious socialism in fact, as he had long intended in principle, came with the lecture "The Christian's Place in Society," delivered at the end of 1919 after he had completed the first edition of *Romans*. What is new in this lecture, as Frei points out,[109] is that for the first time Barth begins to break with his earlier organic or developmental eschatology in favor of one conceived along more strictly dialectical lines. That this conceptual revision accompanies a political revision is apparent from the opening lines: Although "we long for something else," writes Barth, "we are still painfully aware that in spite of all the changes and revolutions, everything is as it was of old."[110] Instead of heavily underscoring a revolutionary imperative, he now recognizes a more substantial place for social reform, yet without losing sight of the absolute goal: It is largely in the field of incremental rather than radical change "that we must work out the problem of opposition to the old order, discover the likeness of the kingdom of God, and prove whether we have understood the problem in its absolute and relative bearings."[111] Within the context of this sober political recognition, Barth moves to a more strictly dialectical eschatology: "There is no objective relation between that which is *meant* and that which *is*, and therefore no objective transition from the one to the other. . . . The synthesis we seek is in *God* alone . . . but in God it *can* be found—the synthesis which is *meant* in the thesis and *sought* in the antithesis."[112]

Barth's employment of a dialectical method developed in distinct stages. In the first edition of *Romans*, he had seen a kind of dialectical identity between divine and human praxis in the historical emergence of God's kingdom. In "The Christian's Place in Society," he had radicalized this dialectic so that no objective transition between human praxis and divine could be posited. Finally, three years later, in the second edition of *Romans*, the dialectical method would emerge full-blown, determining every formal aspect of theological thought. But it was his 1919 essay that brought the decisive break with religious socialism. God and revolution were no longer conceived in relational synthesis. The desired synthesis could be found only beyond history in God. Revolution, in other words, had ceased to be part of a relational nexus by becoming one of God's predicates.[113] Henceforth, the socialist task would receive its ground, limit, and orientation in terms of God's revolution alone.

II. The Radical Becomes a Professor (1920–1931)

A. Radical Theology as Dialectical Theology (1920–1928)

In the second edition of *Romans*, Barth recast his radical theology as dialectically as possible. His basic intention remained the same: All human thought and action was to be grounded, limited, and oriented solely in terms of God's sovereignty. What changed was the method by which Barth sought to carry out this intention. The change in method was, in part, a direct result of political experience.

After his profound disappointment with the outcomes of socialist revolutions, Barth became convinced that God's relationship to man must be expressed in wholly dialectical terms. The failures of socialist "praxis" had shaken its underlying "theory." The absolute goal toward which revolution had so abortively aimed could in no way be directly grasped. Neither theological thought nor socialist action could approximate the content of eschatological hope. God's sovereignty emerged as the absolute limit or "crisis"—not just the ground and orientation—of theological "theory" and socialist "praxis." The socialist crisis had indicated a more fundamental theological crisis, demanding a dialectical approach to both "theory" and "praxis."

Every affirmation about God in theological thought must be counteracted by an equal and opposite negation. Every positive effort to approximate God's kingdom through socialist action must be counteracted by an equal and opposite recognition of the complete sinfulness of that action. *Finitum non capax infiniti* (the finite is not capable of the infinite). Only an unresolved dialectical tension, in which every thesis meets its antithesis, can clear the way for the infinite sovereignty of God. Only the self-negation of theological thought can do justice both to the self-contradiction of socialist action and to the concrete reality of the living God who alone makes all things new. Only a dialectical method applied to all human thinking and acting can honor God's irreversible primacy.

Barth's new dialectical method thus had two basic functions. Negatively, it served to eliminate all vestiges of religious-socialist relationalism. There is no area of human existence—whether inward experience or external history—where God is immediately present. God's immediate presence is a matter of eschatological hope, not of present experience. Far from joining in a relational nexus, God and man are almost totally incongruous, meeting only as a tangent to a circle. Between God and man there is an infinite qualitative difference: God is the agent of something wholly other and wholly new; man is the agent of sin and death. God's act of relating himself to man has nothing to do with man's efforts to establish an immediate relationship to God. All such efforts—whether through experiential religion or socialist action—are merely attempts at self-justification and therefore epitomize sin. There is no point of contact in experience or history with the content of eschatological hope. Experience is the absence of hope. Hope is the contradiction of history.[114]

If God is not present to man through a relational nexus, but separated from him through an infinite qualitative difference, then certain consequences follow for political action. These consequences, as Barth draws them in the second edition of *Romans*, have already been mentioned. What is important to see here is how Barth has withdrawn the directly religious sanction for socialist politics which persisted in the background of the 1919 *Romans*. In spite of, and because of, being so close to the truth, socialist revolution meets its crisis when confronted with the sovereignty of God. Whereas in the earlier *Romans* God was conceived from the standpoint of revolution, revolution in the later *Romans* is conceived from the standpoint of God.[115] God's revolution is the absolute limit to all human revolutions and the judgment which discloses their sin.

While stressing the negative function of God's revolution as limit, crisis, and judgment, however, Barth did not mean to deny its positive function as orientation and ground. He did not urge political passivity, but a new quality of political action which allowed more room for social reform and less for revolutionary hubris.[116] God's eschatological revolution remained as the ground and orientation of human hope—and thus of socialist action. Yet because this hope was more than political, it also entailed "waiting and listening," not just "hurrying and setting to work."[117] This was the strength which enabled hope to transcend every political situation without capitulating to present possibilities. Nonetheless, partly because of the subtlety of his view of hope and partly because of his heavy stress on God's revolution as the crisis of socialist action, Barth's theology in the second edition of *Romans* left the impression of advocating political complacency—an impression Barth did not intend, but one from which his theology was never fully to recover.

Positively, by eliminating relationalism, Barth's dialectical method served to clear the way for the concrete sovereignty of God. This method worked to clarify what Barth had intended to say ever since 1915, that God's relationship to man is grounded in God alone apart from all human efforts. God is wholly separate from man, yet the primary reality of human life, because God gives himself to man in Jesus Christ. This positive content, including its basis in predestination, remained from the first edition of *Romans*. What was new was the dialectical form in which this content was cast.

The content of theology cannot be directly communicated. Direct communication would imply the kind of immediacy between God and man which Barth so vehemently rejected. Any attempt at direct communication would be idolatrous. It would be an attempt to derive theological concepts from some reality of human experience as if it were that of God himself. The positive function of dialectic, therefore, is indirect communication. (Here as elsewhere Barth now draws upon Kierkegaard.) God is identical with no human thought, no human action and no human experience, but only with himself. God is a concrete reality which is given only as that which is not given. God's movement toward man in Jesus Christ is at once concrete and wholly transcendent, defying every attempt at systematic conceptualization. Dialectical concepts point, however imperfectly, to the movement of God by leading to their own dissolution. They indicate that God's act in Jesus Christ cannot be contained by any system of thought. Through self-negation, they point away from themselves to "the bird in flight"—to God's concrete act in Jesus Christ beyond all experience and history.[118]

If God's movement to man is ontologically grounded in God alone, then epistemologically this implies that God can only be known through God. The relationship is again irreversible: There is only a way from God to man, none from man to God. Man on his own can secure no knowledge of God and his promises. Nevertheless, man is not outside, but inside this knowledge, because God has made himself known through his Word, Jesus Christ. God's revelation of himself through his Word can only be known through Scripture. Revelation is the correlation between the Holy Spirit and Scripture, whose content is Jesus Christ. Through Scripture, Jesus Christ bears witness to himself. Between Jesus Christ and Scripture, the Word and the words, there is no systematic correlation. The correlation depends solely on God's free activity in his Word—an activity that is not dialectical, but positive and direct.

Faith's relation to revelation, however, is wholly dialectical and indirect. Faith is not (as in liberalism) the form whose content is revelation. The form of revelation is identical only with its content: God's concrete yet transcendent Word. Faith itself is a conceptual vacuum. It has no content that it has not been given, and the content it has been given is something it cannot contain. Faith must therefore negate itself by pointing away from itself to the revelation which created it and which always completely transcends it. Faith has no prior knowledge or independent information about revelation. Faith is simply obedience to the witness of the Word. Therefore, revelation is the presupposition of faith, but faith remains separated from the content of revelation by an infinite distance. There is no formal correspondence between faith and revelation. If revelation is wholly other, faith must be wholly dialectical.[119]

From Barth's later standpoint, three serious problems were intrinsic to this dialectical version of his radical theology. The first was basically formal. The framework of liberal theology had now been dialectically negated, but not conceptually overcome. Barth had done little more than stand Schleiermacher on his head. Barth had not focused on man at the expense of God, but on God at the expense of man. Liberal theology had not been fundamentally dismantled. It had simply been radically inverted. The stress on "crisis" and on the "infinite qualitative difference"—the denial of every point of immediacy between God and man—had resulted in nothing but a drastic reversal of relationalism. The formal structure of liberal theology had persisted in negative dress.[120]

The second problem was basically material. If God's act in Jesus Christ is placed strictly beyond all experience and history, then it becomes logically impossible to affirm the incarnation. Christology had become a wholly transcendent notion, and dialectical theology had reduced itself to a mere Christological prolegomenon. Whereas the 1919 *Romans* had conflated Jesus Christ with an eschatology of immanence, the 1921 version had conflated him with an eschatology of total transcendence. God's act in Jesus Christ had been grounded in eternity, but virtually banished from history. Even Jesus Christ seemed related to history as a tangent to a circle.[121]

Seen from another perspective, the problem was that Barth still conceived of God too abstractly. His revulsion at the consequences of relationalism had led him to describe God's sovereignty as "wholly other" than the evil existing world. This concept of God, derived over against the world, was more nearly philosophical than Biblical. Later, Barth would connect God's sovereignty more directly with Jesus Christ, only then relating it to the world.[122]

The third problem was basically political. Ragaz had suggested that Barth's dialectical theology was really reactionary, because it tended to justify the autonomy of man. The separation of God from man seemed to result in a secularism not unlike that of the Lutheran two-kingdoms doctrine. God was the absolute limit, but apparently no longer the ground and orientation of socialist action.[123] Barth had not intended this implication, but it would take a new political crisis to force him to reexamine his one-sided mode of expression.

Barth's dialectical period persisted from 1920 to 1928. His last major attempt at dialectical theology was his *Christian Dogmatics* of 1927. In this work Barth continued to insist that the object of theological reflection is the Word of God, not religious experience or faith, and that the form of faith is dialectical, not positive or direct. The knowledge of God is not a direct apprehension of revelation, but of ourselves as being known. We do not recognize the Word, but are recognized in it. Here the consequences of merely inverting relationalism started to become more clear. If the direct knowledge of faith is of itself as being grasped, then is the situation ultimately any different than in liberalism? Doesn't faith know only itself rather than God's objectively grounded Word? Doesn't dialectical theology still succumb to Feuerbach's objection?

B. The Suspension and Recovery of Praxis (1921–1931)

The second edition of *Romans* was begun in 1920 at Safenwil, where Barth was still active as a pastor, and completed in 1921 at Göttingen, where he had accepted an appointment as a professor. The decision to leave the pastorate for a university post was difficult, not only because Barth was personally inclined toward praxis but also because he had never pursued studies for a doctorate. Yet the new theological course on which he had embarked seemed to demand that he test it thoroughly and think it through to the end. Nothing less was at stake than a radically new standpoint which promised to safeguard the integrity of theology. Only a new and more radical standpoint could counteract the disastrous capitulations of liberal theology in the conceptual and political realms.

For Barth personally, the decision to become a professor meant the suspension of political praxis. The man who had once considered becoming a labor organizer would now spend many sleepless nights preparing for classes and studying for lectures. "They were of course sour years," he wrote in 1927, "since I perpetually had not only to learn and to teach at the same time, but also to legitimate myself— that is, to save my skin—as the representative of a new theological direction through lectures and public discussions concerning every possible implication."[124] These were also the years in which Barth was apparently most skeptical about the possibilities of socialist action. The revolutionary failures of 1917 and 1918 had left a lasting impression. Barth's chastened attitude toward socialism during the 1920's receives a detailed discussion above in the essay by Helmut Gollwitzer. Barth's decision to withdraw from praxis and to concentrate on theology's conceptual task coincided with his new political sobriety and his turn toward dialectical theology.

Despite this greater political sobriety, Barth did not abandon his socialist commitment even at the height of his dialectical period. His 1919 slogan—"Social democratic, but not religious socialist!"—remained in force. In 1926 he could still speak of "the justice and necessity" of the socialist struggle while castigating theology and church for not having supported the legitimacy of the socialist cause.[125] In 1928 he not only voted for the socialist party in the May elections (upon which it gained control of the German parliament by forming a coalition with the communists) but afterward considered it important to communicate his decision to his colleagues.[126] In 1932 he joined the socialist party as an act of political witness in the midst of a deteriorating situation.

What was at stake in these decisions for Barth was the meaning of Christian hope. Ever since his encounters with the socialist movement and with Blumhardt, Barth had become convinced that Christian hope must remain true to the earth—or else it would cease to be Christian hope. That is why Barth found himself forced to agree with Feuerbach against the tradition of nineteenth-century liberal theology. In contrast to liberalism, Feuerbach had focused on the needs of the whole man—head, heart, and stomach—and had thus carried "the strong 'plus' " of an "unconscious but evident affinity to the ideology of the socialist workers' movement."[127] This radical realism was closer to the Christian hope for "the resurrection of the flesh" than was liberal theology's abstract, inward idealism.

The liberal surrender of resurrection hope was largely why Barth took Feuerbach's objections so seriously. To Barth, these objections were significant in the realms of both theory and praxis. With regard to "theory," Feuerbach's objection raised the question of whether liberalism's anthropologically based concept of God was not really "a human illusion." Barth could only answer in the affirmative: "Whoever is concerned with the spirit, the heart, the conscience, and the inwardness of man must be confronted with the question of whether he is really concerned with God and not with the apotheosis of man."[128] Only a proper concept of God which was not reducible to religious experience could sustain the radical realism of resurrection hope and so remain true to the earth.

With regard to "praxis," Feuerbach's objection led Barth to the parallel question of whether the church should not really have "shown in practice" that her "God" was not "a means of deceit deliberately sustained to quench the proletarian struggle for freedom."[129] Once again Barth could only answer in the affirmative: The church must not become "pharisaically indignant" at the express atheism of the socialist movement, but "should do penance" for having abandoned the struggle for freedom. "The church will recover from the sting of Feuerbach's question only when her ethics is fundamentally separated from the worship of old and new hypostases and ideologies. Only then will men accept the church's word that her God is not merely an illusion."[130] Against Feuerbach, the credibility of resurrection hope depended not only on a proper concept of the living God but also on putting its political implications into practice by participating in the socialist struggle for freedom. This was Barth's conviction in 1926.

By 1927, however, Barth had still failed to provide this conviction with an adequate basis. Ever since 1915, and especially since 1921, he had been striving for a conceptually consistent theology based objectively on "what God is in himself" rather than subjectively on "what God is for man."[131] Only on such a basis could the decadence of liberal theology be overcome. Only on such a basis could the force of Feuerbach's objection be met. Only on such a basis could the radical realism of resurrection hope be recovered and secured for praxis. Then, after his *Christian Dogmatics* of 1927, Barth discovered that his theology had still not overcome the framework of theological liberalism. His dialectical theology was still in an exposed position with regard to Feuerbach's objection. His withdrawal from the pastorate to concentrate on theological reflection had still not achieved an adequate basis for the theory and praxis of hope.

After 1927, Barth became increasingly dissatisfied with the dialectical cast of his theological thought. Once again, a fundamental revision seemed necessary. He undertook new explorations in the relationship between theology and philosophy as well as between theology and ethics.[132] He immersed himself, among other things, in the study of Anselm. With his book on Anselm in 1931, Barth turned from dialectical to analogical theology, satisfied that he had at last gained a conceptually consistent understanding of "what God is in himself." These same years, 1928 to 1931, marked the opening round of the Church Struggle. As described more fully above in the essay by Marquardt, these were the years when Günter Dehn, a Berlin pastor become professor of practical theology, was subjected to extreme harassment by German nationalists and Nazi students for his attempt to separate Christian theology from the prevailing civil religion. Toward the end of this affair, in 1931, Barth circulated a petition among his colleagues declaring "personal and material solidarity" with Dehn.[133] Despite the fact that only four other signatures could be obtained, this simple but fateful act marked Barth's personal recovery of praxis and his entry into what would become the resistance of the church to Hitler. By 1931, therefore, as disastrous new capitulations once again threatened theology and church, Barth had reentered the realm of praxis and grounded his radical theology.

C. Radical Theology as Christological Theology (1931)

It is little wonder that Barth could write of his 1931 study on Anselm: "Among all my books I regard this as the one written with the greatest satisfaction."[134] This was the study which enabled Barth to overcome theological liberalism, meet the force of Feuerbach's objection and provide a positive basis for the theory and praxis of hope. It was the study which enabled him to leave the negative irrationalism of dialectic behind and to provide a positive basis for the church's resistance to Hitler. Above all, it was the study which enabled him to see that theology must be grounded solely on "Jesus Christ as the living Word of God spoken to us men."[135]

Ever since 1915 Barth's problem had been this: If theology starts from the experience of faith and reflects on it (Schleiermacher), then how does theology ever get beyond the subjectivism, relativism, and anthropocentrism of this object of reflection (Feuerbach)? How can theology get beyond the subjectivity of faith to the objectivity of God as he is in himself and his relationship to man? How can theology find a consistent basis for taking God rather than faith as the concrete reality from which theological concepts are derived? How can theory and praxis be consistently grounded, limited, and oriented in terms of God's sovereignty alone?

The first thing which Anselm enabled Barth to see was that this is primarily a problem of understanding, not of proof. It is a problem of clarifying, not verifying, theological concepts—a problem of meaning first and truth second. Yet the peculiarity of these concepts is precisely that the achievement of understanding functions as the attainment of proof. Clarification leads to verification. To understand the meaning is, in this case, to prove the truth.[136]

Second, Anselm enabled Barth to see the necessity of an affirmative rather than a dialectical theology. Such a theology is necessary, because faith itself seeks rational understanding. Rational understanding is a requirement of faith. The desire for rational understanding presupposes the existence of faith and arises from the nature of faith. There are four reasons why faith seeks understanding:

1. The object of faith, God, is not only a compendium of all rational truth but also the source and cause of this truth. Faith seeks understanding because of the rational nature of its object.

2. The subject of faith, man, is related to God by a movement of the will, and the human exercise of the will depends on the capacity of rational discrimination when making choices. Faith seeks understanding because of the rational nature of its subject.

3. The object of faith (God) actualizes a capacity in the subject of faith (man) to know (and love) the object. Faith seeks understanding because of the rational relation of the object to the subject.

4. The subject of faith (man) perceives its limit in relation to the object of faith (God) by virtue of understanding. Understanding leads to the objective boundary which separates the subjectivity of faith from that of the vision of God in glory. Faith seeks understanding because it needs to know its inexorable limits in relation to God.

Therefore, faith inherently seeks rational understanding because of the nature of its object, the nature of its subject, the relation of its object to its subject, and the relation of its subject to its object.[137]

Third, Anselm enabled Barth to see that a nondialectical theology was not only necessary but also possible. Faith can only be rational, not irrational, because the object of faith is mediated to the subject of faith in a rational form. The object of faith, God's living Word (his Logos), comes to the subject of faith through human words (human logos). Through the Credo of the church, the living Word of God is spoken to man. Faith begins as recognition of God's Word and ends as assent to it. Assent is the result of understanding. Faith is not in conflict with understanding, but differs from it only in degree (not in kind). Understanding starts from the object present in faith and arrives at rational knowledge of it. Theology is possible in the limited sense of moving from recognition to assent, from awareness of the actuality of the object to understanding its inner necessity. Theology is neither a storming of the gates of heaven nor a *sacrificium intellectum*. It does not seek to establish the "general possibility" of the object, nor does it require a surrender of reason. It starts from an actuality and arrives at an understanding of its rational necessity. The possibility of an affirmative theology—based on God's living Word spoken to men—explains "the characteristic absence of crisis in Anselm's theologizing."[138]

Finally, Anselm enabled Barth to see that a rational theology was not only objectively necessary and possible, but also objectively conditioned. The object of faith subjects theological understanding to eight conditions:

1. Theology can only be positive, not negative, because it reflects on the object of faith from within a context of affirmation.

2. The object of faith is actual, inconceivable, and subject to no external necessity. Theology does not seek to show that the object of faith is "possible" because grounded in some external necessity. Theology seeks only to understand this inconceivable actuality according to its inner necessity.

3. Theological statements are always inadequate to their object. God can never be expressed adequately by man, but only by himself in his Word to man. Nevertheless, theological statements are possible by virtue of the object's decision to make its rationality accessible to that of the subject. Through the analogy between object and subject, nondialectical theological statements are possible under the conditions set by the object.

4. The certainty of theological statements is therefore relative, whereas the certainty of faith derives from the absoluteness of its object.

5. The relativity of theological statements implies that progress in theology is possible.

6. The criterion of theological statements is Scripture. Theological statements do not merely quote Scripture, but they may not be in conflict with Scripture. They seek the "inner text" of Scripture (God's Word).

7. A further definite, but more provisional, criterion is praxis. Where faith is really faith it issues in obedience.

8. Theological understanding is both a gift and a task. It is a gift to be sought through prayer and a task to be sought through reason. Theology cannot seek to establish the object of faith, but only to understand it in its very incomprehensibility.[139]

On the basis of these conditions, theology proceeds as follows: It moves from the actuality to the necessity of its object. God cannot be other than he is; therefore, faith cannot conceive of him as other than he is. God exists in a particular way; therefore, faith must conceive of him in this particular way. Faith seeks to understand the rationality of God as he actually exists. Understanding can only be derived from God, not God from understanding. God stands over against understanding and cannot in principle be reduced to understanding or to anything else. "God" is the name of that actuality than which no greater can be conceived. Faith and creation depend on God. God depends on nothing other than himself. It is impossible to conceive of that which exists necessarily as not existing.[140]

With this conclusion Barth, following Anselm, had achieved the conceptually consistent understanding of God's sovereignty he had sought since 1915. First, he had overcome theological liberalism by establishing the objective basis of theology apart from faith. Theology could now be centered on God, not on man. Its ground, limit, and orientation was that of revelation, not subjective experience.

Second, he had met the force of Feuerbach's objection by virtue of a consistently concrete and realistic concept of God. "God" was not a secondary concept derived from the basis of some concrete reality other than himself. The living God was the primary reality on which all other ontic realities and true noetic concepts depended.

Third, Barth had overcome his earlier need for dialectical theology while still retaining the positive intention which dialectical concepts had filled. As in dialectical theology, all theological concepts were fundamentally inadequate to their object. Yet, by virtue of analogy, these concepts could conform to their object because of God's decision to make himself accessible to the understanding inherent in faith. The contrast between faith and reason no longer corresponded to that between God and man. Faith and reason were different only in degree. Through imperfect yet appropriate analogies, the rationality of faith could participate in the rationality of God without becoming identical with it.

Finally, Barth had found a positive basis for the theory and praxis of resurrection hope. Just as theological concepts were properly analogous to God's Word, so the human praxis of obedience was properly analogous to God's praxis in Jesus Christ. Conceptually, Barth's turn to analogy meant that "when the *great* hope is present, *small* hopes must always arise for the immediate future" (CD IV/1, 121 rev.). Practically, it meant that as the emissary of the great hope, the church must fulfill its political task as "a responsible, forward-looking and forward-moving community . . . regarding developments in state and society" (CD IV/1, 153 rev.). To Barth, from the beginning of his career to the end, such a forward-looking attitude could only be described as "socialist."

From a study of this chronological development, two points stand out above all else. First, from 1909 to 1931, Barth was always concerned about "theory" for the sake of "praxis," never about "theory" in itself. Every major development in his theology took place in a political context. His break with theological liberalism in 1915, his break with religious socialism in 1919, and his break with dialectical theology after 1928 can only be fully understood in the light of the outbreak of the First World War, the revolutionary failures of 1917 and 1918, and the rise of Nazism, respectively. In each case it was a political crisis which compelled Barth to rethink the conceptual basis of his theology. In each case, furthermore, he was largely seeking a better basis for his social action—one subject to unconditional norms rather than the capriciousness of the times.

This thoroughgoing political involvement means that it is fundamentally false to portray Barth as a theologian who did his thinking in monkish isolation from the world. It is sheer romanticism to suppose that he was constantly revising his theology simply because of "his persistent listening to the mighty voice of Paul."[141] Karl Barth was a socialist. He took the world as seriously as he took the Bible. His thinking moved from praxis to theology as well as from theology to praxis. The chicken-and-egg question as to which came first was entirely foreign to his theological procedure, when viewed genetically. The conceptual priority of theology over praxis goes without saying. Barth took the conceptual problem so seriously that he virtually recapitulated the major moments of nineteenth-century theology—Schleiermacher, Ritschl, and Kierkegaard—before finally arriving at his mature standpoint. The difference was that whereas nineteenth-century theology was either individualistic (Schleiermacher) or bourgeois (Ritschl) or both (Kierkegaard), Barth's theology was always specifically socialist.

Second, it is as fundamentally false to suppose that there is no conceptual link between Barth's theology and his politics as it is to suppose that his theology leads to political complacency. The relationship between theology and politics in Barth's mature thought is formally analogical, materially socialist, and existentially actualist. Formally, Barth conceives of political praxis as an analogy or parable to God's kingdom. God's kingdom is the ground, limit, and orientation of all human action in the world. As the ground of political praxis, God's kingdom provides a positive orientation for working in society. Political praxis becomes as radical and realistic as the hope that guides it. As the limit of political praxis, moreover, God's kingdom remains as the crisis that places all positive social action under the judgment of sin. It is God alone, not man, who will make all things new. In Barth's mature theology, however, this dialectical element is subordinate to the positive element of analogy.

Materially, Barth conceives of political praxis based on the gospel as socialist. The evangelical orientation of praxis is socialist, because it imitates the praxis of God. God is not neutral in the affairs of men. He is a partisan of the godless, the sinners, the poor, and the oppressed. On this point Barth's early position was never to change. In the first edition of *Romans* Barth wrote:

> God is indeed a God of the Jews *and* the heathen, but not a God of the exalted *and* the lowly. He is one-sidedly a God of the lowly. . . . I can certainly be a Jew to the Jews and a Greek to the Greeks, but not a lord to the lords, an aesthete to the aesthetes, or an academician to the academicians. Where idols are worshiped, I am not allowed to take part. Rather, against all those who want to be great in this world, I must espouse the standpoint of those little people with whom God makes his beginning. . . .[142]

In the *Church Dogmatics* Barth takes up the same theme:

> To establish justice for the innocent who are threatened and the poor, the widows, the orphans and the strangers who are oppressed . . . God stands at every time unconditionally and passionately on this and only on this side: always against the exalted and for the lowly, always against those who already have rights and for those from whom they are robbed and taken away (CD II/1, 386 rev.).[143]

In Barth's view, the socialism of God arises from the humanity of God, which did not shrink back from the cross. This is the deepest moment of the socialism Barth sees in the gospel. It was never in doubt through any of the phases of his theological development. Barth was seeking only its proper conceptual ground. His final position was that at best man's socialism stands in solidarity, but not in identity, with the socialism of God.

Existentially, Barth conceives of political praxis in actualist terms. There can ultimately be no systematic correlation between the praxis of God and the praxis of man. "In every time and situation, and therefore in ours too, the final and concrete verdict is not a matter for Christian ethics, but simply for the living Christian ethos in the community" (CD III/4, 534). The gospel provides no less than a socialist orientation for political praxis, but also no more. Ethical norms come to an end at the place where ethical decisions begin. Decisions must be made with respect for both the living God and the concrete situation. Decisions can therefore only be made in a context of fear and trembling and of the assurance of prayer. Prayer and praxis are bound together: *"Ora!* and therefore *Labora!" (Ibid.)*

The actualism of Barth's political decisions was at stake in his view of communism and was the real conceptual issue in the criticisms of Brunner, Niebuhr, and West. The charge that Barth neglected "empirical analysis" was simply beside the point. There was no more "empirical analysis" in the criticisms than in the position criticized. It was not a question of facts, but of construing the facts. Barth's attitude toward bolshevist socialism had been clear since 1919 and unmistakable since 1921. During the cold war, he defended his refusal to reject communism with the same vehemence as he had Nazism on the grounds that the church is "not bound to abstract principles, but to its living Lord."[144] For this reason his position was labeled "capricious."

Barth's attitude toward communism was simply a part of his larger stance with regard to the relative political dangers posed by East and West. The East, to its credit, gave a formal and material recognition not apparent in the West to the social question. Furthermore, Barth considered Western anticommunism to be at least as grave a danger to the world as Eastern totalitarianism. After the anticommunist impulses behind the recent disastrous events in Vietnam and Chile (not to mention Watergate), Barth's position during the 1940's and 1950's will perhaps not seem so misguided today to those who live in the West as it apparently did at one time. If it should not, then perhaps that would be a sufficient justification for his ethical actualism, then and now.

Barth's insistence that socialism is a predicate of the gospel is bound to seem strange in an American context, in part because we have no real cultural analogues for understanding it. It seems to smack of some peculiar mix between Inter-Varsity Christian Fellowship and the American Friends Service Committee, or between *Christianity Today* and the *New York Review of Books.* Perhaps more to the point, it conjures up something like an odd coalition between the historic Reformed churches and the Democratic Socialist Organizing Committee. Theology and church in America seem as little likely to accept Barth's high Christology as the socialist implications he draws from it. Those inclined toward the one would not be inclined toward the other. Yet at the present time, when many people believe that although the bolshevist "socialism" means the loss of human freedom, the advance of "democratic" capitalism is bringing an increase of world poverty, perhaps Barth's socialist views are not as outmoded as his critics would suggest. And despite the obvious and overwhelming difficulties of trying to reconcile the evangelical gift and the socialist task in theology and church as they exist for us today, those so inclined may take some small comfort in the fact that in the life and work of this century's preeminent theologian, the needed reconciliation has already begun.

NOTES

1. Quoted from manuscript notes of an interview between Karl Barth and Margareta Deschner, April 26, 1956, by John Deschner, "Karl Barth as Political Activist," *Union Seminary Quarterly Review* 28 (Fall 1972), p. 55 n. 3.

2. Reinhold Niebuhr, *Essays in Applied Christianity* (Meridian Living Age Books, 1959), p. 172.

3. *Ibid.,* pp. 186, 184.

4. *Ibid.,* p. 187.

5. *Ibid.*, p. 184.

6. Peter Monsma, *Karl Barth's Idea of Revelation* (Somerset Press, Inc., 1937), p. 162.

7. This Niebuhrian line of criticism is parallel to that of Leonhard Ragaz and other religious socialists in Switzerland. For a similar conclusion, based not on Barth's concept of God's sovereignty and human sin but on his Christocentrism, see Charles West, *Communism and the Theologians* (London: SCM Press, Ltd., 1958), pp. 222 and 211.

8. West, *Communism and the Theologians,* pp. 313 f.

9. *Ibid.*, p. 188; cf. p. 186 n. 1 and p. 317.

10. The conceptual and political validity of this criticism is discussed at the end of this essay.

11. Emil Brunner, "An Open Letter to Karl Barth," in Karl Barth, *Against the Stream: Shorter Post-war Writings: 1946–52* (London: SCM Press, Ltd., 1954), p. 107. West, in *Communism and the Theologians,* refines Brunner's judgment while retaining its point (pp. 312 f., 321, 323).

12. Brunner, "An Open Letter to Karl Barth," *loc. cit.,* p. 113.

13. Niebuhr, *Essays in Applied Christianity,* p. 187.

14. *Ibid.*, p. 184.

15. *Ibid.*, p. 188.

16. *Ibid.*, p. 165.

17. West, *Communism and the Theologians,* p. 186.

18. *Ibid.*, p. 189.

19. *Ibid.*, p. 313.

20. *Ibid.*, p. 288.

21. *Ibid.*, p. 317.

22. *Ibid.*

23. *Ibid.*, p. 319; cf. pp. 179, 288.

24. Friedrich-Wilhelm Marquardt, *Theologie und Sozialismus: Das Beispiel Karl Barths* (Munich: Chr. Kaiser Verlag, 1972), p. 49.

25. Hans Gerth and C. Wright Mills, *Character and Social Structure: The Psychology of Social Institutions* (Harcourt, Brace & World, Inc., 1953, 1964), p. 452.

26. *Ibid.*, p. 451.

27. Marquardt, *Theologie und Sozialismus,* p. 165.

28. Cf. Karl Barth, *The Epistle to the Romans,* 2d ed. (1921), tr. by Edwyn C. Hoskyns (Oxford University Press, 1933, 1968), pp. 476–492; Marquardt, *Theologie und Sozialismus,* pp. 165 ff., 307.

29. Barth, *Romans,* 2d ed., p. 484.

30. *Ibid.*, p. 491.

31. *Ibid.*, p. 485.

32. Cf. Marquardt, *Theologie und Sozialismus*, pp. 305 ff.

33. See above, pp. 48 f.

34. Cf., for example, Karl Barth, "Brief an Professor Hromádka in Prag" (1938), in *Eine Schweizer Stimme* (Zurich: Evangelischer Verlag, 1945), pp. 58–59.

35. Barth, *Romans*, 2d ed., p. 490.

36. Marquardt, *Theologie und Sozialismus*, p. 167. Emphasis added.

37. Cf. Karl Barth, "Past and Future: Friedrich Naumann and Christoph Blumhardt," in *The Beginnings of Dialectic Theology*, ed. by James M. Robinson (John Knox Press, 1968), p. 38.

38. Karl Barth, "Brechen und Bauen," in *Der Götze wackelt* (Berlin: Käthe Vogt Verlag, 1961), pp. 120 f.; cited by Marquardt, *Theologie und Sozialismus*, p. 15.

39. Marquardt, *Theologie und Sozialismus*, pp. 110 ff.

40. *Ibid.*, p. 19.

41. Cf. Karl Barth, *Church Dogmatics* II/1, pp. 257–321.

42. Marquardt, *Theologie und Sozialismus*, p. 236; cf. Barth: "God's loving is concerned to seek and create community for its own sake" (CD II/1, 276 rev.).

43. Marquardt, *Theologie und Sozialismus*, p. 237; cf. Barth: "God is free to be and operate in the created world either as conditioned or as unconditioned. God is free to perform his work within the framework of what we call the laws of nature or outside it in the shape of miracle." (CD II/1, 314.)

44. Karl Barth, *The Word of God and the Word of Man*, tr. by Douglas Horton (Harper & Brothers, 1957), p. 160 rev.; quoted by Marquardt, *Theologie und Sozialismus*, p. 238.

45. Marquardt, *Theologie und Sozialismus*, pp. 238 f. and 159.

46. *Ibid.*, p. 278.

47. *Ibid.*, p. 280.

48. *Ibid.*, p. 150.

49. Karl Barth, *Protestant Theology in the Nineteenth Century* (Judson Press, 1973), pp. 655 ff.

50. Hans W. Frei, "The Doctrine of Revelation in the Thought of Karl Barth, 1909 to 1922: The Nature of Barth's Break with Liberalism," Yale University Ph.D. dissertation, 1956, 588 pp. (referred to hereafter as "Barth's Break with Liberalism"). Pages 174–202 of this work appear in Frei's essay, "Niebuhr's Theological Background," in *Faith and Ethics: The Theology of H. Richard Niebuhr*, ed. by Paul Ramsey (Harper & Row, Publishers, Inc., 1957, 1965), pp. 40–53.

51. Cf. Marquardt, *Theologie und Sozialismus*, p. 299; Hans Urs von Balthasar, the preeminent Barth interpreter, makes this same point in passing: "To the extent that certain of Barth's political positions can stand at the origins of a dogmatic pursuit, to that extent such a pursuit is in a position to lead back once again to practical and political consequences. The more deeply one enters into Barth's thought, the more evident such connections become. . . ." *Karl Barth: Darstellung und Deutung seiner Theologie* (Cologne: Verlag Jakob Hegner, 1962), p. 54. (This passage is omitted from the English translation of von Balthasar's book. It is quoted by Marquardt, *Theologie und Sozialismus*, p. 34.)

52. Karl Barth, "Moderne Theologie und Reichsgottesarbeit," *Zeitschrift für Theologie und Kirche* 19 (1909), pp. 317–321.

53. *Ibid.*, p. 319; quoted by Karl Kupisch, *Karl Barth in Selbstzeugnissen und Bilddokumenten* (Hamburg: Rowohlt Taschenbuch Verlag, 1971), p. 28.

54. Karl Barth, "Der christliche Glaube und die Geschichte," *Schweizerische theologische Zeitschrift*, 1912, pp. 1–18, 49–72.

55. James D. Smart, *The Divided Mind of Modern Theology: Karl Barth and Rudolf Bultmann 1908–1933* (The Westminster Press, 1967), p. 47.

56. Barth, "Der christliche Glaube . . . ," *loc. cit.*, p. 1; quoted by Frei, "Barth's Break with Liberalism," p. 34.

57. Barth, "Der christliche Glaube . . . ," *loc. cit.*, p. 3; quoted by Smart, *Divided Mind*, p. 47 (rev.).

58. Barth, "Der christliche Glaube . . . ," *loc. cit.*, p. 61; quoted by Frei, "Barth's Break with Liberalism," p. 47.

59. Karl Barth, "Der Glaube an den persönlichen Gott," *Zeitschrift für Theologie und Kirche* 24 (1914), pp. 21–32, 65–95.

60. *Ibid.*, p. 22.

61. *Ibid.*, p. 70.

62. *Ibid.*, p. 89.

63. *Ibid.*, p. 94.

64. Frei, "Barth's Break with Liberalism," p. 157.

65. For a report on the hitherto unpublished manuscripts which will now appear, see Uvo A. Wolf, "Der gesamte Barth," *Evangelische Kommentare* 5 (1972), pp. 304 f.

66. Barth, " 'Die Hilfe' 1913," *Christliche Welt* 28 (1914), cols. 774–778.

67. *Ibid.*, col. 777.

68. *Ibid.*, col. 776.

69. *Ibid.*, col. 777.

70. *Ibid.*, col. 776. Barth here employs the terminology of H. Kutter.

71. *Ibid.*, col. 777.

72. *Ibid.*, col. 778.

73. *Ibid.*

74. Cf. Frei, "Barth's Break with Liberalism," p. 160.

75. Karl Barth, *The Humanity of God* (John Knox Press, 1960), p. 14.

76. *Ibid.*

77. Barth, "Moderne Theologie und Reichsgottesarbeit," p. 320; quoted by Kupisch, *Karl Barth*, p. 28.

78. Eduard Thurneysen, *Karl Barth—"Theologie und Sozialismus" in den Briefen seiner Frühzeit* (Zurich: Theologischer Verlag, 1973), pp. 8 f.; Kupisch, *Karl Barth*, pp. 37 f.; Smart, *Divided Mind*, p. 60; cf. Barth, "Past and Future: Friedrich Naumann and Christoph Blumhardt," *loc. cit.*

79. Eduard Thurneysen, letter of October 6, 1921, in Karl Barth and Eduard Thurneysen, *Revolutionary Theology in the Making: Barth-Thurneysen Correspondence, 1914–1925*, tr. by James D. Smart (John Knox Press, 1964), p. 75.

80. Thurneysen, *Karl Barth*, pp. 8 f.; Kupisch, *Karl Barth*, pp. 37 f.; Smart, *Divided Mind*, p. 60.

81. Barth, *The Word of God and the Word of Man*, p. 100.

82. Barth, letter of February 5, 1915, in Barth and Thurneysen, *Revolutionary Theology*, p. 28.

83. Markus Barth, "Current Discussion on the Political Character of Karl Barth's Theology," in *Footnotes to a Theology: The Karl Barth Colloquium of 1972*, ed. by Martin Rumscheidt; supplement to *Studies in Religion / Sciences Religieuses*, 1974, p. 77.

84. Quoted by John Deschner, p. 56 (see note 1 to this essay).

85. Barth, letter of September 4, 1914, in Barth and Thurneysen, *Revolutionary Theology*, p. 26.

86. Barth, *The Word of God and the Word of Man*, p. 18.

87. *Ibid.*, p. 40.

88. Frei, "Barth's Break with Liberalism," pp. 62 ff. and 431 ff.

89. *Ibid.*, pp. 113 ff.

90. *Ibid.*, pp. 131 ff.

91. *Ibid.*, pp. 126 ff.

92. Karl Barth, *Der Römerbrief* (Bern: G. A. Bäschlin, 1919), p. 328; quoted by Smart, *Divided Mind*, p. 84.

93. Frei, "Barth's Break with Liberalism," pp. 136 ff.; Smart, *Divided Mind*, p. 82.

94. Barth, *Römerbrief* (1st ed., 1919), p. 381; quoted by Smart, *Divided Mind*, p. 85.

95. Barth, *Römerbrief* (1st ed., 1919), p. 381; quoted by Marquardt, *Theologie und Sozialismus*, p. 135.

96. Marquardt, *Theologie und Sozialismus*, pp. 126 ff.

97. *Ibid.*, 132.

98. Barth, *Römerbrief* (1st ed., 1919), p. 388; quoted by Marquardt, *Theologie und Sozialismus*, p. 131.

99. Barth, *Römerbrief* (1st ed., 1919), p. 390; quoted by Smart, *Divided Mind*, pp. 85 f.

100. Barth, *Römerbrief* (1st ed., 1919), p. 332; quoted by Gollwitzer above, p. 119, note 39.

101. Barth, *God in Action* (Round Table Press, 1936), p. 125; quoted by John Godsey in his Introduction to Barth's *How I Changed My Mind* (John Knox Press, 1966), p. 23.

102. Cf. Barth's letter of September 8, 1915, in Barth and Thurneysen, *Revolutionary Theology*, pp. 30 ff.

103. Marquardt, *Theologie und Sozialismus*, p. 121.

104. *Ibid.*, pp. 127, 160.

105. Barth, *Römerbrief* (1st ed., 1919), p. 390; quoted by Marquardt, *Theologie und Sozialismus*, p. 131.

106. Barth, *Römerbrief* (1st ed., 1919), p. 377; quoted by Marquardt, *Theologie und Sozialismus*, p. 131.

107. See Barth's letter of October 27, 1920, in Barth and Thurneysen, *Revolutionary Theology*, p. 53.

108. Marquardt, *Theologie und Sozialismus*, p. 166.

109. Frei, "Barth's Break with Liberalism," p. 497n.

110. Barth, *The Word of God and the Word of Man*, p. 273.

111. *Ibid.*, p. 319.

112. *Ibid.*, pp. 321 f.

113. Marquardt, *Theologie und Sozialismus*, p. 159.

114. Frei, "Barth's Break with Liberalism," pp. 112 ff.

115. Marquardt, *Theologie und Sozialismus*, p. 143.

116. Cf. *ibid.*, p. 158.

117. Barth, "Past and Future: Friedrich Naumann and Christoph Blumhardt," *loc. cit.*, p. 45.

118. Frei, "Barth's Break with Liberalism," pp. 101 ff., 120 ff.

119. *Ibid.*, pp. 513–545.

120. Barth, *The Humanity of God*, p. 43; Frei, "Barth's Break with Liberalism," pp. 96 ff., 462 ff.

121. Frei, "Barth's Break with Liberalism," pp. 145 ff., 433, 481.

122. Barth, *The Humanity of God*, pp. 44 f.

123. *Ibid.*, p. 45; letter of March 21, 1923, in Barth and Thurneysen, *Revolutionary Theology*, p. 140.

124. Karl Barth and Rudolf Bultmann, *Briefwechsel 1922–1966*, ed. by B. Jaspert (Zurich: Theologischer Verlag, 1971), p. 310.

125. Karl Barth, "Ludwig Feuerbach," tr. by J. L. Adams; published under the title "An Introductory Essay," in Ludwig Feuerbach, *The Essence of Christianity* (Harper & Brothers, 1957), p. xxvi.

126. Karl Barth and Eduard Thurneysen, *Briefwechsel, Band 2, 1921–1930* (Zurich: Theologischer Verlag, 1974), p. 607.

127. Barth, "Ludwig Feuerbach," *loc. cit.*, p. xxv.

128. *Ibid.* (rev.).

129. *Ibid.*, pp. xxvi, xxvii.

130. *Ibid.*, p. xxvii.

131. *Ibid.*, p. xix.

132. Karl Barth, "Schicksal und Idee in der Theologie," *Zwischen den Zeiten*, 1929, pp. 309–348; "Theologische und philosophische Ethik," unpublished lecture from 1930; *Ethik*, lectures from 1928–1929. Volume I has appeared in the series of hitherto unpublished manuscripts (Zurich: Theologischer Verlag, 1973); a second volume is to follow.

133. Quoted by Kupisch, *Karl Barth*, p. 73.

134. Barth, *How I Changed My Mind*, p. 43.

135. *Ibid.*

136. Karl Barth, *Anselm: Fides Quaerens Intellectum*, tr. by Ian W. Robertson (The World Publishing Company, 1960), p. 14.

137. *Ibid.*, pp. 15–21.

138. *Ibid.*, p. 26; cf. pp. 22–26.

139. *Ibid.*, pp. 26–40.

140. *Ibid.*, pp. 40–59, 73–89.

141. Thomas F. Torrance, *Karl Barth: An Introduction to His Early Theology, 1910–1931* (London: SCM Press Ltd., 1962), p. 48.

142. Barth, *Römerbrief* (1st ed., 1919), p. 366; quoted by Marquardt, *Theologie und Sozialismus*, p. 296.

143. Quoted by Marquardt, *Theologie und Sozialismus*, p. 297; cf. Barth, CD III/2, pp. 241 f.

144. Barth, *Against the Stream*, p. 118.

Contributors

FRIEDRICH-WILHELM MARQUARDT is Professor of Systematic Theology at the Free University of Berlin.

His works include *Die Entdeckung des Judentums für die christliche Theologie: Israel im Denken Karl Barths* (1966); and "Theologische und politische Motivationen Karl Barths im Kirchenkampf," *Junge Kirche* 34 (1973), pp. 283–303.

HELMUT GOLLWITZER is Professor of Systematic Theology at the Free University of Berlin.

His works include *The Rich Christians and Poor Lazarus* (1969); *The Christian Faith and the Marxist Criticism of Religion* (1967); and *The Existence of God as Confessed by Faith* (1965).

HERMANN DIEM (1900–1975) was Emeritus Professor of Systematic Theology at the University of Tübingen.

His works include *Dogmatics* (1959); *Kierkegaard: An Introduction* (1964); and *Kierkegaard's Dialectic of Existence* (1957).

DIETER SCHELLONG is Assistant Professor of Systematic Theology at the University of Münster.

His works include *Karl Barth und die Neuzeit* (with K. G. Steck) (1973); and *Calvins Auslegung der synoptischen Evangelien* (1969).

JOSEPH BETTIS is Distinguished Professor of Humanities and Professor of Religion at the University of Nebraska at Omaha.

He has edited *Phenomenology of Religion* (1969); his articles include "Is Karl Barth a Universalist?" *Scottish Journal of Theology* 20 (1967), pp. 423–436.

GEORGE HUNSINGER is a Ph.D. candidate in Religious Studies at Yale University.

His articles include "A Marxist View of Kierkegaard: George Lukács on the Intellectual Origins of Fascism," *Union Seminary Quarterly Review* 30 (1974–75), pp. 27–40; and "The Crucified God and the Political Theology of Violence: A Critical Survey of Jürgen Moltmann's Recent Thought," *The Heythrop Journal* 14 (1973), pp. 266–279 and 379–395.